THE ILLUSTRATED GUIDE TO

FORENSICS

THIS IS A CARLTON BOOK

Design copyright © Carlton Publishing Group 2004
Text copyright © Dr Zakaria Erzinçlioglu 1999

This edition published in 2004 by Carlton Books Ltd
A Division of the Carlton Publishing Group
20 Mortimer Street
London
W1T 3JW

Text first published by Carlton Books Limited under the title
Every Contact Leaves a Trace

A CIP catalogue for this book is available from the British
Library.

ISBN: 1 84442 698 X

Captions: Dr Sharon Erzinçlioglu
Executive Editor: Stella Caldwell
Senior Art Editor: Vicky Holmes
Editor: Anne McDowall
Designer: Mark Lloyd
Picture Researcher: Steve Behan
Production: Lisa Moore

Printed in Dubai

THE ILLUSTRATED GUIDE TO

FORENSICS

TRUE CRIME SCENE
INVESTIGATIONS

Dr Zakaria Erzinçlioglu

CARLTON
BOOKS

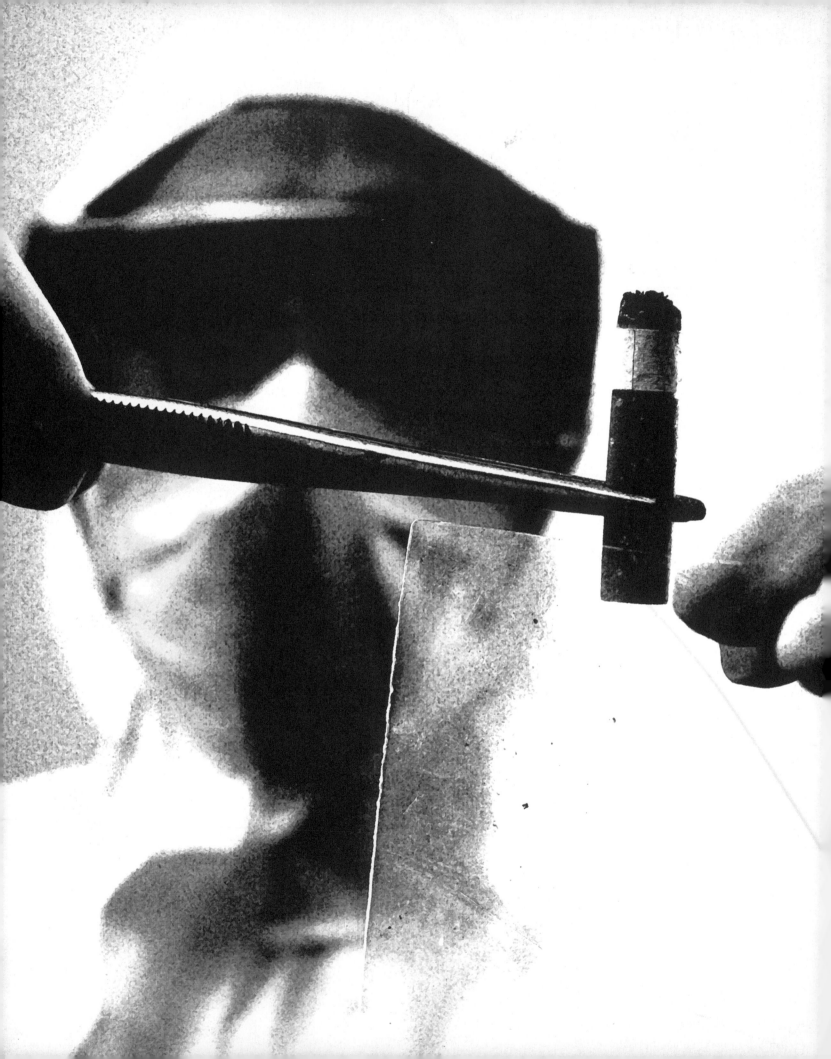

CONTENTS

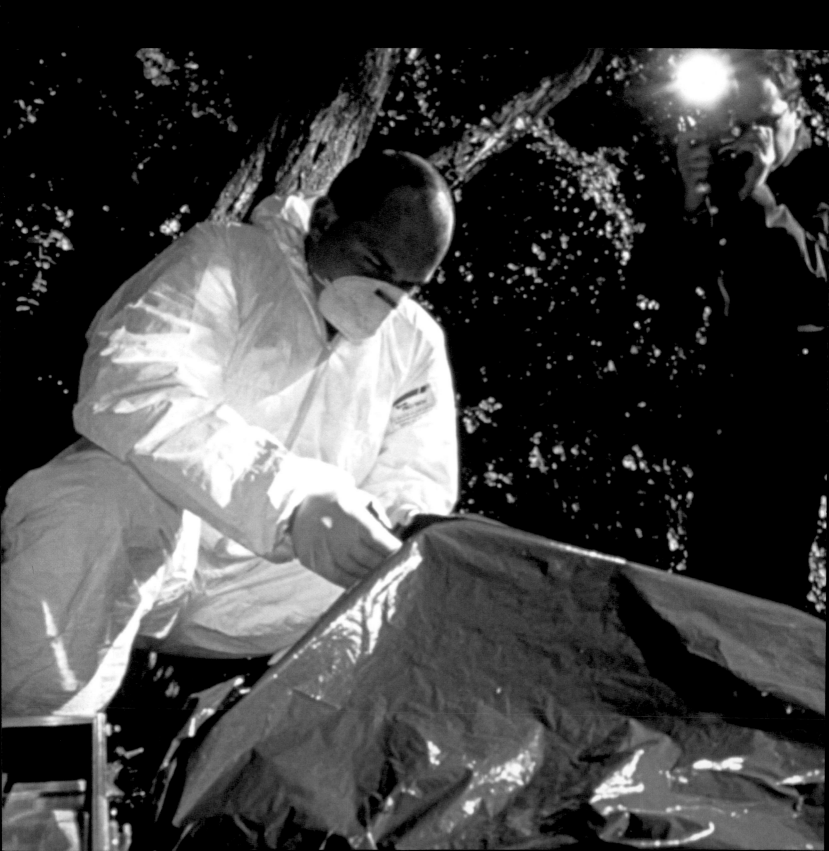

LOCARD'S PRINCIPLE

I was standing by a tree watching a team of policemen digging into the loose soil a few feet away. The dead body of a murder victim had been found not far from this place and there were signs suggesting that it had first been buried, but later exhumed and deposited in the place in which it was discovered.

At last, several things turned up all at once: a human fingernail, some strands of hair, and a few pupal cases of flies, which must have developed from maggots that had been feeding upon the corpse. Later, when the hairs from the burial site were compared with those on the dead body, they were found to match exactly. So that part of the mystery was solved. Once the body was buried, it left its mark. The disturbed soil, the fingernail, the hair, and the tell-tale fly pupal cases were all the result of the burial. The clues left behind were the consequences of the act.

In 1921, some sixty years before these events took place, Sir Arthur Conan Doyle, creator of Sherlock Holmes and Doctor Watson, arrived at Lyons in France, on his way back to England from his travels in Australia. In Lyons he visited Dr Edmond Locard, one of the great names in forensic science, at his famous laboratory behind the Palais de Justice in the city.

Edmond Locard was delighted to meet Conan Doyle, whom he took on a tour of his Black Museum of criminal cases. He showed him the cabinets of weapons and all sorts of physical clues from the cases he had investigated throughout the world. He showed him the photographs of the various criminals who had been arrested by the application of Locard's own techniques.

Suddenly, Sir Arthur Conan Doyle stopped. He was looking at one of the photographs and he appeared puzzled. The photograph was of a young man with a moustache and cold, disdainful eyes. Turning to Dr Locard, Conan Doyle said:

"But that is Jules, my former chauffeur!"

Dr Locard was astounded. "No, you must be mistaken, Sir Arthur, that is Jules Bonnot, the motor-bandit."

And so it was, but Conan Doyle was not mistaken. For Jules Bonnot – murderer, anarchist and terrorist – had, indeed, been his chauffeur in the years before the First World War.

Dr Locard told Conan Doyle the whole story of what was known of the life and death of Jules Bonnot. In one of those odd coincidences that prompt the exclamation that truth is stranger than fiction, it transpired that Bonnot had also served as the chauffeur of another celebrated criminologist, Harry Ashton-Wolfe, who worked as the assistant of Alphonse Bertillon, chief of criminal identification in Paris. In 1911, some time after he left Sir Arthur's employ, Bonnot embarked on a new career of crime. Until that time, he and his associates had attacked the bourgeoisie by stealing their cars. Now, they began to use the car itself as a weapon, driving about the country committing robberies and murders. At last, with the forensic help of Dr Locard, Bonnot and his gang were brought to justice – violently.

In April, 1912, the police besieged a garage in Choisy-le-Roi, near Paris. Inside it were Bonnot and the other members of the gang. Shooting began; one of the gang was killed and Bonnot was mortally wounded. Cursing his captors, he was taken to hospital to die.

Dr Locard was horrified to hear that the creator of Sherlock Holmes had been driven around by the murderous Bonnot. Conan Doyle could have been murdered, he said. "Bonnot chauffeuring Sir Arthur Conan Doyle! The flesh creeps. Think how close we came to not having all we do have of Sherlock Holmes!"

Dr Locard came to be known as the Sherlock Holmes of France, a title of which he was very proud. He practised his skills for a very long time. Born in 1877, he studied medicine and law at Lyons, eventually becoming the assistant of Alexandre Lacassagne, a pioneer criminologist and professor of Forensic Medicine at the University of Lyons. He held this post until 1910, when he began the foundation of his criminal laboratory. He produced a monumental, seven-volume work, *Traité de Criminalistique*, and continued with his researches until his death

Left: *Sir Arthur Conan Doyle (1859–1930). His Sherlock Holmes stories stress the importance of physical evidence in criminal investigations. The French Sûreté Laboratory at Lyons is named after him.*

in 1966, aged almost ninety.

What has all this to do with the excavation of a presumed burial site in an English forest so many years later? There is a link, albeit not a unique one. Edmond Locard, having absorbed the ideas of Lacassagne, Bertillon, Gross* and Conan Doyle, was able to focus his thoughts and formulate the basic principle of forensic science – a principle so simple and, with hindsight, so obvious, that some might say that it is hardly worth spelling out or aggrandising with the title of "Principle". Yet it is the basic idea upon which all forensic science is ultimately based, for Locard's Principle simply states: every contact leaves a trace.

The burglar who touches a window pane with his bare hands leaves his fingerprints behind; the prowler who steps on to the flower-bed leaves his tracks and carries some soil away on his boots; the robber who smashes a window carries minute fragments of glass on his clothes; the murderer may be contaminated by his victim's blood; the victim may retain in his hand some fibres from the murderer's clothes, pulled out during the struggle.

Yes, it is a simple idea, but, like many simple ideas in science, it is a very powerful one. It clears our thoughts and helps us to concentrate our efforts. Newton, observing the apple fall, came up with the simple idea, which seems so obvious to us now, that the Earth pulled it down. Darwin, studying the animals on the various Galapagos Islands, arrived at the simple conclusion that those individuals best suited to their environment would have a greater chance of survival. Archimedes, simply by sitting in his bath and watching the water rise, reached the simple conclusion that the volume of water that was displaced was equal to his own volume (or as much of him

Above: *Edmond Locard (1877–1966): a pioneer forensic scientist who became known as the Sherlock Holmes of France. He formulated the basic principle of forensic science: "Every Contact Leaves a Trace".*

Left: *Fingerprint for analysis. The distinctive pattern of ridges and whorls that is unique for each person can be clearly seen.*

as was under the water). All very simple indeed.

Yet is Locard's Principle really equivalent to these other notions? Is it necessarily true that every contact leaves a trace? The critical reader might say that, although we found a fingernail and a few other things in the forest, it was quite possible that we could have failed to find anything. What if we had simply found nothing? What if the culprit had packed the soil more firmly, making it difficult to discern whether or not it had been disturbed? How could Locard's Principle have applied then?

The answer to this is that, every time a grasshopper jumps, the planet Earth is pushed in the opposite direction, but we may not be able to detect such a movement. By this I mean that Locard's Principle remains true, even if we cannot find a trace. The trace will be there, but the likelihood of our finding it will be limited by our abilities, our knowledge and the degree of refinement of the techniques and equipment at our disposal. Had we found nothing in the forest, chemical analysis of the soil may have revealed the presence of decomposition products from the body. The change in the composition of the microscopic flora and fauna in the soil may have provided a clue, and so on. The idea may be simple, the practical application of it may not be. The trick lies in actually finding the trace.

Formulating a principle, however simple or obvious, is a great boon, for it helps us to think clearly. When I taught students at Cambridge University, I used to tell them, before designing and carrying out an experiment, to write down the question they wanted to answer. However much difficulty they may have had at the outset, they were surprised at how much easier it was to design the experiment when they had actually formulated the problem in writing. They may have already "known" what the question was, but writing it down, as clearly as possible, crystallized it and made the problem much easier to handle. We seem to a great extent to think in language and in words.

Forensic science is concerned with finding out what happened in the, usually, recent past. It is akin to other areas of human endeavour, like history, archaeology and palaeontology, the aim of which is to discover the course of events that took place long ago. The time-scale may be much shorter in forensic science, but the thought processes involved are much the same. In fact, one could say that Locard's Principle forms the basic tenet of all these subjects.

I have always been fascinated by the past and how we can get to grips with it – how we can find out what really happened. This "past" may be the relatively recent past, as when one is conducting a forensic investigation of a murder; the more distant past, as in the reconstruction of historical events during the period of written history; the even more distant past, that which forms the subject matter of archaeology; or the remote past, the realm of the fossil-hunter. During the course of my professional career, I have had the opportunity – the privilege – to contribute to all these fields of study.

Below: *Finding the trace. A forensic scientist at work removing fibre samples from a suspect's clothing. These will then be compared microscopically to fibres found at the crime scene.*

Right: *Interpreting the trace. This skeleton from a graveyard at Withorn Priory is Mediaeval, but a careful study of the bones may provide clues about the diseases that affected our ancestors.*

This book is about finding the traces that can lead us to discover the truth about past events – specifically, past events that are of interest to the law. Finding a buried skeleton that turns out to have belonged to someone who died 30 years ago – or even 75 years – is a matter for the law and the police, but the body of a person who died 100 years earlier is of historical, not legal, interest. Forensic science and history merge at the edges, for where one ends, the other begins. Yet it is as well to bear in mind that forensic science has an applicability far beyond the area of the law, for its techniques and thought processes are widely used to interpret the facts – the traces available to us – in other historical subjects. These traces may not necessarily be physical ones – actual objects that one can hold in one's hand. They may be ideas that took shape, or events that took place, as consequences of earlier ideas or events.

You are standing by a pond and you throw a pebble in the water. There is a splash around the spot where the pebble entered the pond. Ripples are formed; they grow gradually fainter and less discernible towards the edges of the ever-widening circle. If someone else, standing beside you, throws a larger stone into the water, the ripples from it will collide and merge and mingle with the ripples from your pebble and it will be difficult to know the extent to which your action was responsible for the disturbance of the water. Once the pebble has disappeared beneath the surface, all we can observe are the tell-tale signs of the ripples. These ripples – these traces – will be our only clues to the past, so we must make the most of them, knowing that they could easily mislead us. Our task is not only to find these traces, but to find the correct interpretation of them and to attribute to them their true significance.

✻ Hans Gross (1847–1915) was the Austrian author of *System der Kriminalistik*, the first comprehensive work on forensic science, published in 1891. It was translated into English in 1907, under the title of *Criminal Investigation*.

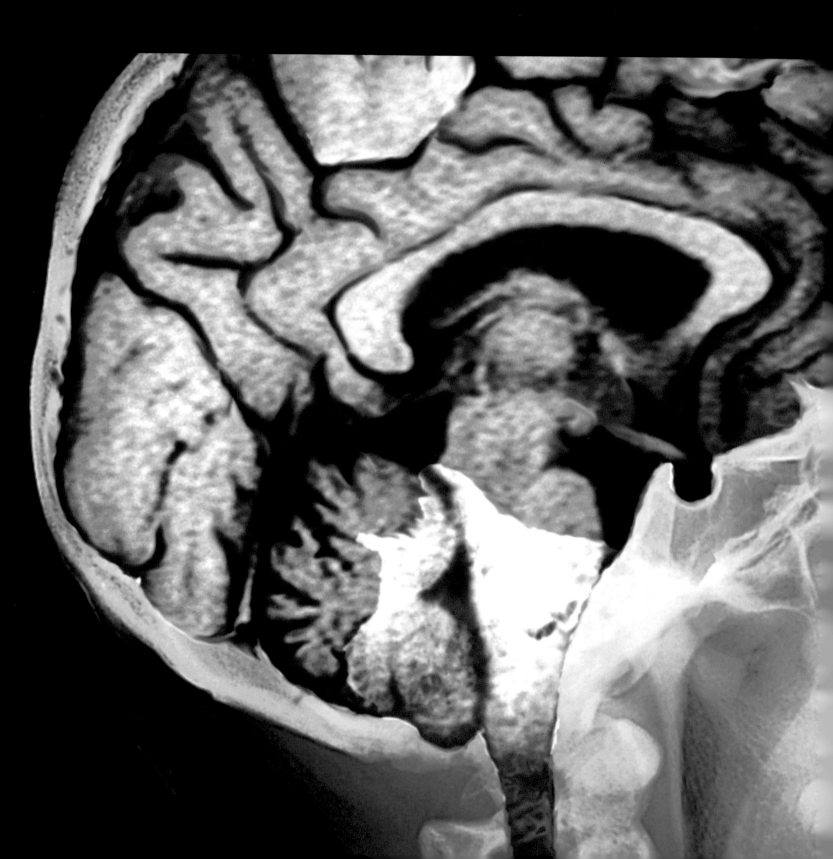

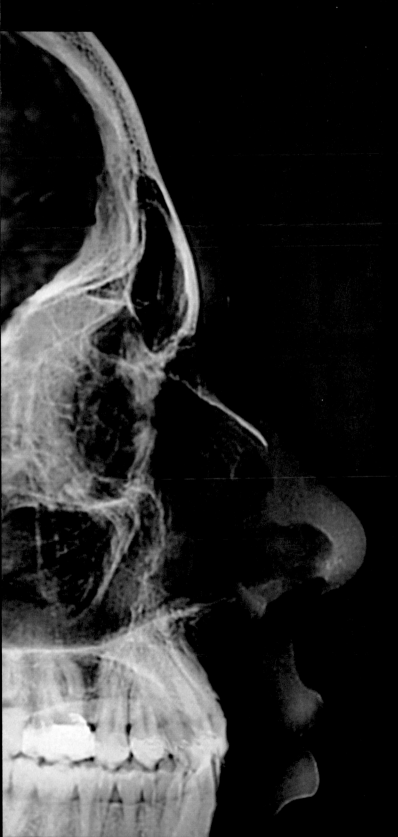

The practice of forensic science is not simply the application of a set of laboratory techniques. It is the acquisition of the habit of starting with a doubt, of being eager and willing to question the unquestioned. It is the cultivation of a suspicious mind.

Suspicion, of course, is of little use on its own. Unfounded or emotionally based suspicion is, indeed, worse than useless and can cause great harm; it is what guides the lynch mob. For suspicion to be productive, it must be based on, and followed up with, sound reasoning. This mixture of suspicion and reason is the forensic scientist's forte. It is essential. Without it, forensic science is reduced to the routine application of scientific recipes. The techniques of forensic science will be discussed in some detail in this book, but the thought processes that lead one to decide which technique is to be used, and in what way, are the subject of this chapter.

Sound Reasoning

Evidence that goes together with other evidence can confuse in many ways. It is possible to present a piece of evidence in isolation, or in conjunction with another piece of evidence. In one kind of situation, presenting the evidence in isolation may be very misleading, yet in other situations presenting the evidence hand in glove, so to speak, with other evidence may be even more misleading.

Consider what your reaction would be if you saw a man walking along the street clutching a knife in his hand. Most people would feel that the man represented a threat; his appearance would seem menacing, even criminal. To put it more formally, the evidence of the knife would suggest that he was a dangerous man.

But what would your reaction have been if the man had been clutching a knife and a fork in one hand? Clearly, he would not have appeared in such an unpleasant light as he did when he was clutching only a knife. In fact, far from appearing menacing or criminal, he would have seemed amusing or even absurd. The evidence of the fork diluted the evidence of the knife, or more accurately, it modified the evidence of the knife. The fork made us look at the knife in a different way, with the result that our opinion of the man changed fundamentally.

Let us look at this man's behaviour more closely. We concluded that he appeared

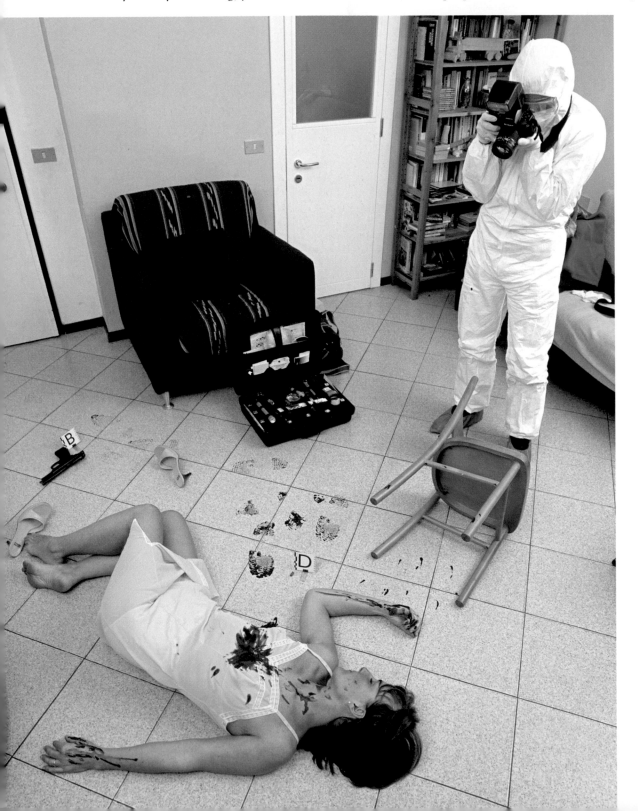

Left: *Gathering the evidence. In this reconstruction of a murder, a detailed photographic record is initially made of the scene, the victim and any potential evidence such as the bloody footprints or the gun.*

threatening when he was walking along with the knife on its own, but this does not necessarily mean that he was a criminal. It is our reaction to him, when he was carrying both knife and fork, that is really interesting. The fork may, indeed, suggest that the knife was an innocent object, but it may have been that very fact that made the man carry the fork in the first place; in other words, he may have carried it to deceive us into believing that he was harmless. On the other hand, if we had rushed to the police station and reported the sighting of a man walking about town with a knife, and withheld the information about the fork, the investigating police officer may subsequently feel that we had misled him by not mentioning that relevant little fact.

It is easy to think of a number of situations in which evidence, when taken in conjunction with other evidence, can give a very different picture from the one that would appear if the evidence had been looked at on its own. If the man in our example had been carrying a happy child in his arms, he would have looked quite harmless, even if he had been clutching the knife without a fork.

Right: *Interpreting the evidence. Trainee forensic scientists examine the bullet hole and blood stain pattern from the victim's dress in order to make judgements about the distance from which she was shot.*

Cause and Effect

WHEN I USED to teach at Cambridge University I often supervised groups of three or four students at a time and we frequently discussed problems of logic and reasoning. In one such group, one of the students sometimes used to appear wearing a bright red jumper. The other students and I noticed that he always appeared quite cheerful when he wore this jumper and that he was never quite so pleased with himself when he was not wearing it. The link between his good spirits and his arrival in the red jumper was so strong that I felt moved to ask the group why they thought this was so. The chap himself was very good-natured and entered into the spirit of the thing, agreeing with my request that he should not divulge the true reason for this link, assuming there was one, until the end of the discussion.

His colleagues came up with a number of ideas. The first was that he wore that jumper whenever he felt happy, hence the correlation. No, our friend replied, this was not the reason. Someone else suggested that the cause and effect were the other way round – he felt happy whenever he wore the jumper; in other words, the jumper made him happy. Again, this was not the case. The jumper did not cause his happiness and his happiness did not make him wear the jumper; neither was the cause of the other. What, then, was the explanation?

The answer was simply that he wore the jumper when he went rowing. On those occasions when the supervision period immediately followed a bout of rowing, he would appear in my room wearing the red jumper. It was the rowing that caused the wearing of the jumper and the young fellow's happiness; both the jumper and his good spirits were the consequences of a cause that was invisible to us. The rowing "chicken" produced the two "eggs" of jumper and cheerfulness.

This kind of situation can arise very frequently in more complicated forms, often causing a great deal of confusion and misunderstanding. The reasonable conclusion that the red jumper and the good spirits were cause and effect, or vice versa, would have caused further confusion if the student had decided, halfway through term, to wear a blue jumper on his rowing excursions instead. The point of all this is that we may often be presented with a number of effects and no causes, but that, in the absence of the latter, we tend to assume that one of the effects is the cause of the others. Such a conclusion would not necessarily stop there, since our reasoning might lead us on to actions or further arguments that would lead us deep into areas of utter confusion.

Too Many Assumptions

Above: *A .45 calibre pistol. In 1997, such handguns were banned from private ownership in the UK after the Dunblane tragedy in Scotland.*

The unconscious selectivity of evidence can often lead us astray. Consider the following remark, variations of which are very commonly heard: "Yesterday I was thinking about Aunt Mary and, bless me, she telephoned that very afternoon. I do believe we are telepathic." The speaker and Aunt Mary may well share a telepathic sense, but Aunt Mary's telephone call is not evidence for it, for is it not true that Aunt Mary is thought about almost every day? The hundreds of occasions in which Aunt Mary came to mind, but after which she did not telephone, are forgotten.

This kind of mental trick, whether consciously or unconsciously adopted, is not confined to ordinary, everyday things, but affects our ideas in criminal trials and about historical events of all kinds. I have even heard eminent barristers argue their cases in court this way and, sadly and disturbingly, political decisions have even been based upon such false reasoning.

An example of recent political action of this kind concerns the ban on private ownership of handguns following the tragedy at the school in Dunblane, Scotland, in which a number of children were shot dead by a killer, Thomas Hamilton, with a handgun. Whether this ban was justified or not is a complex issue and cannot be dealt with summarily in a few sentences. My purpose is to examine the reasoning that led to the decision to impose the ban.

The ban was intended to prevent such an evil from happening again – or at least to minimize the chances of a recurrence. It was argued that if fewer people owned guns, the likelihood of anyone being shot by a gun would be reduced. If Hamilton had not owned a gun, he could not have committed the multiple murder.

Furthermore, gun ownership is high in the United States, a country with a much higher murder rate than Britain, so it would seem reasonable to conclude that the prevalence of handguns in the population leads to more killings than would be the case if fewer guns were available.

However, this reasoning uses only part of the evidence available. For example, there is evidence to suggest that some of those parts of the United States that have the highest levels of gun ownership are blessed with the lowest crime rates in the country. Certainly, the crime rate in the United States is decreasing, while that in Britain is increasing. Furthermore, Switzerland has the highest gun ownership levels in Europe, yet it is the most law-abiding country, at least as far as violent crime is concerned.

There are many other arguments, both for and against the ban on handguns. I do not wish to review these, since the point I wish to make is that choosing some evidence, simply because it supports one's emotional preference, and ignoring other evidence that is not sympathetic to one's preferred solution may lead people, and even governments, into taking the wrong decision, i.e. the decision that is less likely to bring about the desired change. Deciding upon a course of action before examining all the evidence is a very dangerous procedure.

Left: *Thomas Hamilton, who possessed licences for six guns in total. On March 13 1996 he walked into a primary school in Dunblane, Scotland and shot dead 16 children and a teacher before killing himself.*

Occam's Razor

WILLIAM OF OCCAM, a Franciscan monk who lived during the late thirteenth and early fourteenth centuries, had some valuable things to say about reason and evidence. He taught that "entities are not to be multiplied beyond necessity". This turgid philosophical dictum can be expressed more usefully by saying that it is always best to consider the simplest explanation of any problem first. This useful principle has become known as Occam's Razor, with which unnecessary "entities" can be shaved off. If one is faced with a problem it is best to try and explain it without recourse to too many assumptions.

To take a simple example, let us say that you have returned home from work one day and found a book lying open on the table. One explanation is that another member of your family put it there. Another explanation is that it was a guest, admitted into the house by a member of your family, who opened the book. Yet another explanation is that a burglar gained entry and, when he had a free moment, decided to

consult the book but left it on the table when he heard you coming. The first explanation is clearly the most likely. It may be said that this is, in fact, so obvious a conclusion that one does not need a mediaeval philosopher to draw one's attention to it.

But consider again. Although we know "instinctively" what the most likely explanation is, it is instructive to ask ourselves why we think that. The answer is that it is the explanation that makes the fewest assumptions about the situation. In other words, we have no reason to suppose, in the absence of other evidence, that either a guest or a burglar entered the house. To accept these other explanations would require us to assume things that we have no particular reason to believe. The first explanation does not require us to assume anything out of the ordinary; that is why we accept it in favour of the others. If we find that we were mistaken, we may then consider more complicated answers, but it is always logical to start with the simplest answer to our question.

False Arguments

Above: *In this US courtroom, the lawyer explains a point to the jury. The stenographer in the background is making a verbatim record.*

Sitting in court, listening to the proceedings of a criminal trial, I have often heard false arguments presented by barristers and accepted, in all good faith, by juries. Unfortunately, pointing out such errors of thinking does not always result in a withdrawal of the argument. One is hardly ever thanked for doing it. Some barristers are quite determined to win, regardless of the way in which the victory is achieved.

This brings me to a rather sensitive matter. In court it is often difficult to know whether a particular false argument is simply an honest mistake or whether it is an intentional manipulation of the truth. On the face of it, in a discussion of this sort, it may not appear to matter which of the two it is, as long as the illogicality of the argument is demonstrated. Sadly, it does matter. It matters because the empty rhetoric of a barrister of the kind who is impelled by a desire to win at all costs may sway a jury more

certainly than logic. Consequently, the force of the logic used to refute the argument and expose the fallacy needs to be very clear indeed. A courtroom is often a field of battle. This chapter would be incomplete if we failed to look at the less savoury aspects of evidence presentation. It is, in any case, instructive to consider not only the ways in which things should be done, but the ways in which they should not be done. Little good would be achieved if it is claimed that the forensic mind is always perfect.

Although all this may sound perfectly obvious, the underlying point is, nevertheless, often not grasped (or is obfuscated) when evidence is given in court. Astonishingly enough, errors that may appear so simple and obvious in everyday life are often made in the courtroom without being noticed.

How can this happen? Here, I can only give my impressions, since it is almost impossible to collect hard·evidence to support an explanation. We are dealing with the undivulged thoughts and reactions in people's minds and we cannot know what these are. In the case of juries, it is illegal to ask how members arrived at their conclusions. So, the answer to the question must, to a great extent, be speculative.

The atmosphere in a criminal court is always tense. Very serious matters are discussed. Someone's life, or at least future, is at stake. Barristers almost always exude an aura of great and ponderous authority and are usually endowed with enviable oratorial powers. They tend to be believed; few people think they would make such simple mistakes. Furthermore, the point, in a legal situation, is not as simply or as clearly manifested as it can be in more everyday situations. This may have something to do with the fact that scientific evidence tends to be presented and handled as though it were a special kind of evidence, to be assessed in a different way, e.g. not many people know how many people have a particular blood-group. Even when the number of people having a particular blood-group is given in court, the new information is presented in a manner that makes it difficult for the lay person to assess its significance in the real world. Although I cannot speak for jury men and women specifically, scientific evidence seems to be regarded either with great reverence or great hostility by the population at large.

A particularly common error has to do with the evaluation of individual pieces of evidence against the accused. An excellent example of this sort of error took place during the notorious criminal trial of O.J. Simpson, the American football player, who was accused of murdering his former wife and her lover.

The Case of O. J. Simpson

Evidence presented by the prosecution showed that blood found at the scene possessed blood-grouping characteristics that matched Simpson's blood. It was stated in court that only one in 400 people had blood with such characteristics and that, therefore, this was strong evidence that the blood at the scene was Simpson's. The defence retorted by saying that a very large number of people, equivalent to the full complement of spectators at a Los Angeles football stadium, as they dramatically put it, would share the same blood characteristics. Therefore, they said, the findings could hardly be seen as being evidence against Simpson. In fact, they claimed that the evidence was, effectively, useless.

But was it? In principle, the answer to this question in the abstract must be "Yes" or "No", depending on the circumstances. If Simpson had been accused of murder solely on the basis of these findings, then they could not be seen as being evidence against him. For why select him, when many thousands of others could have been chosen with equal validity? On the basis of the findings, the blood could have belonged to any one of them, with equal probability in each case. Under such circumstances, the evidence would, indeed, have been worthless.

But the evidence did not come to light under such circumstances. There was already a *prima facie* case against Simpson – in other words, a certain amount of evidence against him already existed. To put it another way, the case against him could be presented in terms of odds. Let us say, for the sake of the argument, that, from what we already knew about Simpson (i.e. from the existing evidence and before assessing the blood evidence), the odds against him were three to two in favour of him being guilty. Without going into the mathematics of this matter, odds and probabilities can be calculated on the basis of existing evidence. So, we performed such calculations and came up with the odds of three to two; in other words, that the evidence suggests that he is more likely than not to have been guilty. If the calculated odds had been three to two against him being guilty (or three to two in favour of him being innocent, which is the same thing), then the evidence would suggest that he is more likely than not to have been innocent.

The point is that we start with certain odds. These are known as the prior odds. Now we come to the value of the blood evidence. The questions we have to ask are these: How does this new evidence affect the prior odds? Does it strengthen or weaken them? Does it strengthen or weaken the case against Simpson? Or does it not affect our beliefs at all?

In the case of the blood evidence, this new information certainly strengthens our belief in Simpson's guilt. Scientists would say that the posterior odds – the new odds, after the latest evidence had been taken into account – are greater in favour of guilt. So, contrary to the claims of the defence, the blood evidence was far from useless; it strongly affected our opinion about what happened. In other words, each piece of evidence, taken in isolation, may not constitute evidence of guilt or innocence, but it is the multiplicity of evidence that should be used to reach the final conclusion.

Below: *Orenthal James Simpson was accused of the murder, on 12 June 1994, of his ex-wife Nicole and of Ron Goldman, a local waiter.*

There are more subtle ways in which evidence can be misrepresented. Take the following example: say that a motorist is caught speeding by the police. He is stopped and breathalyzed and found to be over the legal limit for driving.

Now, nothing devised by human beings is perfect and it may be that the motorist may register as being over the permitted limit, when, in fact, he was not. Let us say that the chance of this happening is very small; records may show that one per cent of the results of breathalyzing tests are incorrect in this way.

In order to consider the driver's conduct in court, it will have to be stated that there is a one per cent chance of a positive result (i.e. that the driver had been over the limit) when, in fact, he had not been over the limit. This fact may be presented in court in a slightly different way: that there is a one per cent chance that the man was not over the limit, if he had got a positive result.

Are these two statements of probability the same thing? Although they look very similar, they are, in fact, not at all the same thing. Let us look at them again:

1. There is a one per cent chance of a positive result, when the driver was not over the limit.
2. There is a one per cent chance of the driver not being over the limit, if he got a positive result.

The statements are not at all the same, because the emphasis has been shifted from the probability of a positive result to the probability of the driver being over the limit. The difference may not be immediately obvious and it frequently goes unappreciated in court, especially when spoken by an able barrister. The shift in emphasis usually goes totally unnoticed, although that shift may make all the difference in the presentation of the evidence. The two statements are taken to be identical, whereas they are very different indeed, with potentially dire results.

An example from everyday life should make this point very clear. Consider these two statements:

1. All dogs are four-legged animals.
2. All four-legged animals are dogs.

Left: *French gendarmes breathalyse a motorist. Permitted alcohol levels for driving vary from 20mg (Norway, Sweden) to 50mg (Austria, France, Germany, Greece, Spain) to 80mg (Ireland, Italy, UK, USA).*

I think most people would see instantly that these two statements are not the same, although exactly the same words are used in each one; only their order in the sentences is different. It is also clear that one cannot possibly deduce the second from the first. Although the error in our second example is blindingly clear, whereas it may not have been so in the first example, both are exactly the same kind of mistake, logically speaking.

A few years ago I was involved in the investigation of a murder in which a man was stabbed to death. His body was weighted down with bricks and deposited in a canal. I was asked to give an opinion as to the length of time the body had been immersed in the water. For various reasons, this proved very difficult to determine, although I could conclude that the body had been in the water for at least two days. It was possible that it could have been there for longer, but there was no evidence to suggest that it had been in the canal for more than the minimum two days.

When I attended to give evidence at the trial in the Old Bailey, the defence barrister asked me to confirm what I had said in my report, namely, that the evidence showed that the body was not in the canal for more than two days. I replied that I had not said this; what I had said was that there was no evidence to suggest

that the body had been in the canal for more than two days. He retorted, somewhat testily, that that was the same thing, but, once again, I disagreed and pointed out that the two statements were very different. To my amazement, the barrister became somewhat sarcastic and made comments of a kind that suggested that I was either a pedant or a fool.

I had to explain that it was one thing to say that there was no evidence to suggest that the body had been immersed in the canal for more than two days and quite another to say that there was evidence that it had not been there for more than two days. To make the point even clearer, I said that the first statement meant that the body may or may not have been immersed for more than two days, whereas the second statement meant that the body had not been in the canal for two days. In my report I had made the first statement, not the second. Astonishingly, he still could not (or would not) see my point of view. Finally the judge intervened. He had fully grasped the point and was able to make my meaning clear to the jury, but not before a great deal of confusion had been created in the courtroom.

Below: *Recovering a body from water. This can be a difficult operation. Care must be taken to try to retrieve any objects e.g. bricks, stones, ropes, associated with the body as these may yield valuable clues.*

A Valid Conclusion?

As we have seen, it is often not possible to discern whether confusion or manipulation is the cause of the faulty presentation, so both have to be considered together. I should explain that I use the word "manipulation" to mean the presentation of evidence in such a way that weak evidence is made to appear stronger than it really is and strong evidence to appear weaker, with the purpose of influencing the jury's understanding of it. Much of what follows is critical of barristers, but I do not wish to give the impression that I am issuing a blanket condemnation of the behaviour of barristers in court. Many barristers I have known and worked with have been very open and straightforward in their handling of their cases and some shine as excellent examples of how to conduct oneself in a court of law. But I have also known barristers who were quite proficient at manipulating evidence in various ways.

One of the main sources of confusion or means of manipulation comes from the concept of "consistency". This, it has to be said, is a notion that lawyers seem to have acquired from forensic scientists, since it is often invoked by the latter when trying to explain the significance of their findings. Let me explain.

Consider the case of someone who was accused of breaking into a house and committing a burglary with violence. Glass fragments are discovered embedded in his shoes. Scientific tests on the glass show that it has properties similar to the glass of the window that was smashed and through which the burglar gained entry. As far as it goes, this is good evidence, as long as its

Below: *Gathering evidence. A forensic scientist takes various samples from a pair of jeans. Such samples could include glass fragments, fibres, hairs, plant material, soil, blood and DNA.*

strength is not exaggerated.

In court, a barrister, perhaps repeating the conclusion in the forensic scientist's report, may say that this evidence is consistent with the accused having broken the window. Although this is a true statement, it is nonetheless misleading, for it actually tells us very little, while having the effect of appearing to tell us a great deal. Very often, this kind of evidence is not discussed any further. The problem with it is that it does not tell us what else it is consistent with. In our example, the glass findings may

have been consistent with the accused having broken any number of other windows with the same properties, but this is hardly ever pointed out.

There are worse examples. I have known several cases in which injuries to a child were said to have been consistent with sexual abuse, although they were also consistent with a dozen other possible causes. The point is that these other causes are not mentioned; only one is mentioned – the one that a barrister or a witness wants to implant in the jury's mind. There is no other reason for mentioning only one cause that is "consistent with" the evidence, otherwise why not choose at random any other cause? It is the choice of a particular cause and the withholding of other possible causes that makes the pronouncement of consistency dangerously misleading. What should be done in such cases is to present all possible causes or scenarios that could have resulted in the evidence in question, be it an injury or the presence of glass in a shoe. The likelihood of each cause being the true one could then be argued and assessed in court.

Another kind of false reasoning can cause a great deal of trouble in court. Often a psychologist will report that a child who was interviewed exhibited certain attributes or mannerisms; say, he or she tended to avoid looking the psychologist in the eye or bit his or her nails while sitting and listening. The child may also have told the interviewer that he or she had dreams of a particular kind. Referring to the results from his own and other studies, the psychologist may find that 80 per cent of abused

children exhibited the first mannerism, 75 per cent exhibited the second and 90 per cent had dreams of the kind described. He would then conclude that the child he interviewed was very likely to have been abused.

Is this a valid conclusion? On the face of it, it seems reasonable enough, but closer examination will show that it is deeply flawed. Without ever having examined an abused child, I can say, without fear of contradiction, that they all share another attribute in common: 100 per cent of abused children breathe. This attribute – breathing – is even more strongly correlated with abused children than is any one of the other attributes that led the psychologist to conclude that the child had been abused. It is not how often a particular attribute is manifested in the behaviour of abused children that matters, it is whether such a characteristic is shared by other children as well. The question that should be asked is whether, and how often, children that have not been abused also show these characteristics. In the case of breathing the answer is perfectly clear, since we all know that all living children breathe. When it comes to mannerisms or dreams the answer is not so apparent; most people, including jury members, do not know how common such attributes are among children in general. The psychologist's conclusions, presented with statistical support, can appear to be rigorously scientific, when, in fact, they are not. The results and the conclusions present only half the picture; without the other half we cannot possibly arrive at a valid conclusion.

Scientific Method

Contrary to some popular beliefs, science is a highly uncertain endeavour. It does not deal in certainties, but probabilities. Those accustomed to thinking of science as the production of high-tech equipment may be surprised by this assertion. In the minds of many non-scientists, "science" is computers, lasers and rockets to the Moon; but this is to confuse science with technology. While technological advances do, indeed, owe much to scientific research, the two activities are by no means the same thing.

Science is the activity concerned with the rational understanding of the natural world; technology is the production of machines or other processes designed to bring about a particular result. Technology uses science; and science uses technology. I mention this because many people look askance at the assertion that science is concerned with probabilities not certainties; perhaps they feel it is false modesty, or even an affectation, on the part of scientists. They will say that the television always works when it is switched on (unless it is broken); that the light comes on when the switch is flicked. Surely, then, science always works.

This is to misunderstand what scientists (as opposed to developers of technology) are trying to do. Scientists seek to explain why things are the way they are. Such explanations (or hypotheses) are put forward, tested as rigorously as possible and, if they withstand these tests, they are accepted as theories, until such time as they are shown not to work. In other words, scientists do not seek to "prove" theories – they do not believe they can do such a thing – rather, they fail to disprove them. Having bombarded an idea with arguments and experiments, if the idea emerges unscathed, then it is accepted – for the time being.

So, science is concerned with probabilities at all levels of organization. Physicists cannot say where a particular electron will be at a given moment – they can only say where it is most likely to be. Animal behaviourists cannot say which way the antelope will flee when it sees a lion – they can only suggest the most likely direction. Probability is a very common word in the vocabulary of scientists. Forensic scientists are no exception; they, too, must evaluate evidence on the basis of probability.

So, when interpreting the crime scene or the evidence taken from it for laboratory examination, one is looking, not for what happened, but what probably happened. A report is eventually produced that presents the results in terms of probability.

But, you may ask, the probability of what? The scenario, in other words the mentally reconstructed idea of what *may* have happened is, strange to say, often quite a different things in the mind of the police officer and in the mind of the forensic scientist. Police officers are apt to ask whether the story of the accused man is likely to be true, in view of the forensic evidence found at the scene. Forensic scientists ask the question the other way round; they ask whether the evidence is likely, in view of the story of the accused.

Who is right? Is it not all an exercise in semantics anyway? No, it is not; and the forensic scientist is right and the police officer is wrong. Before you say: "He would say that, wouldn't he?", or "The police officer is clearly the one with his feet on the ground", or "Trust a pedantic academic to come up with such nonsense!", consider the following.

The evidence at the scene is a fact; one either did or did not find a smoking gun on the floor. What may have happened is a hypothesis, an opinion, an idea – call it what you will – but is not a fact. So, if the investigating officer asks me whether it is likely that Bloggs was at the scene, in view of the fact that his gun was found there, my answer will have to be yes, it is likely.

How helpful is this? In truth, not much. One does not need a forensic scientist to tell one the obvious. But if the officer had asked me whether the evidence is likely, in view of Bloggs' story, I am able to say much more useful things. Why? Because I am no longer restricted to one possible scenario, namely, that Bloggs went to the scene and left his gun there. I would be left free to consider many other scenarios, many other possibilities and I would be able to assess, not only the possibility of each one, but to offer an opinion as to which one is the most likely – the one with the highest probability. Presenting the question the way the police officer did, leaves no room for manoeuvre – the answer to his question had to be yes, it is probable, but, much more dangerously, it closed the door that could have led to the consideration of other possibilities. It told us that it was, indeed, probable that Bloggs frequented the scene, but what else was probable would never have been known.

Let us now look at the techniques at the disposal of the forensic scientist – the armoury itself. To pursue this military analogy, the choice of weapons will depend upon the nature of the problem. But it is also true that each problem brings with it special challenges to the forensic mind; and we will have occasion to learn more of the forensic mind as we pass through the arsenal.

Left: *Collecting evidence. Paint samples are taken from a car that was involved in a collision. Paint traces from the other vehicle will have been left.*

Right: *The next step. By matching the paint trace (on the glass slide) to known samples, the exact colour can be found. A match to a suspected car justifies further investigation.*

POLICE LINE DO NOT CROSS

The scene. It is a word that has a very special meaning to a forensic scientist. It evokes not a beautiful vista of sea or mountains. Rather, it conjures up a picture of tragedy, misery and squalor, for the "scene" is not scenic.

The scene of a crime is also, usually, a chaotic place. The police would have been the first to arrive there, alerted by a telephone call that something was amiss. What they do in those first few moments may affect everything that happens afterwards. The classic image of policemen trampling all over the evidence before the specialists are called is not wholly unfounded, but these days scene-of-crime officers, or SOCOs as they are called, take a look at the scene from the outset, with the aim of avoiding any such damage from taking place.

Examining the Scene

The SOCO takes a general look at the situation. The dead body clearly requires the attendance of a pathologist; the blood splattered on the walls and floor suggests that a specialist in these matters be called in; the maggots in the body point to the need for an entomologist. Fingerprints too will have to be sought and, if found, "lifted". All the relevant specialists are briefed over the telephone and they arrive as soon as they can.

The photographer will have taken a number of preliminary photographs, starting from the outside of the house, working inwards toward the spot where the body is lying. But his task does not end there. He waits for the specialists, who will ask him to take further photographs of this or that. The SOCO prepares a diagram of the scene, makes notes, records the presence of items of interest, hopefully with the minimum of disturbance to the situation as he found it. Nowadays video-recording of the scene is becoming the norm, but this is in addition to, not instead of, "still" photography.

In a case of murder or suspicious death the first person to examine the body is usually a police surgeon or other doctor, not a forensic pathologist. The doctor must establish whether the person in question is, indeed, dead. In many, perhaps most, cases this will be perfectly obvious, but in some cases it will not. The police surgeon will examine the body, perhaps feeling for a pulse. Then a stethoscope will be used to detect any sounds of breathing and of the heart beating. Contrary to popular images, the doctor will not use a mirror or a feather to determine whether there is life in the body; there is no alternative to a proper medical examination.

Once the specialists, or "experts", as the police, with touching faith, call them, start to arrive, what happens next? The textbook account will say that the expert will don protective clothing and, knowing what evidence to look for, will set to work at once, collecting items and placing them in polythene bags, labelling them, getting photographic records, making supplementary notes

Below: *Examining the scene. In this reconstruction of a murder scene, a permanent photographic record of the scene is made before removing the victim or collecting any other evidence. A ruler provides a scale.*

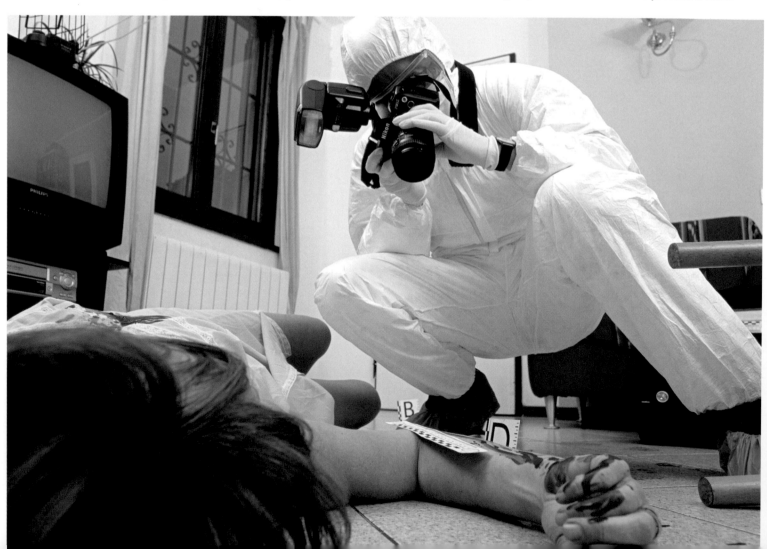

and generally behaving as though this scene was much like the last, with the evidence obligingly obvious. The reality is very different. A crime is not a laboratory experiment, with everything in its proper place and all the conditions known. Indeed, great care must be taken to ensure that evidence is not mishandled or contaminated. It will be the task of the forensic scientist, faced with the end results of a series of events, to deduce what those conditions might have been. In this sense, it is the reverse process to a classic laboratory experiment.

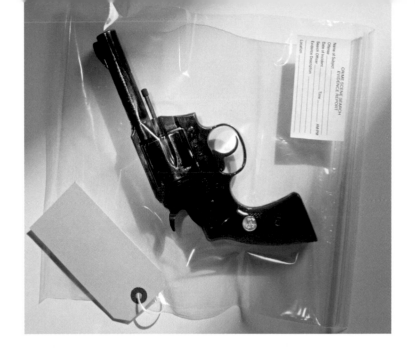

Right: *A handgun in an evidence bag. Note the labels for collection details (where, when, how, who) and the chain of custody signatures.*

Below: *A New York City police officer inspects a murder scene. The victim was shot by serial killer Darnell Collins. The area has been cordoned off to facilitate the search for evidence.*

Continuity of Evidence

A MOST IMPORTANT matter associated with scene investigation is the continuity of evidence. Any mistakes made during the initial examination of the scene will affect the rest of the investigation, so it must be absolutely clear where, when and how a particular item of evidence was taken; and by whom. The evidence must be packaged and labelled in such a way that there can be no doubt as to its "history". This chain of custody is maintained by keeping a record of signatures on the label on the container – bag or glass tube – when it is handed from person to person. Thus, the SOCO signs the container when the evidence is taken and packaged; when he hands it to a forensic scientist, both people sign and date it. When the scientist returns the item to the police, it is again signed by both parties; and so on. This ensures that the court will be satisfied that the piece of evidence being discussed at the trial is, in reality, the same as the piece of evidence taken from the scene. This does not, of course, guarantee that the evidence has not been switched at some point, but it makes it a good deal less likely. At any rate, it is the most that can be done.

Expect the Unexpected

Above: *The specialists take over. Italian forensic entomologist Margherita Turchetto collects insect evidence from a corpse. Once the body is removed, the ground beneath can be checked for further clues.*

A good look at the scene, with the least disturbance to it, is essential. There then follows some talking, the scientist asking the police officer and the SOCO for further information about one or other aspect. The specialists will often consult with one another, coming to some agreement as to who should conduct an examination first. Should it be the pathologist? Or would that damage the possible fingerprint evidence that may be retrieved? Should it be the entomologist? Or would that make the pathologist's examination more difficult? Perhaps the blood-splattering specialist should go first, since the patterns on the floor would be trampled upon, if someone else were to go before him. And so on.

Things are often not at all what they seem and it is very easy to make incorrect interpretations as a result of preconceived ideas.

To counter this tendency, there is only one thing that can and should be done; one must expect the unexpected.

I was once taken to task for making that remark. What an affectation! I was told. Only an academic could say something so silly! The unexpected is, by definition, unexpected, so how could one expect it? The answer is that one can quite easily expect things not to be what they seem to be, even if, at the outset, one does not know what the truth is. One can tell oneself that there may be more than one interpretation, even if one is, initially, totally at a loss.

Consider the following crossword puzzle clue: "More Work".

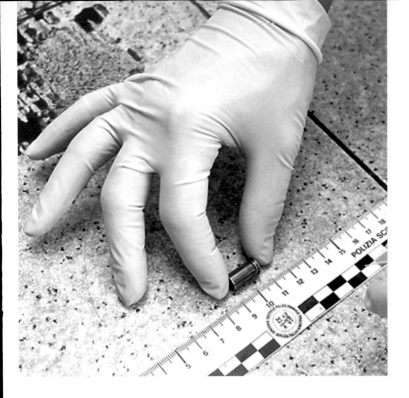

The answer is a word of six letters. The devotees of crossword puzzles will have no difficulty in seeing that the answer may be not at all what it might appear to be. They will tell themselves that the answer may well have nothing to do with additional tasks to be performed, even though it may take them some time to discover what the clue really means. The answer, in fact, is: "Utopia".

The reason this clue presented a challenge is because the answer, while perfectly straightforward, was unexpected. If the answer was elusive it was because not all possible meanings of the two words were considered. The mind has a tendency to select the evidence most in keeping with its expectations and to ignore the evidence that is not.

Left: *Things are not always what they seem. Meticulous recording of every piece of evidence is vital. This spent cartridge shell was photographed where found, then measured, bagged and labelled.*

CASE HISTORY

A Miscarriage of Justice

A woman was found murdered in her house on a Thursday morning; she had been beaten to death. It was known that she had returned home from work at about six o'clock on Tuesday evening. Her husband did not have an alibi for the period between six o'clock and eight o'clock and suspicion fell on him. The prosecution alleged that the murder took place some time during those two hours on Tuesday, since, when her body was discovered, the woman had still been wearing her formal clothes and her work badge. (She worked in a department store.) Evidence had been presented in court that she was in the habit of removing her badge and changing into casual clothes as soon as she returned home. This suggested that she was murdered a little after six o'clock.

I was not involved in this case from the outset; I only became involved after the husband was put on trial, convicted and sent to prison. I was asked by some friends of the convicted man to look into the forensic evidence, since they were convinced of his innocence. I read all the available documentation, both scientific and legal, and examined the photographs taken at the scene. It immediately became clear that a central piece of evidence from the scene had been overlooked, presumably because its significance was not grasped. If it had been, the whole reconstruction of events would have had to be revised.

The documentation revealed that several people testified that the woman was wearing a white blouse on Tuesday afternoon. The photographs of her body showed her wearing a black blouse, with the work badge appended to it. Since it is hardly likely that she changed her clothes, removing the white blouse and putting on, uncharacteristically, a formal black blouse, on Tuesday evening, then appended the badge once again after she changed, her death must have happened on the following morning, Wednesday. However, it was known that she did not go to work on Wednesday, so the conclusion one has to arrive at is that she was killed just before she was about to leave for work that Wednesday morning, not on Tuesday evening. The badge was appended because she was about to go to work, not because she had just returned from work. I can see no other possible explanation.

It is worth mentioning, as a matter of interest, that the husband did have an alibi for Wednesday morning. In spite of the emergence of this new evidence, he has not been released from prison.

This example shows how things may not be what they seem to be at a scene. No-one considered the evidence of the blouse; everyone was concerned wholly with the evidence of the badge. The result was a miscarriage of justice.

Arousing Suspicion

A doctor will arrive at any scene of death in order to certify that the person is actually dead. In most cases the matter will be quite straightforward. The police will be involved only if the doctor notices anything that arouses suspicion. However, in most murder cases, the police arrive before the doctor, because they are alerted by someone, or something, else. But, in cases that are not at first regarded as suspicious, much depends on the certifying doctor's ability to recognize suspicious signs and to notify the police.

What is a suspicious sign? There are no rules for this kind of thing. Some signs are so obviously suspicious that there is no difficulty at all in recognizing them. An empty bottle of poison lying beside the bed is an example. However, there are more subtle signs; the doctor might feel that the body is not lying in an altogether natural manner. Inquiries may reveal that the deceased had collapsed and died and fell to the floor, whereupon his family picked up the body and placed it on the bed, showing that there was an innocent explanation. In other cases there may be no convincing explanation for the body's unnatural position. The doctor may notice a bruise on the deceased's neck, or what may appear initially to be a minor injury on the head. Were these caused by foul play, or can they, too, be innocently explained? Much depends on the doctor's ability and readiness to look for such signs; in the words of one forensic pathologist, the late Professor Keith Simpson, "the doctor is the watchdog of the public, and must keep an ever-open eye for the kinds of death that require an explanation."

In cases in which suspicion is aroused, the doctor must refer the matter to the Coroner without delay. The referral is usually made through the police. The Coroner's duty is to order an investigation. However, there are some cases of suspicious death – or "sussy" deaths, to use the somewhat grotesque patois of forensic pathologists – that are automatically regarded as suspicious; these are the sudden deaths of young people, previously not known to have suffered from a life-threatening illness. Such a death is treated with suspicion from the outset and is investigated accordingly.

I have often felt it odd that so many people seem to be unaware that post-mortems are obligatory in cases of suspicious death. This point was made very well in the television production of an Inspector Morse story, *Service Of All The Dead*, by Colin Dexter.

The victim was found dead, with a knife in his back, but forensic examination revealed that he had received an overdose of morphine as well. The murderer had drugged his victim, unwittingly using a lethal dose of morphine, with the purpose of changing his clothes (this is much easier to do with a living person than a dead one), then stabbed him. The forensic findings were important in the story, but the point here is that the culprit did not realize that a post-mortem examination would take place.

Removing a body from the scene is not always a straightforward matter. During daylight hours a group of ghoulishly interested by-standers may collect outside the door of a house and the policeman outside has the duty of persuading them to maintain a respectful distance. The body itself may not be easy to move without damaging some of the evidence, not least that concerned with the very position of the body when it was found. Inevitably, lifting the body and moving it to the ambulance will alter the position to a greater or lesser extent. The chalkline drawn around the body before removal, often featured in crime films, is what actually happens, wherever this is feasible. (It is not always feasible, however, such as when a body is lying on a crumpled-up white sheet.)

The body is usually removed to a mortuary or to a hospital equipped to deal with post-mortem examinations. The work of the pathologist and other specialists at this stage will be discussed in later chapters; for the present we will concern ourselves only with the scene.

And yet, again, what exactly is the scene? Is the scene simply where the body was found, or is it where the murder actually took place? The two are not necessarily the same. Very often, a body is removed by the murderer from the place in which the deed was committed. An important part of the investigation must be to find out whether the body had been moved from another place and, if so, where that other place might be.

There are two questions here; we will start with the simpler one – has the body been moved? After death, the blood stops circulating and, under the force of gravity, it sinks to those parts of the body that are lying lowermost, causing purplish patches to appear. This phenomenon is known as hypostasis. So, if one finds a body with purple blotches on that side of the body that is uppermost, one can conclude that the body had been moved after death.

Left: *A difficult removal of a body. The dismembered remains of Sandra Lecœuche were recovered from the Deule Canal, France.*

Right: *If at all possible, the position of a body is marked with a chalkline before removing it for post-mortem examination.*

Looking for Clues

Like so much else in criminal investigation, one has to look for clues wherever one can find them. Certain changes that take place when a body is placed in a particular environment can be used to determine not only whether a body has been moved, but from where it has been moved. For example, a body that had been lying in water is easily recognisable as such, even if it is found on dry land. Many of the changes we notice in ourselves after having a bath also occur in a dead body. These include the "goose-flesh" appearance of the skin, which is caused by the cold making the muscles that erect the small hairs on the body contract. In water, the head sinks low, causing the blood to gravitate toward the head and neck, making it more likely for decomposition to start in those areas.

Adipocere formation is another tell-tale sign that the body had been immersed in water or in a very moist place. Adipocere is a waxy substance formed by the action of water on the fatty acid, known as oleic acid, in the tissues. The "hydrogenation" of this acid produces stearic acid; it is essentially the conversion of an oily substance into a harder, more "fatty" substance. It is the same process that turns vegetable oils into margarine.

A mummified body, i.e. one that has dried out with the minimum of decomposition, indicates that it has lain in a dry place. Mummification takes place because the dryness prevents, or at least greatly retards, bacterial decomposition. Dry conditions, aided by air currents, such as one might expect in a chimney or in the desert, make mummification much more likely. The bodies of new-born babies tend to mummify more rapidly than those of adults, because they are, to all intents and purposes, free of bacteria.

Below: *Maggots can provide vital clues. Bluebottles lay their eggs on dead flesh. The age of the resulting maggots gives a minimum time since death. The infestation pattern can give clues about wound positions.*

It is clear that these post-mortem changes can indicate that a body had been moved from a certain type of locality, but they cannot, in themselves, tell us what the actual geographical locality was. Depending on the circumstances of the case, certain actual localities may be suggested, such as when a body showing adipocere formation is found in a house not far from a lake. Clearly, the lake would seem to be the most likely place in which the body had been immersed, but the changes themselves do not allow that conclusion to be reached.

In many cases the insects that infest a body after death can give very valuable clues to the place of death. Insects have known habitat preferences and known geographical distributions, so it is often possible to arrive at conclusions about the kind of place (woodland, grassland, indoors, etc.) in which a body has been previously lying, as well as the part of the country in which it has been. For example, I was consulted on the question of time of death in the famous case of Karen Price, the girl whose skeleton was found wrapped in a carpet and buried in the garden of a house in Cardiff. The insect fauna on the body was mostly of a kind that one would expect on a buried body, but there were also some bluebottle pupal cases. These revealed that Karen's body had lain exposed above ground for some hours before burial, since bluebottles have no means of reaching a buried body. Moreover, despite the fact that they can easily detect a buried body, they will not lay eggs on the surface of the soil in the "expectation", so to speak, that the hatching maggots will burrow through the soil to reach the body. Some flies can do this, but not bluebottles.

Buried bodies have a very characteristic kind of associated insect fauna, which varies according to soil types. A body that had been buried, then exhumed and placed above ground, will carry with it the tell-tale signs of burial. I have had many cases of this sort, in which the presence of a typically subterranean fauna on an exposed corpse revealed the truth. One very common indicator of previous burial is a minute fly, known, quite appropriately, as the Coffin Fly. It hardly ever fails to turn up on buried corpses, whether or not they were coffined.

Above: *This piece of raw beefsteak left exposed quickly attracted the attention of a female bluebottle fly, but the absence of eggs or maggots on a corpse can provide an equally important clue.*

CASE HISTORY

Blood Stains as Clues

The murdered body of a woman was found in a moorland. The police wanted to know whether the murder had taken place at that spot, or whether it had been committed elsewhere, the body being dumped on the moor later. The woman had an injury to the head, which would have bled profusely. (Wounds to the head usually result in much bleeding.) Therefore, if the woman had died on the moor, there would have been a great deal of blood in the soil beneath her head. The forensic scientist consulted on the matter took two squares of turf from beneath the head and another two squares from the ground some distance away from the body. Chemical testing revealed the extent of blood-staining in the first two squares. Animal blood was added to the uncontaminated pieces of turf until the extent of staining matched that in the samples taken from beneath the body. This enabled the investigators to determine how much blood had soaked into the ground. The answer was about half a pint – a good deal, in other words. It was concluded that the murder must have taken place on the spot, since a body dumped there from another place could not possibly have bled to that extent.

Above: *John George Haigh (1909–1949). He admitted to killing nine people in total by shooting them and then dissolving their bodies in acid.*

Even an incompetent investigator is bound to find some clues at the scene. The real challenge comes when there is, initially at least, no scene and no body. The legal dictum of *corpus delicti* means "the body of the crime", but the "body" referred to here is the body of evidence, not the body of a human being. People have been found guilty of murder without the discovery of a body. For example, James Camb was found guilty of the murder of Gay Gibson, whose body he tipped out of a porthole into the sea.

The case of "Acid Bath" Haigh (opposite) has often been used to make two points, neither one of which is strictly, or wholly, true. First, as we have seen, it is said that someone can be tried for murder in the absence of a body. While true in principle, in fact this very rarely happens, the Camb case being one of the notable exceptions. I have known a case in which the body was stolen subsequent to my post-mortem examination; the case never came to trial.

The second point is that it is very difficult, if not impossible, to get rid of a dead body. Again, this is true in the sense that it is certainly no easy matter, but statements of this sort are, in fact, back to front – we know only about those bodies that have been discovered, despite all attempts to destroy them, but we know nothing about those bodies that were never discovered. After all, the bodies of Haigh's first five victims were never found.

Acid is not the only agent that has been used by murderers to dispose of their victims. Quicklime is another such substance, much favoured by writers of whodunits, although, in truth, quicklime is quite useless for the purpose. Lime is an oxide of calcium, having the chemical formula, CaO. When it comes into contact with water it turns into calcium hydroxide, with the formula, $Ca(OH)_2$. This compound, known as slaked lime, is indeed very corrosive, but its effect on buried bodies is not at all what one would expect.

When a body is buried and covered in quicklime, the oxide quickly reacts with water in the soil and in the body itself, turning into the corrosive slaked lime. Some corrosion of the body surface will take place, but the heat from the reaction is so intense that the body becomes quickly dehydrated – mummified, in effect. Mummified bodies, as we have seen, will not easily decompose.

The notorious nineteenth-century murderer, Henry Wainwright, who shot his mistress, Harriet Lane, in 1874, tried to dispose of her body by burying it in half a hundredweight of another form of lime, known as chlorinated lime. The body was so well preserved as a result of this treatment that it was quite easily identified when it was exhumed. Wainwright was hanged.

The Case of "Acid Bath" Haigh

John George Haigh, known to history as "Acid Bath" Haigh, claimed on his arrest for the murder of Olive Durand-Deacon that he could not be found guilty, since the police would not succeed in finding the body. He boasted to Detective Inspector Webb "I have destroyed her with acid. You will find the sludge that remains in Leopold Road. Every trace has gone. How can you prove murder if there is no body?"

Haigh robbed his wealthy victims and put their bodies in a tank of sulphuric acid on the premises of his plastic fingernail-making business. He had already murdered five people before he committed the murder that would end his career. On Friday February 18, 1949, he invited Mrs Olive Durand-Deacon to visit his factory. She was never seen again; and her friend, a Mrs Lane, was worried. She told Haigh that she was going to the police, whereupon he replied: "I'll come along to the police station. I might be able to help." In the words of Professor Keith Simpson, the pathologist who worked on the case, it was "an outsize understatement".

The officer put on the case was a woman police sergeant named Lambourne, who instantly distrusted Haigh. Inquiries into his background revealed that he had a record of theft, fraud and shady dealing, but he had never been suspected of violent crime. After his boast to Inspector Webb, Professor Simpson was asked to pay a visit to the "factory", which was, in fact, nothing but a warehouse. On arrival, he looked at the rough, pebbled ground outside the warehouse and, almost instantly, he stooped and picked up what looked like one of the pebbles.

But it was not a pebble; it was a gallstone; laboratory examination subsequently confirmed that it was a human gallstone – an important point, since animals get them, too. Mrs Durand-Deacon had not disappeared without trace after all.

Professor Simpson, ever ready to give credit where it was due, pronounced his immediate discovery of the gallstone as "impressive"; and I suppose it was.

Further examination of the site revealed some human bones, as well as a set of dentures. These last were shown to Miss Helen Mayo, Mrs Durand-Deacon's dentist. She had no doubt; they were the very dentures she had made for Mrs Durand-Deacon. The case against Haigh was complete. He was put on trial, convicted and hanged at Wandsworth Prison.

Below: *Sightseers outside Haigh's "workshop" in Leopold Road, Crawley where he kept oil drums, sulphuric acid and other equipment.*

In cases like that of "Acid Bath" Haigh, there is no body, but there is a scene. In other words, there is a fairly well-defined area in which one could look for clues. But what can one possibly do if there is no body and no scene? What if someone disappears and is presumed murdered? Where does one begin?

Clearly, such a situation presents considerable practical difficulties, although, in the eye of the law, this does not necessarily mean that no conviction of a suspect can be made. Very frequently, the mysterious disappearance of a person can be linked to the activities of some other person. The police will make inquiries about the missing person by interviewing friends, relations, work-mates and others, one of which, for one reason or another, may well come to be suspected by the police. Nevertheless, it is must be remembered that many people disappear without trace every year and are never found. It is said that about 25,000 such people go missing annually in the United Kingdom alone.

Once the police have a suspect, they will begin by searching his house and garden; as well as any other places he might frequent. Is the body anywhere in the vicinity? This is the time for heavy spadework, quite literally. Although there is no substitute for digging, many new forensic techniques have been developed that narrow down considerably the area that needs to be searched.

An example of such a method is ground-penetrating radar. A short pulse of electromagnetic energy is transmitted into the ground and, if there is an object present in the soil, a characteristic reflection will be received. This happens because the buried object will cause an alteration in the electrical properties of the soil. The information appears on a monitor that shows the pattern of the pulses. This technique was used successfully in the notorious Frederick West case in Gloucester, England, where the buried bodies of nine murder victims were recovered.

In this case the technique saved a great deal of time, effort and money, but the location of the bodies was never really in doubt. When a very large area is concerned, such as an area covering, say, half a county, other techniques have to be used. Aerial reconnaissance is very useful in such cases. It is much easier to discern a pattern on the landscape from a distance, much as one would "see" a painting better if one stood some feet away from it. A feature visible from the air may not be visible on the ground. Aerial reconnaissance is particularly valuable if older aerial photographs of the area are available, since these could be compared with the newer photographs taken during the

Above: *Frederick West (1941–1995). Using ground-penetrating radar the bodies of nine murder victims were found at his home in Gloucester: six were buried under the cellar and bathroom and three under the patio.*

investigation. Any differences in the landscape, such as vegetational or structural differences, may help to focus the search on an area that seems to have been disturbed. Spy-plane and satellite photographs were used to detect the presence of mass graves in Bosnia-Herzegovina, in particular the mass graves at Srebrenica.

Aerial photographs for forensic purposes are much more useful if they can be taken from different angles, in order to exploit the fact that differences in shading may highlight certain features. Also, regardless of shadows, some surface features may be more easily visible from one angle than from another.

Various methods of enhancing the contrast between different areas of the landscape have been in use in geological surveying and for military purposes for many years, although their application to forensic investigations is very recent. Thermal imaging is one such technique. It makes use of the fact that the heat lost from disturbed soil (such as a burial pit) and that lost from undisturbed soil is different. A buried, decomposing body would release more heat than the surrounding soil. Clearly, this would help to narrow down the area of, say, a large field that needs to be investigated.

Multispectral imaging is based on the fact that different materials absorb and reflect the various bands in the electromagnetic spectrum differently. This information can be presented visually on a monitor and it is possible, at least in principle, to use this technique to locate spots on the landscape whose spectral pattern is not explicable on the basis of the known characteristics of the area. To my knowledge, this method

Right: *Aerial view of a murder scene. In 2003, 17-year-old Hannah Foster's body was found beside the hedge, centre left, where the undergrowth has been cleared. Aerial photos can help in the search for clues.*

Below: *This aerial shot gives an overall view of the scene in Surrey, England where the body of a murdered company director was found. On the ground, the photographer is taking more detailed close-up shots.*

has hardly been exploited at all in forensic science, although it has long been used in the study of the fabric of old buildings, especially churches.

The methods of geophysical prospection, long used by geologists and archaeologists, have also been applied to forensic science. One method involves the measurement of soil resistance.

Above: *Specialized techniques. Magnetometers can be used to locate buried bodies. Here, one is being used to locate unmarked graves in an abandoned overgrown poorhouse cemetery in Washington, DC.*

Here, the investigator pushes two metal probes into the ground, then passes an electrical current between them. The resistance is measured; it will be lower in moist soils than in drier, stonier soils, since water is a good conductor of electricity. The characteristics of a grave can be detected, since the resistance of the soil in it will be different from the surrounding soil. This resistance will often be lower than the surroundings, since the grave is likely to be more moisture-retaining than the adjacent areas, but it may sometimes be higher if the grave is filled with rubble or stones and if the body itself is wrapped, say, in a polythene bag.

Magnetometry is a technique that detects local changes in the Earth's magnetic field. A magnetometer is a device carried at a constant height above ground; it can register magnetic differences in iron-bearing soils. If the soil at a particular spot contains a buried body, it will contain fewer magnetic particles than the surrounding soil, thus registering a difference on the magnetometer.

These methods, which detect differences in the electrical resistance or magnetic properties of different areas of the ground, are not metal detectors as such. The classic metal detector of the amateur treasure-hunter is an electromagnetic device that can detect the presence of metallic objects, such as coins, buttons and watches. The finding of such artefacts, if modern, may give an indication as to whether a body is in the vicinity, although the presence of such objects does not, of course, mean that a body is lying buried in the area. In any case, the object being sought may not necessarily be a body; it may be a stolen item of jewellery, for example.

It is an interesting – and useful – fact that buried objects do not soon disappear into the structure of the subterranean soil and stones, as is generally supposed. The surface of the Earth is formed of stratified layers, although these layers may often be disturbed by human activity, which itself creates new layers. A buried body will create a new such layer, which will persist – and remain detectable – for a very long time. Another interesting fact that archaeologists often point out is that an object discovered

buried very deeply in the soil is not necessarily older than one that is found nearer the surface. Areas that have been intensively used be human beings may have relatively recent layers lying very deep in the ground; conversely, some very ancient layers in areas that have seen very little human activity may lie very near the surface. Also, although it is generally true that murder victims are usually buried in very shallow graves, this is not always the case by any means.

Searching for a buried body requires more than a set of sophisticated techniques. At any rate, the search investigators should be very flexible in their approach, using whatever methods or evidence come to hand. In Colorado, USA, an interesting series of experiments was carried out some years ago. Using buried pig carcasses, various methods were brought to bear to discover their whereabouts. The study showed the need to use a multi-disciplinary approach in the search for concealed bodies. As so often in forensic science, there are few easy routes to the answer; it is as Thomas Edison said: genius is one per cent inspiration and 99 per cent perspiration.

High-tech methodology is not always used in the search for bodies; in fact, it is still the norm not to use them. Such techniques are expensive to use and are conducted by highly paid practitioners, so the initial stages, at least, of a search are usually conducted using low-budget techniques. In any case, high-tech methods are not always applicable to the actual circumstances of a case.

Dogs are, famously, used to find both living people and dead bodies, buried or exposed. They can even detect bodies that are lying underwater and are routinely used in some parts of the USA for this purpose. During the Arab-Israeli Wars, dogs were used to find the bodies of soldiers buried up to one metre (more than three feet) deep. The olfactory abilities of dogs, although well-known, are actually much more developed and impressive than is usually supposed, as we shall see in chapter four.

CASE HISTORY

The Abduction Of Stephanie Slater

Stephanie Slater was abducted by Michael Samms in 1992 and kept alive for eight days in a cold coffin in Newark in Nottinghamshire, England. The ransom for her safe return was found buried in a field in Lincolnshire. The hoard of bank notes, totalling about £150,000, was eventually discovered, after a painstaking investigation. The known movements of the suspect, eyewitness accounts, the advice of archaeologists and the military, and even psychological reports, were all used to narrow down the area of search. When the "suspect" field was identified, the cache was found using ground-penetrating radar. Miss Slater was later released unharmed.

Buried Bodies

Let us consider what one might actually do when searching for a buried body in a field. What tell-tale signs would one expect to find? Most soil is covered by vegetation of one kind or another and this would have been disturbed by the digging of the grave, so it makes sense to look for such disturbed areas. However, the burial may have taken place some time earlier and the vegetation may have regrown. But would it be the same vegetation? The presence of a body beneath the surface will encourage the growth of some plant species and retard the growth of others, since some plants prefer a highly fertile soil while others do not. Also, the high moisture content above the grave would also favour some species at the expense of others. Alternatively, if the buried body had been wrapped in polythene wrapping, or covered with stones, the moisture content may well be depressed, a fact that would be reflected in the type of vegetation above it.

More often, it is not so much the species of plant, but the vigour of vegetational growth, that will reveal the site of a grave. Again, one would expect a stronger vegetation growth above a body buried unwrapped and covered only with soil; while a wrapped body placed beneath stones will result in a less vigorous growth. Either way, any change of growth vigour or species composition from the general surroundings will indicate that the spot had been disturbed and was worth investigating. Differences in plant growth may be seen in drought-afflicted areas, where the area above a shallowly buried and uncovered body will reveal a much lusher plant growth. Such changes, however, are not always easily discernible from the ground; as we have seen, aerial reconnaissance is more likely to reveal such differences, but, in practice, climbing a tree and examining the surroundings from that vantage point is often very effective. Examination of such sites when the sun is low (either rising or setting) is more likely to show up the differences more clearly, because of the shadows that are cast.

When a grave is dug, much more soil is removed than can be put back in, since the body itself will fill much of the hole. Therefore, the surrounding area is likely to be covered, to a greater or lesser extent, by the removed soil. Also, the deeper the grave, the wider the adjacent area of disturbance is likely to be, since there will be much more soil lying about. Footprints and other marks may be discernible around the grave. In order to address this problem of excess soil, the perpetrator might compact the refilled soil with foot or spade, but this in itself will bring about a difference in vegetation growth.

Usually, a small mound of earth is apparent over the grave. With time, this will be compacted and sink, to become a depression. Compaction will be greater in deeper graves, resulting in a deeper depressions. Another event that causes compaction is the decay of the body itself and the collapse of its skeletal structure. Indeed, two depressions, separated in time, may occur; one due to the compaction of the soil and another due to the collapse of the abdominal cavity of the body. The impression left is of a smaller depression within a larger one. Moreover, when compaction of the soil takes place, cracks will appear at the edges of the grave where it meets the undisturbed ground – another sign of the presence of a pit.

The examination of such sites with artificial light in the dark might make it easier to detect them, because of the shadows that will be cast. Snow-covered ground is particularly revealing of irregularities.

When searching for a burial place all sorts of factors and kinds of evidence have to be taken into account. For example,

Below: The Moors Murders. Lesley Ann Downey's body was found near Greenfield, UK in 1965. Here police are searching for further evidence by probing the ground with sticks, and by straightforward digging.

geological records of the area to be searched may reveal that large tracts cannot hold a buried body, since the bedrock is shallow and very hard, confining the probable site of burial to a more limited section of the suspected area. The kind of soil trapped in the tyres of the suspect's car should reveal valuable clues. Gullies and ravines on the landscape are usually worth searching, since they are often used to bury bodies, because their depth allows easy burial. This fact was used to good effect during the investigation of the Moors Murders.

It is by no means easy to construct and camouflage a hastily and clandestinely dug grave. The perpetrators of crimes almost always try to dispose of the bodies of their victims in the easiest way and in a place that they believe is unlikely to be examined. For example, the bodies of many murder victims are concealed beneath the floorboards of houses, presumably in the belief that no-one would think of looking there. In fact, it is the first place one looks – I have looked under more floorboards than I care to remember. The attraction of the floorboards is that they are usually invisible in most modern houses with fitted carpets; this, together with the presence of tables, chairs and other furniture, tends to make the space under the floorboards appear remote and, as a hiding place of a body, unthinkable.

Hiding a body indoors has the advantage of allowing the perpetrator to work undisturbed, so bodies buried under the floorboards are usually, but not always, very well buried. I have known cases in which the body had been placed directly under the floorboards – in such cases the odour, if nothing else, betrays the crime. In other cases, the body is not simply deposited in the space beneath the floorboards, but under the concrete base that lies about a foot or so below them. The concrete has to be broken first, of course; then a pit is dug, the body buried and,

Above: *The Moors Murderers, Ian Brady and Myra Hindley. Between 1963 and 1965 they killed five children and buried four of them on Saddleworth Moor. To this day, Keith Bennett's body has not been found.*

finally, new concrete put in place. Even these measures fail to deceive, this method of concealing a body being so common.

People's physical abilities and psychological tendencies must also be considered when searching for a clandestine grave. For example, most people cannot carry a dead body very far. A corpse is usually heavy and unwieldy, as well as being something that people generally do not want to carry. This means that corpses are disposed of as soon and as easily as possible. It is a good deal more likely to find a buried body downhill than uphill, simply because people find it much easier to dump a body down a slope, rather than carry it up a hill. Indeed, published work indicates that about 90 per cent of bodies are discovered downhill.

Excavating the Grave

THE EXCAVATION OF A GRAVE has to be carried out carefully. Until the very recent past, suspected graves were dug, rather than excavated, by policemen with spades and shovels, resulting in the destruction or loss of much of the evidence. Nowadays, archaeological methods of excavation are employed. It is important to limit the excavation to the genuine space of the burial pit, recognized by the difference in soil structure and compaction. As we have seen, the edge of the dug-out area of soil is often visible when the soil settles with the passage of time. This "cut" may not be easily discernible, since hastily-dug graves almost always have a jagged outline, making careful excavation more difficult. If digging is carried out indiscriminately, ignoring the delimitation of the dug area, extraneous evidence may be dug up, confusing the investigation. For example, a button may be unearthed; if it had come out of the genuine grave space, it would be evidence relevant to the case, but if it had come from that part of the soil outside the confines of the pit, then it is clearly not relevant, or at least highly unlikely to be relevant. At any rate, it is essential to document exactly where the item came from, so that a proper reconstruction can be made.

The Disappearance of Two Lovers

Hashmat Ali and Sharifan Bibi had been cohabiting in a manner that incurred the severe disapproval of their families. At first, it was thought that the couple had gone to Pakistan, but inquiries revealed that this was not so, and it soon became obvious that they had been murdered. Suspicion fell on the girl's two brothers. A house that used to belong to the family was examined and it was found that the flagstones in the cellar had been concreted over. Removal of the concrete revealed that the flagstones had been disturbed and broken. A bad smell emanated from the floor; and excavation work revealed the presence of a pit. This was systematically investigated and, although no bodies were found, some suggestive items came to light. A finger nail was recovered and, more significantly, soap and ice-cream wrappers were found. These had on them the batch numbers that could be dated by the manufacturers, thus narrowing down the time of death.

The above work was carried out by specialist forensic archaeologists skilled in the proper excavation of graves. My own involvement came when I was asked to examine large quantities of the rather heavy clay soil removed from the pit, with the purpose of finding any living things that might shed light on the crime. Alas, after several days of very messy work, nothing was found. This may seem a somewhat sterile end to the story, but it serves to show the reality of forensic investigation – sometimes a great deal of hard work comes to nothing. This does not mean that the investigation, as a whole, failed. Far from it; the two brothers were tried for murder and convicted.

Mass Graves

A murder is a horrific thing; a multiple murder more horrific still. The genocide of the Jews by the Nazis; the Bosnian massacres of recent years; the events in Kosova, Cambodia and Rwanda – these must be among the most dreadful things imaginable.

In Rwanda, behind the church at Kibuye on the shore of lake Kivu, a large number of bodies were buried after their massacre. No-one knew exactly how many bodies were there; estimates ranged from a few hundred to 2,000. Six months after the massacre, the grave was opened. In situations like this, the investigators must try to arrive at an estimate of the least number of people interred; in other words, the smallest number of people that had definitely been killed. The difficulty over what may appear a simple matter of counting the bodies lies in the fact that the bodies are usually decomposed; parts are missing and the bones are broken into small fragments and mixed up together in such a way that it is impossible, in most cases, to determine any discrete bodies.

A particular bone, often the bones of the skull collectively, is used as a marker. If one can find a definite number of separately recognisable skulls, then the number of bodies in the grave must be at least that number, possibly more. In Kibuye, the figure arrived at was 460. Other grim facts emerged; from a study of the way the wounds were inflicted, it was concluded that at least 65 per cent were bludgeoned to death – about 300 people. Another conclusion was that 44 per cent were children – about 202 children. Thus, the detached methods of forensic science reveal the extent of human barbarity.

The bones of the dead, if left exposed above ground, will scatter over the surface, as a result of the activity of wild animals. The study of such scattering is called taphonomy, and it is a subject that, until very recently, was the province of palaeontologists interested in the patterns of distribution of fossil bones and what such patterns can reveal about the past. The extent to which skeletons are disarticulated and scattered is often correlated with time since death. Although such estimates are necessarily very general or vague, forensic science now uses such techniques to arrive at a general reconstruction, before the reconstruction can be fine-tuned using more precise methods. But it is not only the activity of wild animals that affects the positions of bones; the results of human activity can often explain what happened before death.

The Bosnian countryside is littered with such bones. Reconstructing events prior to the death of the individuals concerned is all-too-often an easy matter. Near Kravica, the bones of a youth, who could not have been more than 17, lie on a stretcher, the long bones jutting out of the trouser leg. The bones of older men lie beside the stretcher. All were shot as they were trying to take the injured boy to safety. Down the hill, toward some woods, there are more skeletons. People had been fleeing to the woods for safety and were shot in the back as they fled.

It is estimated that 5,000 people died in the massacre at Srebrenica; and that about 8,000 are still missing, probably dead. John Gearns, an American forensic scientist investigating the Bosnian massacres, ordered the placing of plastic sheeting, weighed down with soil, over all the burial sites in the area, since the bodies of the dead had attracted the attentions of scavenging wild animals.

Dr William Haglund, an American forensic anthropologist, investigating mass graves near Nova Kasaba, used a T-shaped rod, one inch in diameter, to find bodies. Pushing it into the soil, then taking it out and sniffing it, he tried to detect the odour of human decay. When such an odour is detected, the digging

Below: *In April 1994, civil war erupted in Rwanda. Refugees fled to camps such as this in Goma, Zaire. Initially, thousands died of cholera and were buried in mass graves. International aid eased their plight.*

begins. Many of the victims had their hands tied behind their backs, to be thrown "ignobly in a hole" in the words of Dr Haglund. Many had their skulls shattered by high velocity bullets. The shell casings found among tightly packed bodies suggest that some of the wounded were shot as they lay among the dead. The way the bodies were lying suggested to Dr Haglund that the "scene is consistent with these people having been lined up along the side of the road and shot". It was dangerous work; mines had to be cleared and the excavation had to be conducted under the protection of NATO guards. It was also harrowing work. "You use one part heart and whole part brain", said the Chilean forensic scientist, David Del Pino.

Dr Haglund and his colleague, Dr Clyde Snow, have also investigated mass graves near Vukovar, Croatia. At the Ovcara Farm outside the town, a detailed map was drawn of every

Above: *This badly decomposed victim of the civil war in Croatia was one of many from a mass grave site on the river Danube.*

Right: *A mass grave being uncovered in Vlasenica, Bosnia in 2003. Investigators must try to piece together the bodies to get an estimated tally before attempting to identify the victims.*

object found – every bone, every bullet was documented. Snow took down the descriptions of missing people from friends and relations and entered them into a computer database for later comparison with reconstructed individuals. It is slow and painstaking work; and very little of it has reached the scientific journals.

Such is the spirit of place. Forensic investigators must adapt – scientifically and emotionally – to the special requirements of each scene of tragedy as though it were unique. No two murders are the same.

TIME WILL TELL

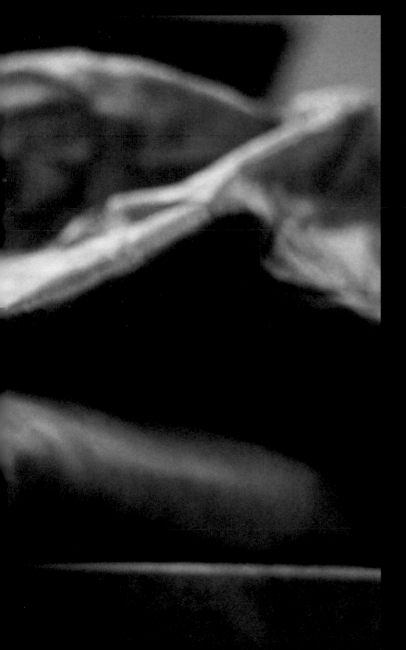

When was the murder committed? This question is one of the most frequently asked during a murder investigation. Whodunits and mystery novels almost always have an answer, which is usually provided by the doctor at the scene.

So widespread is the perception that estimating the time of death is a simple, routine matter, that it might come as a shock to learn that, of all forensic science questions, it is probably the most difficult to answer. In fact, when the first few days after death have passed, conventional forensic pathology has little to contribute to this question.

This does not mean that there are no methods available for dating the time of death. In fact, there is a whole armoury of techniques, but none of them can be applied routinely to any and all cases, except, perhaps, for some of the conventional pathology methods.

Body Temperature and Decomposition

In principle, anything that changes with time can be used as a clock, as long as we understand how that clock works. Almost as soon as someone dies, their body begins to cool down. The relationship between the rate of cooling and the passage of time is reasonably well understood, although practical problems do arise. Under what may be called "room temperature", a dead body will lose heat at a rate of about 1.5 degrees Celsius an hour during the first six hours after death. The rate of cooling slows down very slightly during the following 12 hours, being about 1–1.5 degrees per hour. By the time 24 hours have elapsed, the body temperature will be the same as that of the surrounding air. The body usually feels cold to the touch about 12 hours after death.

This describes a fairly "typical" situation, but conditions are not always typical. If the deceased had died of asphyxiation or a cerebral haemorrhage, the initial temperature may actually be raised. A naked body will lose heat faster than a clothed body; and one submerged in water will cool more rapidly than one lying on land. In general, larger people lose heat more slowly than ones of slighter build, although this is not always the case.

It is important to take the body temperature – usually taken at the rectum – at the scene, i.e. before removing the body to the mortuary. The air temperature is also taken, so that the

Below: German forensic entomologist Mark Benecke (1970–) examines a corpse for insects and/or their larvae. The age of any larvae present will provide an estimate of minimum time since death.

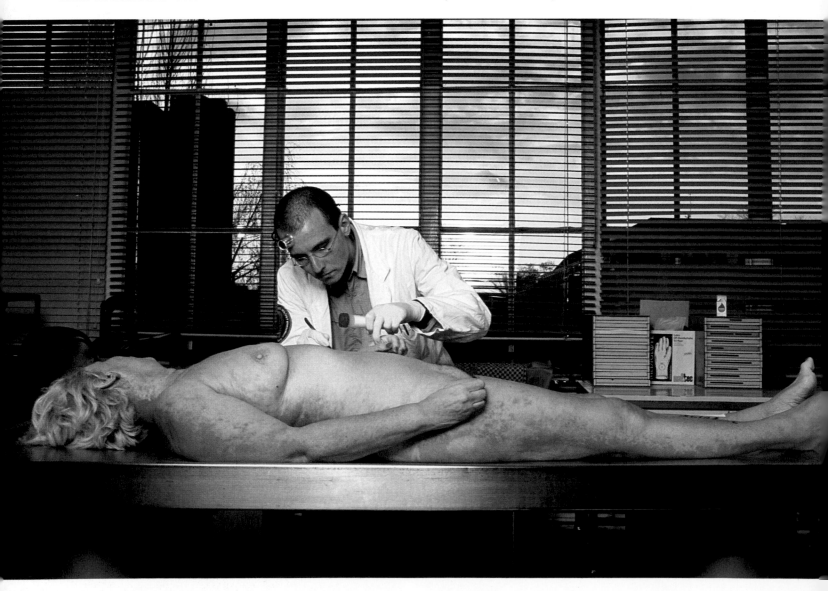

relationship between the two can be established. Ideally, two sets of temperatures should be taken about one hour apart, since this would make the relationship between body and air temperatures clearer. As a general, somewhat rough-and-ready guide to time of death based on temperature, the following formula is sometimes used:

(normal body temperature minus measured body temperature) divided by 1.5 = number of hours since death.

Cooling rate is the classic method of determining time of death in the early stages, but, as we have seen, this method can only be used during a very short period after death. Another change often used is hypostasis, also known as post mortem lividity, which involves the appearance of reddish-purplish coloration in the skin. Hypostasis takes place because blood ceases to circulate after death and, obeying the law of gravity, it sinks to those parts of the body that are lowermost, the red blood cells sinking first. In other words, a body lying face down will exhibit lividity in the abdomen, whereas one lying on its back will show livid patches on the back and the backs of the thighs. Those parts of the body lying compressed against the ground will appear white, since the blood vessels will not be able to fill up. Lividity appears within two hours after death and becomes marked after about four or five hours later, when the initial patches of lividity fuse into a more continuous discoloured area. In the early stages the pressure of the hand will whiten the skin, since the blood will be forced away, but later, when the blood has coagulated, the purplish stain will not disappear under pressure. Like post mortem cooling, hypostasis is a very limited guide to time of death.

Rigor mortis is, perhaps, the best known post mortem change, yet it, too, is highly unreliable as a means of establishing when a person died. Stiffening of the muscles, caused by the accumulation of certain salts in the muscle fibres, appears about 12 hours after death. The face muscles stiffen first, then the shoulders and arms and, finally, the legs. Rigor is at its most pronounced during the next 12 hours, after which it takes another 12 hours to disappear completely, the body losing its rigidity from the face first, followed by the other muscles in the same order as rigidity took place.

A particular form of muscular rigidity, sometimes incorrectly interpreted as rigor, is the phenomenon known as cadaveric spasm, an event much used by writers of whodunits. This occurs at the very moment of death and is expressed as a sudden tightening of muscles, especially of the hand, in which an object, such as a weapon or a piece of paper, may be grasped. This is a rare occurrence and it is not understood why it

Above: *A civilian casualty of the Cambodian War (1970–75) floating in the Mekong River. The bloating of the body shows that he died several days before this picture was taken.*

happens, although when it does occur, it may shed light on the course of events.

The decomposition of the body can give some clues about time of death. About two days after death a "marbling" pattern appears at the neck and shoulders and runs down the arms and sides of the abdomen. At first, this appears red in colour, turning green later. These changes are caused by the invasion of bacteria from the tissues into the blood vessels. At this time the body becomes bloated, filling with gases generated by bacterial metabolism, and the features become unrecognisable. The internal organs are now decomposing and the order in which they decompose may give some pointers to time of death.

At first the stomach and intestines, as well as the heart and the blood in the liver, begin to decompose. Next the lungs and the liver itself break down. This is followed by the brain and the spinal cord. Next, the kidneys, bladder and testis begin to decay, followed by the general body musculature. The uterus and the prostate gland break down last. These, then, are the main gross changes in the body that could be used, in a broad brush-stroke kind of way, to narrow down the time of death. Let us now look at some more specialised techniques.

greenbottles. The flies will lay their eggs in the natural body orifices (ears, nose, eyes, etc.) and the maggots that eventually hatch will feed on the muscle tissues of the remains. They will grow, shed their skins, feed a bit more, shed their skins again, then feed and grow until they have extracted enough nutrients from the body to enable them to pupate. The last maggot stage will then leave the body, burrow in the soil (or crawl under an object, such as a carpet, if indoors) and pupate. Its outer skin becomes hard and it darkens and contracts, forming the pupal case, or puparium. Eventually, the adult fly will emerge from its case and the cycle will start all over again.

As it happens, maggots of various kinds are very intensively studied creatures, not only because of their forensic interest, but also for their relevance to medical and veterinary problems and for the simple fact that, being easy to keep in laboratory colonies, they are used for studies on development and genetics. This knowledge is put to good use in forensic investigations.

The basic question that a maggot can help us to answer is this: "What is the minimum time that has elapsed since death?" In other words, what is the time after which death could not have occurred? For example, if we can estimate the age of a maggot as being, say, five days old, then we can say that death could not have happened later than five days before discovery of the body. Knowing the age of the maggot cannot tell us the actual date of death, since we do not know when the fly arrived at the body, only the minimum time that must have passed since the crime was committed.

If we have reason to believe that the body had been exposed to fly activity almost as soon as it was dead, then we can say that the minimum time since death is the actual time of death. The ability of flies to detect the odour of a dead body, even at the very earliest stages, is so well developed that they will reach it well within an hour after death.

How does one determine the age of a maggot? Like all living things, with the exception of birds and mammals, the rate of development of maggots is determined by the external temperature, since they cannot control their body temperature by internal physiological mechanisms, as we can. Therefore, in order to estimate a maggot's age one has to have a very good idea of the temperatures that prevailed during the course of its

Whten a dead body is exposed in nature it soon becomes attractive to other forms of life. Carnivorous animals will come to eat; insects will arrive to lay their eggs; crows, rats and mice may come to peck or nibble at the remains. All this may sound macabre, but it is a fact of life; moreover, it is a fact that can enable us to estimate the time of death.

Flies of one kind or another are usually the first to arrive at a dead body. Such a body, exposed above ground during the warmer months of the year, will attract bluebottles and development. So, one needs to take the temperature of the maggots in the body, which can be many degrees above the surrounding temperature, adding another complication to the estimation of time of death based on body cooling. In some cases, the air temperature may be of the order of 20°C, whereas the maggot-infested body may have a temperature as high as 40°C.

While it is an easy matter to measure the temperature of the maggots and the surrounding air at the scene, it is much more difficult to estimate the temperatures that prevailed in the days before the body was discovered. Consequently, one has to find another source of information, which is provided by the meteorological offices. Unfortunately, this is only the beginning of the solution.

As we have seen, it is important to take at least two sets of temperature measurements at the scene, in order to establish the relationship between them. Despite the fact that we know a great deal about the way surrounding temperatures affect the temperature within a maggot-infested body, there are always surprises in store, since local conditions may not reflect the conditions under which laboratory studies were conducted. Another complication is that weather stations offer only a general guide to temperatures, since meteorologists are concerned mainly with the "big" weather picture and avoid the confusing details of the climate near the ground. Unfortunately, in forensic work of this kind it is the temperature near the ground – the microclimatic temperature – that is of interest. However, temperatures of the air far above the ground can help us to reconstruct the temperatures near the ground, or what meteorologists like to call the boundary layer. One can then reconstruct the temperatures within the maggot-infested body.

The next step is to dissect the maggot and determine its stage of development. A maggot's stage and its age are not the same thing: the stage is the degree of its development; the age is how long it has been alive. At low temperatures maggots generally develop more slowly than they do at higher temperatures; in other words, they live longer at low temperatures. It is the stage and the temperature, taken together, that will reveal the age of the maggot.

Below: *Scanning electron micrograph of a blowfly (Calliphora vicina) maggot feeding on liver. The prevailing temperature determines how quickly such larvae grow through the various stages from egg to pupa.*

As time passes and decomposition progresses, different insect species will be attracted to the body at different times. This succession of fauna is impossible to predict, but is quite useful in the reconstruction of events after the event.

I am often asked how can an unpredictable phenomenon be used as a forensic tool? The answer is that forensic science, unlike much other science, is not concerned with predicting the future, but reconstructing the past. If, at the crime scene, one finds a cigarette-end and a used match, one is entitled to conclude that a smoker had been there. One could not possibly have predicted such a thing beforehand, but finding the evidence enabled us to arrive at that conclusion. The same is true of the insects, or their remains, found on a body. If we should find, say, the pupal cases of a fly that is active only in the spring, then that fact will help us to narrow down the time of death.

This reasoning, of course, applies to much forensic thinking. If, in December, one finds some shrivelled seeds of oilseed rape in the jacket pocket of a murder victim, one would naturally reflect on what could have happened in May, when the plant was growing and setting seed. If the deceased had been wearing a shirt of a kind that was first manufactured only

Left: *This car boot is being carefully searched. Vital clues can come from seemingly trivial items: a few seeds, a pupal case, or a scrap of cloth.*

Unlawful Killing of Animals

IT IS NOT ONLY THE UNLAWFUL killing of human beings that can result in prosecution; the unlawful killing of animals, domestic and wild, may also bring about the interest of the police. The application of methods of time-of-death estimation in those cases of killings of endangered species is increasing, especially in North America. As the protection of rare animals is now a legal matter, many issues of wildlife conservation are becoming part of forensic science investigations.

One case brought to me concerned a badger that was found in a wire snare in Scotland. The badger, although still alive, was heavily infested with maggots. Certain fly species can cause this condition by laying eggs on the living animal. The police wanted to know whether unnecessary suffering was caused to the badger by the negligent behaviour of the person who laid the trap. Under the law, such traps should be inspected every day. The maggots in the badger's body were almost fully-grown, so it was clear that the trap had not been inspected for up to a week. In the end, the animal was too badly injured and had to be put down.

six months ago, then one is entitled to conclude that death occurred after that date. Forensic scientists should not be too fussy about the kind of evidence available; they must use to maximum effect whatever comes to hand. Evidence involving the use of high-tech apparatus is not always the most revealing; very often the simplest of simple clues can be the most revealing.

This brings me to another point: the forensic scientist must look for clues wherever they may be found. In an earlier chapter I emphasised that it is the way forensic scientists think that matters, not so much the techniques at their disposal. A microscope and a computer no more make a forensic scientist than a brush and paints make an artist.

With these thoughts in mind, let us pause for a moment and ask why it is so necessary to determine the time of death. The answer is that the time of death will tell us so many other things. Could Bloggs have been the murderer? No, he was elsewhere during the critical minimum time since death period. Could Jones have done it? Possibly, since he was in the vicinity at the time; so he remains under investigation. So, the time of death can either include some suspects in, or exclude them from, an investigation. It can tell us other things, even how death occurred. Overleaf, we will look at an example of how this can be.

CASE HISTORY

The Body in the Woods

The body of Jason Swift, a 14-year-old boy, was discovered by a gamekeeper in a thicket inside a woodland early in December, 1985. The body had some maggots in it and, on the basis of these, the police asked for a time of death estimation. The weather had been very cold, dropping to well below freezing during the days before the body was found. On the day of discovery, it rained and the temperatures rose to above freezing.

The problem here was how any maggots could have been in the body at all, since the temperatures prevailing between the time of the boy's disappearance to the time his body was discovered would have prevented any flies from being active and laying eggs.

Therefore, the body could not have been lying out of doors when the flies arrived to lay their eggs on it. The maggots, at their second stage of development, were too old to have been derived from eggs laid on the day the temperatures rose and the body was discovered, so they must have been developing indoors. I concluded that death must have occurred at least two days prior to discovery and that the body must have lain indoors for some time. These facts, slight though they are, were corroborated by other evidence and the minimum time since death estimation turned out to be the actual time of death. The murder itself – by Sidney Cooke and his paedophile gang – took place in a car.

A Very Famous Case

Our example is concerned with a crime that was committed almost 2,000 years ago, yet it is a crime that has affected, in one way or another, everyone who has lived since then. It is the crucifixion of Jesus Christ. What is the truth? Can we really tell what happened, at this great remove in time? I believe we can.

On the whole, the accounts of the four Gospels agree about what happened. After his arrest and torture, Jesus was sent to Pontius Pilate and, subsequently, to the High Priest, Caiaphas, for interrogation. He was then sentenced to death, the mob having chosen Barabbas for release, rather than Jesus, who was then crucified.

The events up to this point are quite straightforward, but a puzzling event takes place while Jesus is on the cross. It is this: he dies, quickly. This is most unusual, since crucified people normally lingered on for days in a slow, truly agonising death. It is true that Jesus was much weakened by a severe whipping before his crucifixion, but so were other condemned people. Why did Jesus die so quickly?

When Pilate is told that Jesus has died so soon after he was crucified, his reaction is one of scepticism, for he knows that his crucified victims normally take several days to die and he asks a centurion to check and report back to him (St Mark's Gospel, chapter 15, verses 43-45). There is another source of evidence that tells us that Jesus' early death was unexpected by the Romans. This is supplied by St John (chapter 19, verses 31-34) who tells us that when the soldiers arrived to break the legs of the three that had been crucified (so that they would die quickly and their bodies could therefore be removed before the Jewish holy day), they broke the legs of the two criminals but discovered that Jesus was already dead.

One of the soldiers then pierced Jesus' side with a spear. This unnecessary and barbaric mutilation of a dead body has not, to my knowledge, been explained. It seems reasonable to speculate that the Roman soldier, having come on his leg-breaking mission with some glee, felt cheated that one of his intended victims was dead. Why else would he do such a vile thing as stab a dead body with a spear? I submit that this vicious deed was carried out because the soldier found the early death totally unexpected and saw fit to vent his spleen on the victim who cheated him. I cannot think of a better explanation.

Let us now turn back to the last horrific moments before Jesus' death. In agony, he was praying to God: "My God, my God, why hast

Left: The Virgin, John and Mary Magdalene by the Cross by Niccolo dell' Abate (1509-1572).

thou forsaken me?" A man, carrying a sponge soaked in sour wine or vinegar at the end of a long cane, rushed up and pushed the sponge at the face of Jesus. Jesus then gave a loud cry, and died (St Mark's Gospel, chapter 15, verses 35-37).

What is the significance of all this? When a man is crucified, his arms are stretched along the horizontal bar of the cross, making breathing difficult. The breath comes in short inhalations and exhalations, since it is difficult and uncomfortable to take a deep breath in such a position. When the vinegar-soaked sponge was put against his face, Jesus, because of the shock of the pungent smell, must have inhaled deeply, which is the natural reaction under such circumstances. But, having done so, it would have been very difficult for him to exhale once more. The muscular anatomy of the chest makes this effectively impossible. A painful death from asphyxiation would follow soon after. The last, loud cry of Jesus was probably the sudden, painful inhalation.

This is probably why Jesus died so quickly on the cross. Other victims were, presumably, left alone to die slowly, since most such people would have had the sympathy of the Jewish population, all crucifixions or sentences of death being carried out by the Romans, who alone could pass a sentence of death. Jesus, however, was resented as the man who claimed to be the "King of the Jews", and was tormented as he died. The incident of the sponge was the last straw.

What does all this mean? Why should such a seemingly trivial event as the sponge incident help us to understand whether or not the whole episode really happened? The reason is this. The Gospels are essentially religious writings. They were written to spread the news of Jesus' life, death and resurrection. They were not written as historical treatises. Those who wrote them would not have taken the trouble to add irrelevant information, unless the events had actually been witnessed. The point here is that nothing turns on the early death of Jesus; the event is not used by the authors of the Gospels to prove anything. It simply does not matter, theologically. It happened and was recorded, although nobody knew, or claimed to know, why or how it happened. To put it bluntly, Jesus' early death is such strong evidence that the crucifixion did happen as described because it could not have been fabricated, since its significance could not have been appreciated at the time the Gospels were written. It is significant to us, because it was not significant to the authors of the Gospels. The time of death revealed the truth.

What other factors affect the decomposition of a corpse in a way that can help with time of death determination? We know that humidity speeds decomposition and dry conditions retard it. In buried bodies, it is said that soil pH (the degree of acidity or alkalinity) does not affect the rate of decomposition, an assertion I find hard to believe. It may be true to some extent as far as whole bodies are concerned, but it is not true in relation to skeletons, as we shall see. Some substances, such as quicklime added to the soil, certainly do affect the rate and manner of decomposition.

The time of death of buried bodies can be estimated using entomological (i.e. insect biology) techniques, very much as can exposed bodies, although the fauna involved is quite different. The fauna in the soil beneath a buried body (i.e. a body buried without a coffin) will change in certain predictable ways. First, the existing fauna will decrease, both in number of species and

Above: *Leyte Island, Phillipines. In December 2003, week-long rains triggered a landslide that left 200 people dead or missing. Decomposition of the victim's bodies was rapid making removal more difficult.*

number of individuals. This happens because the decaying body releases decomposition products with such evocative names as cadaverine and putrescine, which are highly toxic. The fauna slowly disappears, a process that takes something of the order of two months. After that a new fauna begins to appear; it will be different from the original fauna and will gradually develop to its maximum extent. The exact order of events will depend on the nature of the soil and the time of year; and it is not possible to be very precise in all cases.

One of the main biological events occurring in soil is the growth of plant roots. It sometimes happens that the roots of a tree penetrate through the skeleton of a buried body and knowledge of the speed of their development will give an indication of time of death. Also, the number of growth rings in roots that had been damaged while the grave was being dug will reveal the time of burial. These methods were used in a case in Bedfordshire, England, in 1978 and it was concluded that the body had been buried three years earlier. Also, the absence of fly pupal cases indicated that the body must have been buried very soon after death.

Taphonomy, the pattern of bone scattering discussed in the last chapter, can also give a general idea of time of death, since a correlation has been found between time of death and extent of disarticulation and scattering of the bones. Bone scattering is said to begin at about five weeks after death, although I do not doubt that much will depend on the time of year in which the person died, as well as on the local conditions, such as the species of wild animal present. Such things cannot be timed to perfection – too many factors and unknowns are involved.

Teeth often acquire a pinkish pigmentation after death, this colour appearing a few weeks post mortem. The discoloration is caused by the accumulation of haem compounds, but how this arises is not understood. It seems that the discoloration usually takes place in victims of violent death. These facts can be useful in time-of-death estimation, but their potential has not been fully developed. Interestingly, the aorta also develops a pinkish colour after death, although this starts days, rather than weeks, after death.

It might seem surprising that all the techniques so far examined are somewhat vague and uncertain, lacking the "Yes" or "No" character that the public in general – and lawyers in particular – expect of science. Are there, then, no such techniques that can be applied to this vexed question of time of death?

Well, yes there are, but they, too, are limited in their own ways. Most can be applied only under special circumstances and, even then, their precision of measurement does not necessarily mean that they will give us a precise answer. If this sounds self-contradictory, let us look at some of these techniques and see what they can do.

Human remains are often found as skeletons. In such cases it is possible to analyse the chemical composition of the bones with a view to establishing time of death. The rate at which nitrogen is lost from buried bones has been used as a time marker in the technique known, wonderfully, as FUN analysis. The letters stand

Below: *A well-preserved Roman skeleton from Fishbourne, near Chichester, UK.* It is important to date skeletons accurately, since bones more than 100 years old are no longer of legal interest.

for fluorine, uranium and nitrogen. Nitrogen loss is essentially protein loss, since proteins are the only nitrogenous compounds found in bone. More specifically, most bone protein is collagen, which accounts for 90 per cent of skeletal protein and for about a third of the protein in the body as a whole. It is the main component of tough tissues like tendons and is the substance that yields gelatine when boiled. Its rate of loss, together with the rate of uptake into the bones of the chemical elements fluorine and uranium from water in the soil can give an approximate time since death. It was FUN analysis that enabled Dr Kenneth Oakley and his colleagues at the Natural History Museum in London to expose the Piltdown hoax, demonstrating that the bones were modern and not ancient, as had been claimed.

The nitrogen content of bone is measured using the micro-Kjeldahl technique, in which the dried bone is treated with sulphuric acid to yield ammonium sulphate. This salt is in turn treated with sodium hydroxide to release the ammonia from the sulphate. The ammonia, which is a nitrogenous compound with the formula NH_3, is then absorbed into hydrochloric acid. The residual acid is then titrated. This allows the amount of ammonia produced to be calculated and hence the amount of nitrogen in the bone.

This very precise method of estimating the amount of nitrogen in a bone sample is not matched by a great precision of dating the remains. The reason is that we do not know how much nitrogen is lost from bones over a particular period of time. This is because the rate of nitrogen loss is greatly influenced by temperature and the amount of water in the soil during the period in which the bones had been buried. Nitrogen forms about four per cent of bone by weight and the rate of its loss is also affected by the size of the bone fragments, the smaller fragments losing nitrogen more rapidly. Protein in bones survives for longer in cold, dry conditions, especially if there is little oxygen present and the soil pH is high (i.e. non-acidic). Conversely, it lasts for a much shorter time in wet, warm conditions that encourage microbial growth. Bone will be destroyed very quickly in highly acidic soils.

Protein is made up of chemical building blocks called amino acids. These are lost selectively over time. In other words, some amino acids disappear before others. These facts have been used as a technique of time-of-death estimation by archaeologists and attempts have been made to apply them to forensic problems. The technique involves the breaking down of collagen in the laboratory, then identifying the various amino acids found. The basic idea here is that, the longer the post mortem period, the fewer amino acids will be found. Fresh bone yields between 10 and 15 different amino acids, whereas bones that are over 100

years old have less than seven. The absence of two amino acids, proline and hydroxyproline, indicates that the bones had been in the ground for hundreds, even thousands, of years.

The relative proportions of amino acids in the bone has also been used as a dating technique. In general, is has been found that the relative proportions of amino acids in old bones is roughly similar to modern bones, as long as more than 10 per cent of the original amount remains. At lower proportions the amino acid "profile" will look very different. The reason some amino acids are lost faster than others lies in the fact that they are more easily dissolved in water than others. This applies to proline and hydroxyproline, which, as we have seen, are lost relatively quickly. Some amino acids are more susceptible to destruction by acids than others; this is the case with tryptophan and threonine, for example.

There are three problems associated with the application of this technique to forensic science. First, the obvious reason that it is highly unreliable. Secondly, there are unresolved chemical problems with the method of extracting the amino acids in the laboratory. Thirdly, the timescales involved are too great, rendering it of little use in modern case-work. However, it is not entirely without interest to the forensic scientist, since it can, at least in many cases, distinguish between a recent death and one that happened several hundred years ago. This is important, since the discovery of, say, a 500-year-old skeleton is of no legal interest and need not be investigated by the police. Also, we must not forget that some cases of forensic interest are historical ones, as we shall see more clearly in later chapters.

When bone is exposed under ultra-violet light it fluoresces a blue colour. Older bones have been found to fluoresce a yellowish-green colour; this latter is attributed to the presence of the metabolic products of bacteria and moulds. Other old bones, such as those excavated from an Etruscan site in Italy, fluoresced only very weakly. More recent samples from Mediaeval times fluoresced bluish-white, but more weakly than modern samples and the distribution of fluorescence was patchy; moreover, it was restricted largely to the centre of the bone. It seems that the ability to fluoresce is lost with the lapse of time from the outside of the bone inwards. It is generally thought that bones that fluoresce across the whole of their cross-section are less than 100 years old. Older bones, up to 800 years old, will have completely lost their ability to fluoresce.

These findings are very promising, but the exact relationship between loss of fluorescence and passage of time is not understood. It is not yet established what it is that fluoresces in bone; some researchers believe it to be the organic (protein) parts, while others believe it to be the inorganic (mineral) part.

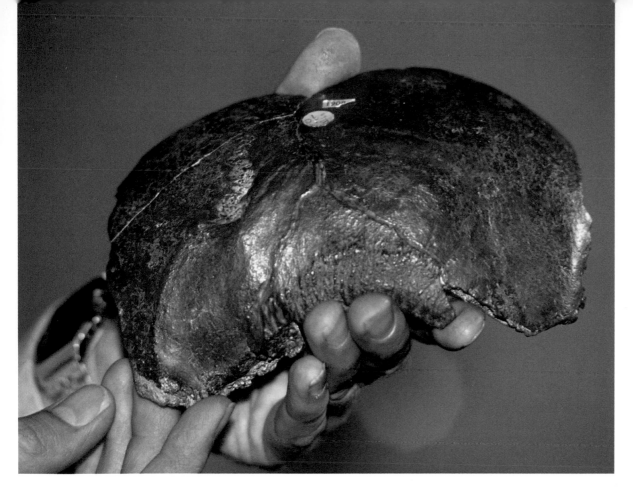

Left: *Piltdown man. A supposedly apelike ancestral fossil found to be a fake, made from a human cranium and ape's jawbone.*

Right: *Modern skeleton from Argentina. Between 1976 and 1983, many people were abducted and murdered during the military rule. The task here will be to identify the remains.*

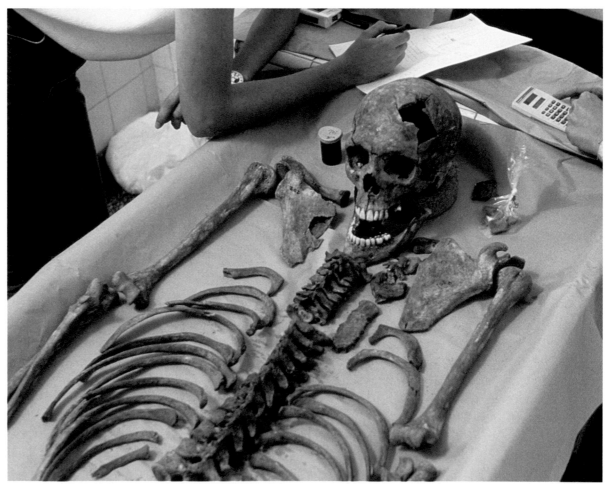

Above: *Radiocarbon dating. Carbon dioxide samples are put into a linear accelerator which analyses the amount of carbon-14 (^{14}C) present. The ratio of radioactive ^{14}C to stable ^{12}C is related to the age of the sample.*

This uncertainty introduces another problem. Bones lying in the ground are exposed to the process of remineralisation. Such changes in the mineral content of the bone would then confuse the picture, since one would not know whether the presence of strong fluorescence is due to the original mineral components, or to later additions. Furthermore, some of the mineralogical changes that take place in buried bones are well understood, such as the increase in size of the hydroxyapatite crystals, but other changes are not at all understood.

Aminobenzidine is a chemical that stains haemoglobin, the purple pigment in red blood cells. (Blood appears red only when it is oxygenated.) Applying this stain to old bones shows that, generally speaking, bones older than 50 years do not react positively. Nevertheless, exceptions are known, since some bones as old as 150 years have exhibited a positive reaction. Other tests for haemoglobin usually fail to show its presence after about five years. Confusingly, blood remains have been detected in bones that are as much as 90,000 years old. So, this technique, too, is severely limited in its applicability.

There are other dating techniques, many of which are at present in greater or lesser degrees of development. The most promising of these is the analysis of the presence of the body's decomposition products in the soil. It would be tedious to

catalogue all the work done in this area, but one example will make the point. The increasing concentration of inorganic ions (i.e. ions lacking carbon) in the soil has been developed in the United States. Interestingly, a way round the common problem that so many natural processes are dependent on temperature was found. It was calculated that the concentration of inorganic ions* increased, not simply in relation to time, but in relation to accumulated day degrees (ADDs), which is the product of the temperature and the number of days. (This method is used in other techniques, such as the study of maggot development above.) In other words, the same change would take place over 10 days at 20°C, as would take place over 20 days at 10°C, the ADD being 200 in both cases. So, some kind of indication is given, but not in absolute time terms. Peaks of decomposition products could be shown to occur at predictable ADD intervals. Moreover, the time scales involved, whichever way one "read" the ADD, were applicable forensically, being of the order of hundreds of days.

These results, although interesting, cannot be applied universally, since the nature of the soil and, hence, the rate of loss of decomposition products, will vary from place to place. This is a problem that affects all techniques involving the soil surrounding the body.

Having come this far, it may seem that there is no absolutely reliable time-of-death dating technique. One problem that bedevils all the methods discussed above is the fact that they are all temperature-dependent. Before we can interpret our findings, we have to reach some conclusion about the temperatures prevailing during the relevant period. This is no easy matter.

What, then? People are accustomed to hearing about such success stories as the use of radiocarbon dating of the Turin Shroud, which was shown to have been of Mediaeval, not ancient, origin**, that I am often faced with a look of disbelief when I say that dating the time of death is so difficult. These days everyone is familiar, not only with radiocarbon dating, but with other such high-tech methods as accelerated mass spectroscopy, thermoluminescence and electron spin resonance, all of which sound wonderfully infallible as dating techniques. Why, then, are there no fail-safe methods of determining the time of death? Is it true that there are no available techniques that do not depend on phenomena of natural change that take place at a known rate and totally independently of temperature? The answer is, no, it is not wholly true, but such techniques as are available have problems of their own, too.

First, a technique like radiocarbon dating comes into its own only when we are concerned with very long periods of time, because it cannot be used to detect or interpret the changes that occur over short, more recent periods of time. It would be like trying to time a race that lasts for a few seconds using a clock with only an hour hand, or like weighing a button using a steelyard. Even over long periods of time, radiocarbon dating has correspondingly large margins of error, although, over the time periods in question, they may not appear important to us. For these reasons it cannot be used as a forensic dating technique. It is generally agreed that radiocarbon cannot be used to date events that took place more recently than 400 years ago.

Radiocarbon dating exploits the fact that carbon-fourteen (^{14}C) decays (i.e. becomes non-radioactive) at a known rate. It has a half-life of 5,730 years, the half-life being the time it takes for half the nuclei to decay. It is this change that can be used as a measure of time.

Yet there are other radioactive techniques that can be used in forensic science, two of the most important being the consequences of two of the great disasters of the twentieth century: the Second World War and the explosion at the Chernobyl Nuclear Power Station in the Ukraine. Both events produced peaks of radioactivity, the decline from which can be used as date markers since those events took place.

The numerous nuclear arms tests that took place after the Second World War increased the levels of radiocarbon, or ^{14}C, in the atmosphere. The peak was reached in 1963 and the levels have been declining ever since. This radioactive carbon has ramified throughout the living world and its presence and exact level in human bones can be used to determine whether a person died after 1950, the year in which nuclear testing began.

Let us look at one last, relatively recent, development. It was found that the rate that potassium enters the vitreous humor (the jelly-like substance filling the eyeball behind the lens) takes place at a constant rate and, moreover, is a change that is independent of temperature. The potassium derives from the breakdown of the red blood cells. Have we, at last, found the ideal indicator of time of death? Alas, no. First, like the conventional post mortem changes, it is detectable only during the first few days after death. Moreover, I am far from convinced that the process is as wholly independent of temperature as has been believed, but I keep an open mind about it. Time will tell.

*An ion is one of the two electrically charged "halves" of an inorganic compound. The word "inorganic" refers to a compound lacking in carbon, with the exception of such common compounds as carbon dioxide and various carbonates.

** The date of the Turin Shroud has not, in fact, been conclusively demonstrated.

Below: *Chernobyl Nuclear Power Station, Ukraine. In 1986, an explosion in Reactor No 4 released tons of radioactive material.*

A QUESTION OF IDENTITY

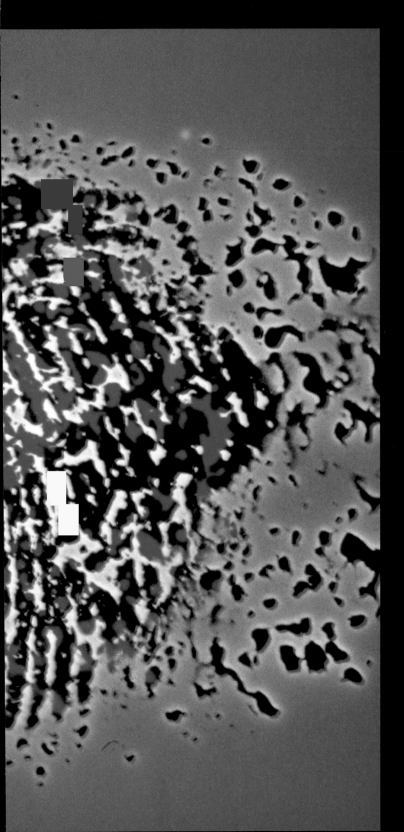

We have dealt with the "where" and the "when" in earlier chapters; now we ask "Who?". Who was the victim; and, equally importantly, who was the criminal – the classic question, "whodunit?"

We began this book by looking at Locard's Principle, the fundamental tenet of forensic science that "every contact leaves a trace"; but there are other tenets of comparable importance. One of these is the Principle of Individuality, which states that no two objects can be identical. No two people, no two documents, no two skulls, no two fingerprints, even those from the same person, are exactly alike. This does not mean that they are, perforce, distinguishable in practice, but crucially they are distinguishable in principle. Forensic assistance for identification is frequently needed by the police and, happily, many techniques are now available. These techniques are constantly being developed to increase our powers to distinguish between things or people.

The first attempt to identify people on a rational, scientific basis was developed during the second half of the nineteenth century by the French forensic scientist, Alphonse Bertillon. Anthropometry was a system based on a number of measurements of key facial and body features. It was a good beginning and it had some successes, as when Bertillon asserted that a criminal named Dupont was the same person as a man named Martin – Dupont later admitted that he was, indeed, Martin.

In spite of its successes, anthropometry suffered from a number of flaws, the most important of which was the fact that it was impossible to assess the probability of two people having the same sets of measurements. Also, it could only be used comparatively, to say whether a person had similar features to a known criminal. For these reasons, as well as the cost involved in training police officers to apply it routinely, anthropometry gradually fell out of favour.

Bertillon developed another technique, called *portrait parlé* – a "word" or "speaking" portrait. This system involved the use of

various forms of the facial features and building them up to make a "picture" in words. For example, the forehead might be broad or narrow, the nose high-bridged or concave and so on. The various states in which each facial feature could occur were much more numerous and fine-tuned than the example given in the last sentence, but it serves to make the point. It was useful in enabling police officers to describe a person in a way that would allow others to form a very good idea of their appearance.

The obvious step from a "word" picture to a real picture happened when the Identikit was invented by Hugh McDonald in California during the Second World War. This system employed a number of transparencies of different forms of mouth, nose, chin, etc., which could be superimposed on one another to produce a facial representation. The number of variations of each feature differed from feature to feature; for example, there were 102 eye forms, but only 52 chin forms. Nevertheless, Identikit proved to

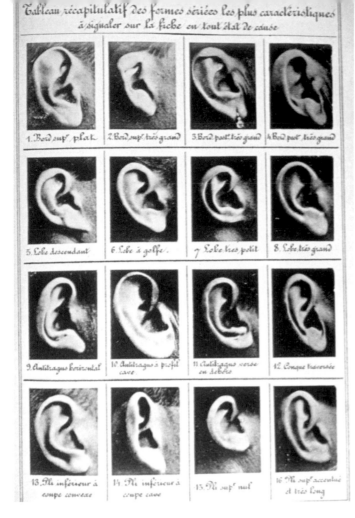

be a valuable method in producing a more or less accurate visual representation of a face from a description given by a witness. Publication of the Identikit in newspapers has resulted in the identification and arrest of many a criminal.

The logical next step came when Jacques Penry in Britain developed the technique known as Photo-FIT – the last three letters standing for Facial Identification Technique. It is essentially the same as Identikit, but uses photographs rather than drawings. It is also more detailed, including, for example, 101 mouth forms and 89 nose forms, compared with Identikit's 33 and 32, respectively. It is possible to construct 15 billion different faces using Photo-FIT.

With the advent of computers it is now possible to reconstruct faces in three dimensions and to introduce other kinds of feature, such as colour. Computers have also played an important role in the development of techniques of identifying not only the living, but the dead, as we shall see later in this chapter.

Left: *Images of human ears from Dr Bertillon's 1893 book* Indentification Anthropometrique Instructions Signaletiques.

Below: *Wanted! From the witness's description, standard facial shapes are used to generate the basic picture. The police artist (right) modifies this as directed to produce a recognisable appearance.*

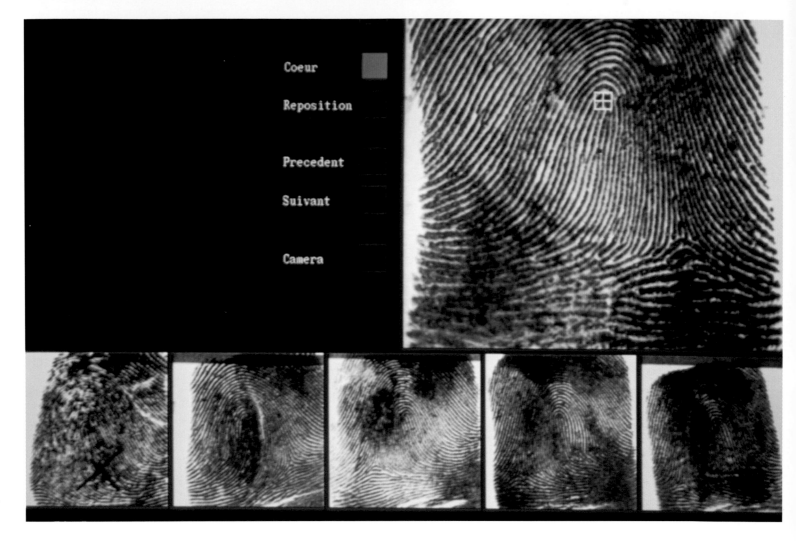

Above: *Digitised fingerprint from French police files. A hand-held scanner is used to convert paper copies of fingerprints from criminal records into computer records, building a database for future comparisons.*

Fingerprint analysis is the classic tool of crime detection, yet it is a technique that is little understood, not only by the public at large, but by the law courts as well. Surprisingly, fingerprint specialists themselves often give the impression that they are not wholly aware of the full power of their methods.

Fingerprints are made up of many ridges, arranged in rough, concentric circles. Some of the ridges end abruptly, others end in forks and yet others fork and close up again. The full number of permutations is infinite, hence the perfectly justified belief that no two individuals have identical fingerprints. The various features of a fingerprint, together with their relative positions on the print, are what enable the fingerprint examiner to identify a particular set as belonging to a specific individual. In Britain, the traditional way of doing this is to match 16 points of the print with the suspect's fingerprint; if they match exactly, then an identification can be made.

Yet there is no reason to suppose that the number 16 has any special significance. The number was not arrived at through any process of logical reasoning, it simply appeared to be a safe number of points upon which to arrive at a conclusion. In Paris, 17 points of congruence are required to prove identification, whereas only 12 are required in the rest of France. Again, only 12 points are required in Australia and New Zealand, whereas only eight points of agreement are used to prove identity in Turkey. In India the figure varies from six to 12, depending on the particular state. The United States no longer has a fixed number of points.

Does this mean that standards are highest in Paris and Britain and lower elsewhere? No; in fact, in one sense, it may mean the

Above: *Collecting fingerprints. A fine brush is used to apply fingerprinting dust, which adheres to oil left by any prints on the cup. An adhesive plastic strip is then used to "lift" the fingerprint.*

Right: *Once lifted, the fingerprint is digitized (scanned) and saved for comparison. Here, 32 characteristic features have been marked.*

exact opposite. To explain this apparently self-contradictory statement it is necessary first to look at the way fingerprint analysts actually identify fingerprints.

The examiner usually begins by studying the prints as a whole. He then makes comparisons between equivalent parts of the prints to see whether they match. Next, having made up his mind that the two prints came from the same individual, he draws up a list of the matching 16 points and presents his report. Note that I have written that the identification is made first, the listing of the points of congruence being made after the fingerprint analyst has satisfied himself of his identification. I do not mean by this that these examiners are in any way dishonest about their conclusions. What I do mean is that they actually arrive at their conclusions on the basis of experience and not on the basis of the counting of points of similarity. The following

results from a Home Office study should make the point clear.

In this inquiry, pairs of prints from the same individual were sent to fingerprint examiners throughout England and Wales. In addition to the true pairs of prints, one pair of unidentical prints (i.e. not from the same individual), which were altered to make them appear to be the same, were sent to the examiners, who were asked to determine whether the prints in each pair came from the same individual and to give the number of points of similarity.

All the examiners saw through the deception of the doctored pair of prints, none misidentified the closest pair of similar prints that could be produced by any fingerprint bureau in the country. On the other hand, they disagreed widely among themselves as to the number of points of similarity between the genuine pairs; in one case the number of perceived points of resemblance varied from 11 to 40.

The conclusion that can be drawn from this study is very clear. Fingerprint examiners are extremely good at matching two prints successfully, but their ability has very little to do with the counting of points. Although this may sound a rather startling conclusion, in fact, it should not surprise us, for recognition and description are quite different things. You and I may be able to recognise our friends and relations with ease, but, if asked how we were so sure that they were not other, very similar people, we would probably falter and hesitate. We are sure of our identification and that's that. We know, but we do not know how we know. The analytical ability to "dissect" a pattern and produce a description is a power that not many people possess.

So, what is the answer to our question, "Are standards higher in countries that demand a larger number of matching points?". The answer must be that, while a sledgehammer will crack any nut, a nutcracker would do just as well. In other words, the desire for a high number of matching points does not raise standards, it merely makes it look as though one is erring on the side of safety. Since we know that fingerprint examiners identify fingerprints on the basis of their experience and not on the basis of point-counting, this excessive caution is not only unjustified, it excludes good evidence from the courtroom. This is because a fingerprint examiner may be sure that two prints came from the same individual, but may not be able to find the required 16 points of similarity. It must be remembered that many fingerprints found at scenes of crimes are only partial prints.

It is odd that fingerprint examiners themselves have not been able to accept these conclusions, perhaps fearing that their subject would be seen as being unscientific if they did so*. But this is to miss the point completely. Although one cannot attach any great significance to the number of matching points in two fingerprints,

one can measure the probability of a fingerprint examiner arriving at the correct answer. This is perfectly respectable and scientific. It does not matter how fingerprint examiners arrive at their conclusions, as long as studies show that they are almost always correct.

It has been pointed out many times, notably by Dr Ian Evett and his colleagues, that one should concentrate on professional standards, that is, on the demonstrated ability of fingerprint examiners, rather than on the counting of matching points. This is sound advice and I hope that both fingerprint examiners and the courts take it on board.

The examination of fingerprints is usually done at the scene and, until recently, British police forces did not "lift", i.e. remove an impression from the scene, in case it damaged the evidence. Despite the fact that other countries routinely lifted prints from the scene to the laboratory, this attitude continued in Britain until 1970, when "lifting" became acceptable.

There are various ways in which a print can be enhanced or lifted. Anyone familiar with cinematic whodunits will be familiar with the use of carbon or aluminium powders to enhance fingerprints for subsequent photography or lifting. According to the nature of the surface upon which the print has been left, different kinds of dye are used to render the impression clear enough for analysis.

"Lifting" itself is a very straightforward operation, although it has to be carried out carefully. It is done by placing low-adhesive tape on top of the enhanced print, then carefully removing it and sticking it down again on a piece of white card, on which the details of the case are recorded.

Taking fingerprints from known individuals – living or dead – is again a reasonably straightforward matter; everyone is more or less familiar with the process of coating the fingers with ink and taking an impression. A certain protocol is followed when doing this; for example, there is an established order in which the prints from the different fingers are taken and deposited on a form with a number of boxes, each box being reserved for a different finger. Occasionally difficulties arise, especially when fingerprinting the dead, since the fingerprints may be damaged as a result of mummification, decomposition or excessive wetting. Special techniques are available to deal with such situations, although it is usually a matter of intelligent improvisation.

It is not only the tips of the fingers that can leave tell-tale signs; the whole hand and the bare foot can do so too. Various systems have been developed to identify individuals using hand and foot prints.

CASE HISTORY

The First Use of Fingerprints in a Criminal Case

Two children, who lived with their mother in a shack near Buenos Aires, were found bludgeoned to death in 1892. The mother was slightly injured, but not badly hurt. The police suspected a man named Velasquez, since the children's mother, Francesca Rojas, had accused him of the crime. However, fingerprints left on blood splashed on the shack door matched those of Francesca herself.

At that time, fingerprints would probably not have been accepted as evidence in court, but, when confronted with the police findings, Francesca Rojas broke down and admitted that she had indeed murdered her children. The reason for her foul deed was that her lover said he would have married her, if only she hadn't had any children.

Sniffing Out Evidence

Everyone knows that dogs have an uncanny ability, through their sense of smell, to recognise individual human beings. Their ability to follow a scent over great distances, over wet fields in the pouring rain, is a matter of common human knowledge. They can also transmit this information to us; their subsequent behaviour leaves us in no doubt that they have successfully accomplished the task they had set out to do.

It may come as a surprise to learn that in Britain, a great dog-loving nation, dogs are not used to identify people in criminal investigations. The evidence of a dog is inadmissible as evidence in British courts, although one or two exceptions to this general statement are known. It is true that dogs are used to find people and dead bodies, but this is not the same thing as identifying a person. When the police search for a missing person they use dogs to track them down. When the person is found that is the end of the matter. The dog's discovery of the person is not used as evidence in any way; the animal was simply being used as a tool to find the person. Should the identity of the found individual be in doubt, then other ways of establishing his or her identity are used.

Above: *A bloodhound's sense of smell is at least 1,000 times better than a human's. Generally used for tracking scents less than a week old, they can also be trained to find bodies underwater.*

Similarly, dogs are often used to find people lost on mountains or buried beneath the rubble of a landslide or an avalanche, but, again, the dog is merely a device to achieve an end, much as a police officer might use a car to go from one place to another.

If, on the other hand, a dog snarls at an individual who is suspected of having burgled the premises of the dog's owner, this is not seen to be evidence of the person's identity; in other words, it cannot be used as evidence that the man was the burglar. This is the case even if the dog barked at the man after being allowed to sniff, say, a glove that was left behind by the burglar.

Why is such evidence not allowed in British courts? It is acceptable evidence in Holland, Germany, Hungary and some parts of the United States, but not in Britain. Could it be that the ability of dogs to identify people is exaggerated, that they are not really as proficient at this task as they are claimed to be?

Let us look first at the evidence for the power of dogs to recognise people through their sense of smell, before answering the question about the legal use of their abilities. The police force that has done more than any other to develop the use of dogs as identifiers of human beings is the Rotterdam police in Holland, where the use of dogs is now routine. Experiments carried out at

Rotterdam have contributed immensely to our knowledge of the smelling abilities of dogs. It is worth looking at these experiments and their results.

To test the ability of a dog to identify a specific person, a cloth that had been previously handled by that person is given to the dog to smell. Together with a number of other people, the man who had handled the cloth is required to have a shower, using a particular brand of soap. They are then required to wear identical garments that had been washed in the same way and with the same washing powder. Next, they each stand in a separate cubicle in a row inside a room. A screen in front of each man prevents the dog from seeing them. Fans, one behind each man, are switched on.

The dog is now taken into the room, together with its handler. The handler is not told of the position of the man who had handled the cloth, so that he cannot influence the dog's choice, however unconsciously. The dog, having smelt the cloth, is walked back and forth in front of the row of cubicles by the handler. Eventually, usually very quickly, the dog stops in front of one cubicle and barks. It has identified the person and hardly ever makes a mistake.

The dog is taken out of the room and the people in the cubicles change positions. The man playing the part of the culprit is now in another cubicle and the experiment is repeated. Again, the dog finds the right man. Next, another experiment is conducted. Cloths are handed to each of the people involved in the experiment; they handle them and then place them in special jars, with each cloth in a separate jar. The jars are placed in a row in the experiment room and the dog and handler come in. The dog sniffs each jar in turn and then identifies correctly the jar with the right cloth. As with the earlier experiment, the jars are moved around in the absence of the dog, who returns with his handler and correctly identifies the cloth.

These results are very impressive, but, to my mind, the results of the next experiment are the most impressive of all. The jar with the "right" cloth is removed completely, leaving all the other jars, plus another to keep the number constant. What will the dog do now?

As with the other experiments, the dog is led by its handler into the room. The dog sniffs each jar in turn. It is puzzled. It starts again, sniffing each jar diligently. It stops and looks up at its handler and then looks back at the jars. It then starts to whine to its owner and walks away from the jar; no doubt it feels that it has failed in its task.

But it has not; it has succeeded brilliantly, for the dog has not chosen a second best, a nearest odour to the one it was seeking. The smell was

Left: *Search and rescue. This volunteer and his dog, members of the Soccorso Alpino (Mountain Rescue) are searching for a person buried in the snow as part of a training exercise in the Italian Alps.*

Above: *Searching for evidence. The dog is allowed to search the scene where two pizza delivery men were killed in Franklin, NJ. It will draw its handler's attention to anything with an unusual scent.*

either present in one of the jars or it was not. It is as simple as that. The dog would not identify a false jar even to please its handler; it would rather fail than do that.

A great deal of experimental work of this kind has been carried out, but the above experiments suffice to show that the sniffing abilities of dogs and their power to identify individuals with almost unerring accuracy are very great. In Britain, my colleague Dr Barbara Sommerville of the Department of Clinical Veterinary Medicine at Cambridge University, has been conducting similar experiments and has been able to demonstrate that dogs can even distinguish between identical twins. In Norway, scientific investigations showed that dogs that have been oriented at an angle of 90° to the direction in which a person has walked will turn in the right direction within two to five seconds. Some dogs have been able to track people 48 hours after

they had crossed a field in winter.

All this shows that there can be no doubt that dogs have formidable powers to find and identify people. Such powers ought to be harnessed for the benefit of the criminal justice system in Britain, but the courts continue to resist their use.

Why? The reason is that, if one accepts the evidence of a dog it would be tantamount to saying that a dog is the equal of a human being. One judge is reported to have said that he would not accept the evidence of a dog against the evidence of a man and many commentators have ridiculed the idea of a dog appearing in court answering the questions of a magistrate. It is seen as a fairy tale or science fiction. "What next?", such people have asked, "Are we to have cats and horses and cows giving evidence in courts of law? Such ideas are ridiculous and not worthy of further discussion."

And so they are, but such things are not being proposed. Nobody is suggesting that dogs should give evidence in court, only people. Dog evidence is no different from any other kind of evidence; courts have accepted the evidence of blood, glass, textile fibres and a whole host of other things, but nobody, to my knowledge, has ever said that they would not accept the evidence of a fibre or a piece of glass in favour of that of a human being. Nobody suggests that the evidence obtained through a chemical reaction in a test tube requires us to accept the evidence of the test tube or that the test tube should stand in the witness box and give evidence. The evidence lies in the interpretation by a human being of the analysis of the blood or glass or fibre or whatever it happens to be. It is the chemist or the biologist or the fibre specialist who gives evidence. And so it is with dog evidence. It is the person knowledgeable about dogs and dog behaviour who analyses and interprets the dog's behaviour, on the basis of scientifically acquired knowledge, and who stands in the witness box and gives evidence.

It is a simple case of being at cross purposes. Dogs are much more like human beings than are test tubes or pieces of glass. When the idea of dog evidence is raised, some people, who have

Below: *Tracker dog training. The "suspect" walked a pre-determined course. The bloodhound must pick up the scent from the jacket and follow that course to earn his reward.*

not thought the matter through, think it amusing and unreal that a dog should give evidence. This confusion would, indeed, be amusing were it not for the fact that it is depriving the legal system of a very powerful line of evidence and the police of a very effective weapon in their crime-detection armoury.

I believe that the use of dog evidence in British courts would be a great step forward in the fight against crime. The value of dog evidence, I make no apology for repeating, would be enormous, especially in cases of burglary. Burglars almost always leave behind a trace of their body odour, which could be identified by a dog and used as a tool against such criminals. The intellectual confusion surrounding the use of dogs as evidence must be seen as a fallacious and simplistic argument against a highly desirable new resource in crime detection in Britain.

Attempts have been made to produce a machine – an electronic nose – that can do what a dog does. These devices have been very successful in determining whether a food product, such as wine or cheese, is fresh and in a fit condition to be consumed. However, their application to criminal investigation has not yet been demonstrated. A dog is still the more reliable tool.

Tracking the Culprit

WE HAVE SEEN HOW a dog can identify a human with unerring accuracy, although the animal does not know how it does it. Moreover, beyond realising that certain odours are involved, we, too, do not understand fully how the dog does it. This in no way undermines the validity or the efficacy of the dog as a tool. Unfortunately, it is often stated that, if the mechanism underlying a piece of behaviour is not understood, then it cannot be considered "scientific". This is not true, since the proof of the pudding is in the eating, not in how it is made.

There are many techniques waiting to be used forensically, but, because we do not understand how they work, they are largely ignored. One such technique is tracking – not by dogs, but by men.

During the 1920s in Egypt a postman was murdered as he was walking between two villages in the desert. He was shot dead, the bullet passing through his head from right to left, although there was no trace of the bullet itself. The description of the wound in the post-mortem report suggested to Sir Sydney Smith, who was consulted on the case, that the bullet came from a high-velocity weapon, such as a .303 rifle. At first, no motive for the murder could be discerned.

Sir Thomas Russell, Commandant of the Cairo police, had great faith in the tracking skills of the Bedouin. They were brought in and asked to find any tracks that might shed light on what had happened, although the police had already made a search for a track, but had found none. The Bedouin trackers did find some tracks – of a man wearing sandals, they said. The tracks led to where the body had lain on the sand. The trackers then traced the footprints back to a place about 40 yards away; here, they said, someone had knelt down. One of the Bedouin picked up something from the sand and handed it to the police. It was an empty .303 rifle cartridge.

The trackers then said that the man who had left his tracks took off his sandals after inspecting the victim's body, then ran barefooted to the road. They followed the trail, which led to a fort in which were stationed six members of the Camel Corps. There the trail stopped.

Clearly, one of the men in the fort was the murderer, at least according to the Bedouin. The police arranged a march across the desert, in which all six Camel Corps members, as well as a number of other men, took part. The Bedouin examined the tracks and pointed out one set as belonging to the murderer. The experiment was repeated – with the same result. A third time the experiment was carried and, again, the Bedouin picked out the same man's tracks. A fourth and final test was carried out, this time without the man whose tracks the Bedouin always picked out. After their examination of the marks in the shifting sands, the Bedouin said they could not find the tracks that resembled those near the murdered man; and they insisted that the man could not have taken part in the march.

Although the police were now fairly sure that they had their man, trackers' evidence is not usually accepted in court. Everything now depended on the evidence of the cartridge, which was sent to Sir Sydney Smith. Samples of cartridge cases were obtained from the rifles of all six men – six rounds were fired from each rifle. These were examined under the microscope and compared with the one found at the scene. From various marks on the cartridge cases, each uniquely caused by the rifle from which they were fired, it was possible to say which rifle had been used to murder the postman. It was the rifle belonging to the man whose tracks the Bedouin had picked out.

In the words of Sir Sydney Smith: "Two sciences, one very ancient and the other very modern, led to exactly the same conclusion." Ballistics and Bedouin tracking both identified the same individual.

Below: *Human trackers. Arab Bedouins serve on the Israeli Defence Force as trackers. If they find evidence that someone has crossed the border into Israel they will follow the trail.*

Forensic Anthropology

Physical anthropology – as opposed to social anthropology – is the study of the variation in the anatomy of the human body, especially the form of its bones. Its aims include the determination of the sex, age, stature and general physical condition of bones, particularly those that have been excavated during archaeological or palaeontological work. Forensic anthropology is essentially the same kind of work in a legal context.

When the bones of a totally unknown person are discovered, attempts are first made to establish what kind of person they were. Were they male or female, old or young, white or black? When an initial physical description of the person is made, one can then set to work trying to find a specific identification and to answer the question: "Who was he or she?"

Establishing the sex of the skeleton is usually the most straightforward part of the first stages of the investigation, unless the person in question was a child or, at any rate, a youngster still in the process of growing to adulthood. The fact that sexual differences are not as readily apparent in very young people as they are in adults makes the determination of sex in the very young problematic. In adults, various bones usually indicate the sex of the deceased very clearly. The most obvious of these is the pelvic girdle, which has a different and very characteristic form in adult males and females, related to the child-bearing ability in the female.

However, other bones, such as the skull and the long bones, can also be used to determine the sex of the skeleton. Clearly, the more complete the skeleton, the more

accurate one can be; and it is seldom difficult to determine the sex of a complete adult skeleton. The pelvic girdle or the skull alone can be used with a high degree of certainty, but the use of them together increases the confidence that one has made a correct determination.

Conversely, estimating the age at death of a person is easier in youngsters than it is in adults, because there are many more

Below: *An Argentinian cemetery. Forensic anthropologists dig up a body, one of the 30,000 to die or disappear after the 1976 military coup. Careful examination of the bones can reveal their sex and age.*

changes in the morphology and anatomy of children. So, such events as when bones fuse or when teeth erupt can be used with a reasonable degree of accuracy to determine age. In adults, such changes do not occur, so age determination is more difficult. The degree of dental wear, the extent of the deposition of cement on the teeth, as well as certain changes in the bones – such as the degeneration of sternal ends of the ribs with age – can be used tentatively to determine age and, more often than not, it is a matter of the experience of the particular anthropologist, whose work in this area may be more of an art than a science; and it is no less worthy for that.

The height of an individual during life is fairly easy to determine when a complete skeleton is available. In such a case, measurement of the bones, plus the addition of a "correction factor" to adjust for the presence of soft tissues, will determine stature. Problems arise when the skeleton is incomplete. Individual bones will give an indication of height, but the reliability of the information differs from bone to bone. For example, the bones of the lower limbs are a better guide to height than the upper limbs.

The skeletons of young people present difficulties in this area, if only because of the fact that different children grow at different rates. In fact, in order to determine the stature of a child from a skeleton, it is necessary to know both the age and the sex beforehand, which is not always possible and is usually difficult, at least as far as sex is concerned, as we have seen.

Other problems arise in the determination of stature. The base-line data collected from living people is often itself incomplete or erroneous. For example, measuring a person who habitually adopts a slumped posture, or an aged person (height is reduced with age) may result in misleading interpretations. Even the time of day on which the measurements were taken may make a difference, since people are shorter in the evening than they are earlier in the day.

Next comes the question of race or ethnic group – the most problematic question of all. The problem here is many-faceted; first, because the concept of race is not clearly defined and differs from person to person. Also, much more intermarriage between different racial groups occurs today than ever before, confusing the question further. Nevertheless, certain generalisations can be made about differences in the morphology of the skull between, say, Europeans and black Africans. These have to be interpreted with care by an anthropologist familiar with at least one of the racial groups concerned.

More general conclusions about a person's appearance or habits can be deduced by other, more obvious, means. Remains of clothes or shoes, the colour of the hair, the presence of such things as jewellery, watches or keys, can all help with identification. The erosion of the teeth may suggest a particular kind of diet; heavily eroded teeth may suggest a diet that included much gritty material. Even the destruction of identifying features may suggest an identity. When Dr Buck Ruxton removed the identifying features – eyes, ears, fingertips, teeth, etc. – of his victims (his wife and her maid) the police suspected him all the more, as one who had medical knowledge and who was aware that such features would assist the investigators.

The patterns of the frontal sinuses – the hollows at the front of the skull – are known to vary from person to person; and their description can be an aid to identification. Various diseases present in life may leave their mark on the skeleton; and their presence will add another aspect to the description of the living person. For example, degenerative joint diseases may leave their mark as massive new bone formation. The bones of one who habitually rode horses during life can be identified as such from a study of their skeleton.

Once a general description of a person is made, the question of specific identification can then be tackled. In this context, the teeth are particularly useful, not only because they are the most persistent and indestructible of all body parts, but because they vary so much between individuals. Also, the fact that dental records (i.e. the history of their dental treatment, including fillings) of most people are held by dentists, means that there is a reference point that can be used to check the identification.

Dental identification is the norm in mass disasters. For example, the identification of the victims of the King's Cross Underground fire in London was made by the comparison of dental records with the teeth of the deceased. In such a situation the method is particularly effective, since the records of missing people (i.e. people who might have been travelling on the train) could be consulted and compared with those of the deceased individuals.

In practice, the identification of human skeletons can be wildly successful, or disappointingly inconclusive, according to the nature of the evidence to hand. I was once involved in a case in which the identification of the skeleton was a matter of great importance. Many specialists were called, but the age, sex and race of the victim were never definitely established.

Before we look at further methods of personal identification, let us examine a case of old bones, whose identity is still a matter of dispute.

Right: *Measuring a hominid skull. The probe is moved over the surface of the skull and a picture is drawn on the paper beneath enabling accurate measurement. Skull morphology can help to determine race.*

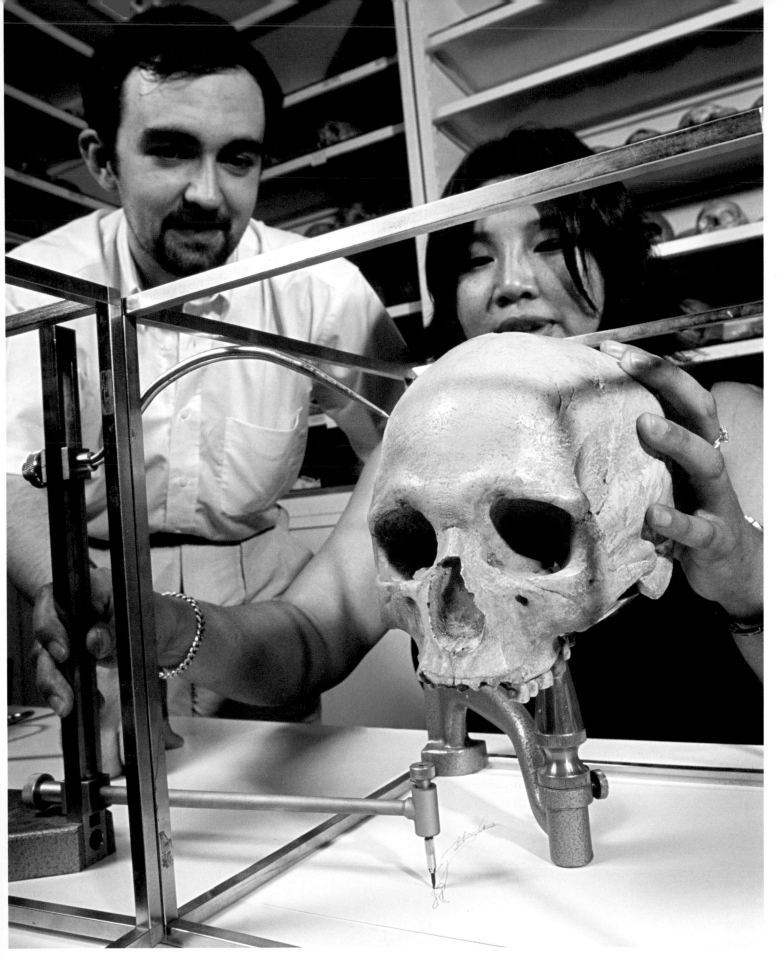

Overleaf: *Vital clues can be yielded from clothes; these include fibres, stains, pattern of rips etc. Often the style can be dated or traced to a specific maker or outlet.*

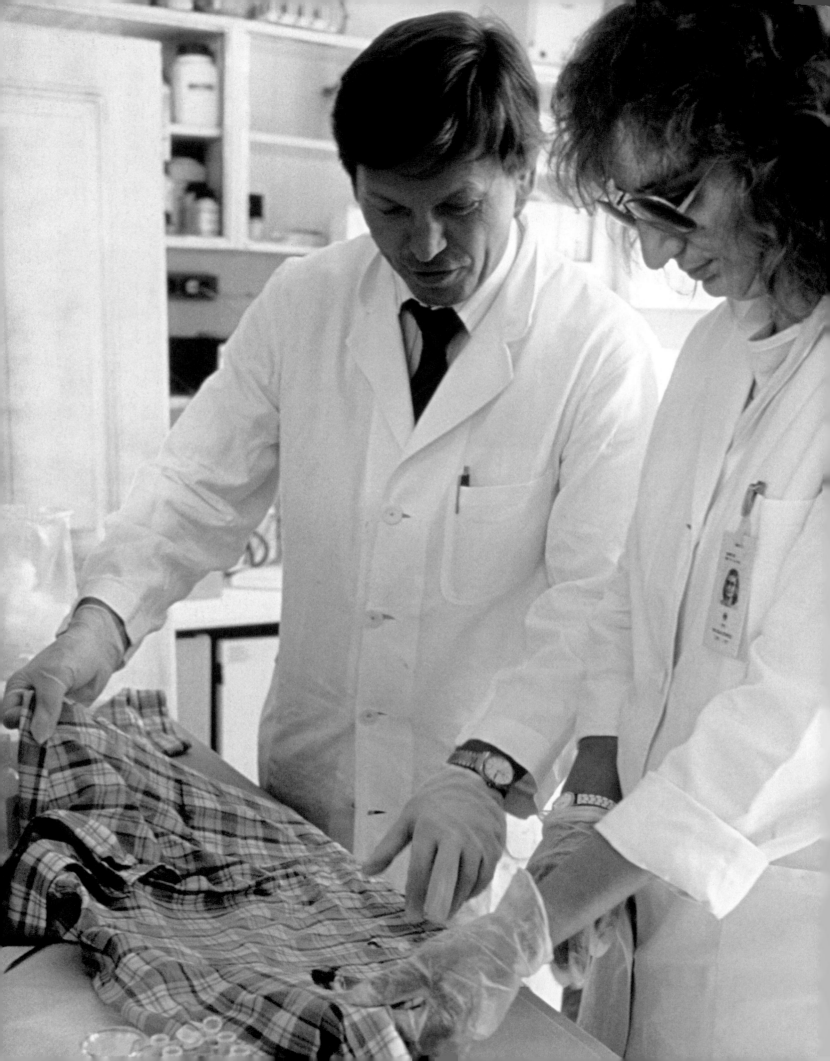

The Princes In The Tower

When the bones of two children were discovered buried 10 feet below the surface at the foot of the stairs in the White Tower in 1674, it was immediately concluded that the skeletons were those of the princes who had disappeared in the Tower of London in 1483. In 1933 the skeletons were subjected to a forensic examination. A basic flaw of this investigation is that it was carried out on the assumption that the remains were those of the two princes, whereas this was the very question that needed to be answered. Nevertheless, the findings were of some interest. It was concluded that the skeletons were those of young people of roughly the ages of the princes when they died, although margins of error were given. The sexes of the skeletons were not established nor was their age (i.e. the period of history in which they died).

Were these skeletons those of the princes? In view of the very precise position given by Sir Thomas More in his account of the reign of King Richard III, it seems very likely. At the very least, it is a most uncanny coincidence. Dental evidence seems to support the idea that the skeletons were those of the princes. The older child's teeth suggested that he (or she) was aged between 12 years nine months and 14 years five months. This fits in with the age of Edward V, who was 13 years old in 1483. Moreover, the skeleton of this child showed that it had a congenital dental abnormality, for both upper second premolar teeth are absent; Edward suffered from pain in the jaw. Lady Anne Mowbray, a close relation of Edward, also had congenitally missing teeth.

It is important to remember that the Tower of London contains many skeletons. For example, two skeletons, similar to those found under the White Tower, were found walled up in an old chamber. These could equally well have been the skeletons of the princes. Another discovery was that of an Iron Age youth, found during excavations of the Inner Ward.

Two other points are worth considering. First, the depth at which the skeletons were found. It has been suggested that 10 feet is quite deep, even for a secret grave, and that this depth suggests a much older burial. Yet, once again, Sir Thomas More was emphatic about the great depth of the grave. The second point is that, when the skeletons were first discovered in 1674, they were described as being found with "pieces of rag and velvet about them". Velvet was invented in Italy in the fifteenth century and was not manufactured in England until the sixteenth. (Velvet would have been imported into England in the fifteenth century.) Of course, it is quite possible that the person who gave this description used the word velvet to mean any kind of expensive cloth, but if the material was, indeed, velvet, then there is a strong probability that the remains are those of the Princes, not only because of the timing, but because only those of the very highest rank would have worn clothes made of this material.

With the modern techniques at the disposal of forensic scientists, many questions could be answered if a new examination of the remains took place. However, it seems unlikely that permission for a fresh investigation will be given. The bones are interred in an urn in Westminster Abbey.

Apart from being of intrinsic historical and scientific interest, this case shows how an investigation can be mishandled as a result of an incorrect approach from the outset. The "correct" answer was "known" before the forensic investigation began, with the result that the very question being asked could not be answered. This is not uncommon, as we shall see later in this chapter.

Below: *Engraving of* The Princes in the Tower *by Sir John Everett Millais RA. In October 1483, Prince Edward V and Prince Richard disappeared from the White Tower and were never seen alive again.*

Mark of the Beast

Bite marks inflicted on the victims of murder, especially women, leave a particularly unpleasant impression on the mind. Professor Keith Simpson, England's first Professor of Forensic Pathology, called it the "Mark of the Beast".

The silver lining of this unsavoury cloud is that the bite marks may betray the perpetrator. One of the first cases in which a conviction was brought about by bite-mark evidence began when a young couple, Mr and Mrs Gorringe, left a dance hall in Tunbridge Wells, Kent, England just before midnight on December 31, 1947. They were quarrelling as they left.

In the small hours of New Year's Day, 1948, Mrs Gorringe's dead body was found in a yard behind a lorry; she was still wearing her dance frock. Detective Superintendent Frank Smeed, head of the Kent CID, took charge of the case and asked Professor Simpson to help him in the investigation. The woman's head had been battered in and she had been strangled; and, significantly, she had a bite mark on her right breast.

Wax impressions of the mark were taken, revealing a set of teeth that were so badly spaced and angled that they seemed quite distinctive. They were compared with the teeth of Mr Gorringe, the prime suspect; and they fitted exactly. Gorringe was put on trial, convicted and sentenced to death, although he was later reprieved.

Below: *Professor Sir Keith Simpson (1907-1985), Professor of Forensic Pathology, photographed in 1975 after giving evidence at the inquest into the death of Lady Lucan's children's nanny.*

The Case of Gordon Hay

Although the Gorringe case was a pioneering one, it was relatively straightforward. A subsequent case, in which Professor Simpson was also involved, was more complex. On August 7, 1957, the body of Linda Peacock was found battered and strangled in a cemetery in Biggar, halfway between Edinburgh and Glasgow in Scotland. She was found by two policemen, lying between a tombstone and a yew tree. Again, she bore bite marks on her right breast.

Working in collaboration with Dr Warren Harvey of the Scottish Detective Training School, Professor Simpson took impressions of the marks. Meanwhile, the police interviewed 3,000 people and excluded all but 29 individuals from the investigation; they were all young men from a nearby detention centre. When asked, they all agreed to allow the police to take impressions of their teeth. One set of teeth, designated number 14, looked the most likely, but they didn't quite fit. Indeed, the marks left by the teeth looked decidedly odd. Number 14 was, eventually, eliminated.

The investigators, convinced that one of the men from the detention centre was the murderer, were puzzled by the lack of a definite "fit" by any one of the sets of teeth. But the problem was solved in a most startling way. Professor Simpson and Dr Harvey had assumed that the assailant's head was oriented in the same way as the head of the girl, but, by turning the cast impression round through an angle of 180°, the teeth of number 11 fitted perfectly; the man had bitten his victim by approaching her from behind – the heads had been upside down in relation to one another.

Gordon Hay, a 17-year-old youth, was number 11. He was known to have met Linda and had been with her the day before the murder. Dr Harvey wanted to make absolutely certain of the identification. Hay's teeth had strange crater-shaped pits on his canines; and Dr Harvey wanted to see how common this condition was. He examined 1,000 canines in 342 boys aged 16 or 17 and found only two with pits resembling those on Hay's teeth. Moreover, not one of the boys had more than one such pit, whereas Hay had several. He was found guilty of murder, but, because of his age, was sentenced to be detained at Her Majesty's pleasure.

Below: *Impression mould of teeth. Such moulds are routinely used by dentists when making crowns or dentures. They are also useful in forensic cases that involve mutilation by biting.*

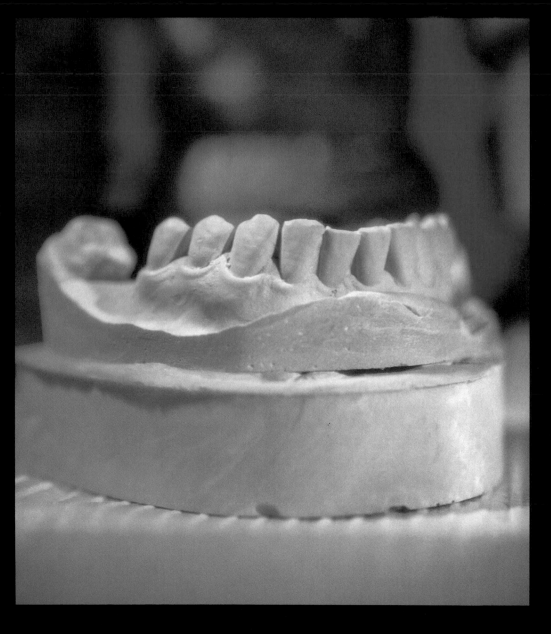

Cranio-facial Reconstruction

One of the techniques of human identification which is still being developed is video-superimposition. This grew out of photographic superimposition, which is simply the laying of a radiograph of a skull over a photograph to see whether the two would fit. Video-superimposition is essentially the same technique, but here the images can be manipulated by computer.

These methods have been used in several forensic cases, but for some reason they do not seem to have "caught on". One reason is the ease with which skulls and photographs can be made to match; and the exponents of this technique are themselves aware of this problem and advocate further research into the subject.

Cranio-facial reconstruction, on the other hand, is rapidly becoming an indispensable tool in forensic identification. This is a technique that produces an actual, three-dimensional model of the head and face from a skull. It is a very complex technique, requiring both the strict adherence to scientific facts, as well as an artistic flair in producing an actual model that people can look at and, hopefully, recognise.

While the application of this technique requires great skill and experience, the basic idea is simple enough. The muscles of the face "reflect" the shape of the skull beneath them; in other words, the thickness of the flesh at any given point will be largely dictated by the shape of the bone on which it lies. When a cranio-facial reconstructionist sets to work, he fixes little pegs at various key points on the skull, the height of the pegs being equal to the calculated thickness of the flesh at that point. Layers of clay, simulating the muscles, are then placed over the pegs and eventually a face appears.

The actual skull is not used in the reconstruction, but a cast made from the original is; this is because the skull itself may provide other kinds of evidence that would disappear under a layer of clay. Sometimes it is not even necessary to make a cast. When reconstructing the face of Peten Amen, an Ancient Egyptian mummy, Dr William Aulsebrook and his co-workers in South Africa took sectioned images of the skull as it lay within its wrappings. This was done using a technique called cat-scanning, in which the skull is "sliced" into a number of pieces that can be rebuilt on a computer. In this

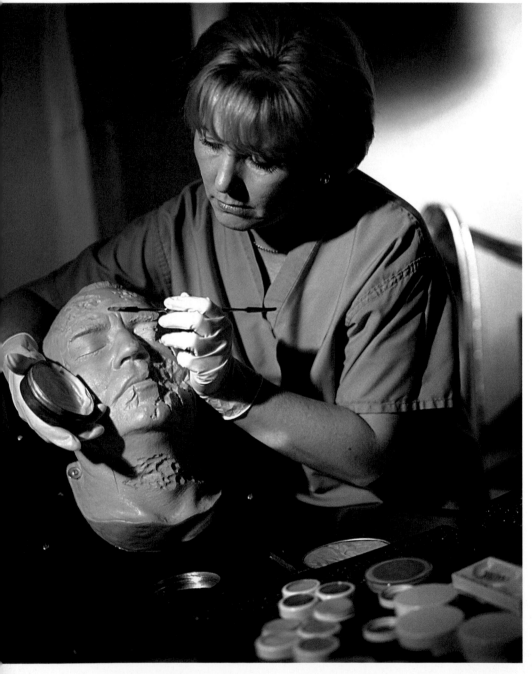

Left: *A face's appearance depends on the shape of the skull beneath. When reconstructing a face, a cast of the skull is used. Layers of clay are added until the face begins to appear.*

way, a three-dimensional computer image was produced. It was then used to make an actual model of the skull, which was used to produce the cranio-facial reconstruction.

Britain's foremost exponent of cranio-facial reconstruction is Richard Neave of the University of Manchester. One of his most famous cases is the reconstruction of the head and face of King Philip of Macedon, the father of Alexander the Great. An interesting point about this case is the fact that Philip received a dreadful battle wound on the forehead and right eye, features that are visible in some of the contemporary images made of him. We have seen above how anthropology can shed light on the medical history of a skeleton; and Philip is a case in point. The skull showed that the king had, indeed, received a horrendous wound in the right place.

Much of the efforts of cranio-facial reconstructionists have been directed toward the production of faces of historical characters, whose physical appearance was unknown. Inevitably, there have been doubts about the accuracy of the finished face, since there was no way in which they could be compared to the original face, or to a known visual representation of it. It was the application of the technique to forensic science that placed cranio-facial reconstruction on a firm footing, since now the faces could be checked against originals. In fact, independent studies on the reconstruction of faces from skulls whose "owners" appearance was known have shown that the technique is generally very successful, although the application to forensic science was the acid test.

Right: *Richard Neave in 2001 with a cast of the representative Semitic skull he used to recreate the face of Jesus. This was a composite generated from three well-preserved skulls from Jerusalem at the time of Jesus.*

CASE HISTORY

The Disappearance of Johann Boucher

In March, 1973, a young man named Johann Boucher disappeared after a car accident near Ladysmith, South Africa. No trace of him was found, although a picture of him was published in the local newspaper, *Die Nataller*. Boucher had been a storeman working for the South African Railways, but his employers and work-mates were unable to shed any light on his likely whereabouts.

In 1987 staff of the Durban Department of Parks, Recreation and Beaches found a skeleton lying under shrubs in the vicinity of Burman Bush. The skeleton remained unidentified for two years, all

attempts at matching dental records with the teeth having failed. Eventually, the police approached Dr Aulsebrook, who proceeded to reconstruct the skull's features. It was only after he had done this that the police showed him a photograph of Johann Boucher – the resemblance between the two was remarkable.

A newspaper, the *Mercury*, published a picture of Aulsebrook's reconstruction of Boucher's face; shortly after that the newspaper received a telephone call from a man who said that he recognised the face as being that of Boucher.

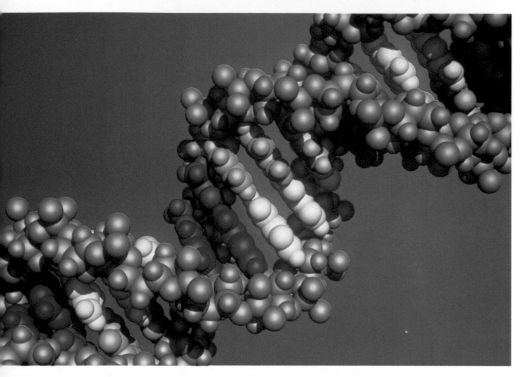

Above: *Model of a DNA molecule. Two atom strands twist into a helix. Each has a sugar-phosphate backbone (dark blue) and bases (guanine, cyan; cytosine, green; adenine, red; thymine, light blue) projecting inwards.*

We come now to that almost magical technique known as DNA fingerprinting. This technique is seen as being the most powerful and reliable tool in the forensic scientist's human identification armoury. Yet it is a much misunderstood technique, as we shall see.

DNA is the genetic material of the cell. It largely determines our physical characteristics, although much depends on the way in which environmental factors affect the way genes are expressed in the individual. This point need not concern us further here.

DNA, short for deoxyribonucleic acid, is present in the cell nucleus and in extra-nuclear organelles of the cell, known as mitochondria (singular: mitochondrion). We inherit half of our nuclear DNA from our fathers and half from our mothers, but we receive all our mitochondrial DNA (known as mtDNA) from our mothers. Thus, nuclear DNA can yield information about our paternal and maternal relations, while mtDNA can shed light only on our matrilineal descent.

The basic idea is that certain stretches of DNA are believed to be unique to an individual – no-one else will have the same DNA along those particular stretches, unless they were the identical twin of the individual in question. When a sample of tissue – be it blood, semen, skin, etc. – is found at the scene, it can be collected and used as a source of DNA. Once the DNA is extracted it is cut into little pieces by certain enzymes that act as chemical scissors. This mixture of DNA pieces is placed on a plate in a gel through which an electric current is passed. The different pieces will separate from one another as they move along the gel, the larger ones will move faster and farther than the smaller ones. The result is still invisible to the human eye, so radioactively labelled pieces of DNA are added; these adhere to the pieces already separated. The radioactivity makes the pieces visible when an X-ray film of the gel is made. In this way a "picture" of the DNA can be made and compared with a similarly-prepared "picture" of the DNA from the suspect. If the samples match exactly, one has a positive identification. The now-famous DNA profile is this picture, which is a series of bands resembling the bar code on supermarket products.

The perceived infallibility of DNA evidence has had a remarkable effect, not only on police officers eager to believe that they had a guaranteed method of identification, but also on criminals themselves. In a British case of murder and rape, the criminal involved paid a man to impersonate him when DNA samples were taken from people living in the area. The deception was luckily discovered, and the man was arrested and convicted.

DNA fingerprinting has had many other notable successes; its failures, on the other hand, have not always received publicity.

"Get me every 'ologist under the sun!" These were the words of Detective Chief Superintendent John Williams, the officer in charge of the case of Karen Price, the girl whose skeleton was found wrapped in a carpet and buried in the garden of a derelict house in Cardiff in 1989.

John Williams' order was obeyed by his staff, with the result that the investigation of the murder of Karen Price became a classic of forensic detection. I was involved in the case, but the star of the show was Richard Neave, who reconstructed the girl's face, with the result that she was recognized and identified by several people. DNA samples taken from the bones and compared with Karen's parents confirmed the identification.

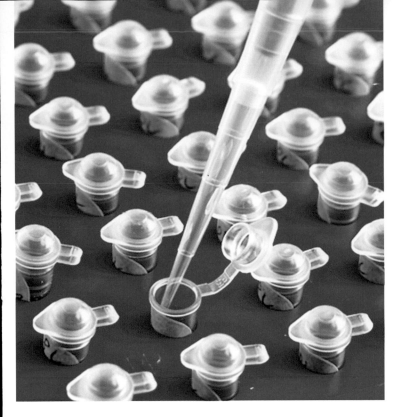

DNA had been extracted and a profile made, no-one would have been able to make any sense of it. People do not recognize DNA profiles as things they have seen before. It was only when Neave came up with the face – an idea or a hypothesis that could be tested – did DNA come into its own.

No evidence is infallible – not even DNA or old-fashioned fingerprints. Arriving at the truth in a forensic investigation is a matter of attacking the problem from many different angles. If the story that emerges is supported by all the strands of evidence, one can then have good reason to believe that it is the truth.

Left: *Modern procedures can amplify and quickly process trace amounts of DNA from blood, saliva, skin, hair, etc found at a scene.*

Below: *The DNA sequence or "fingerprint" resembles a series of supermarket bar codes.*

I applaud Williams' approach to the task, as expressed in his instruction to his staff, not only because it displays a thoroughness, but mainly because it demonstrated an understanding of the nature of evidence. I am sometimes asked why we need to bother with techniques such as blood-typing, fingerprinting (the old kind), anthropology and all such methods, when we now have the highly scientific and infallible DNA testing.

The answer, of course, is that DNA fingerprinting is of absolutely no use, unless one has some idea as to whom the victim or the culprit may have been. In the Karen Price case, if

CASE HISTORY

The Case of Tommie Lee Andrews

On February 21, 1987, in Orlando, Florida, USA, a woman, asleep at home, was viciously beaten and repeatedly raped by an intruder. Later, the police found two fingerprints on the window-sill. They then arranged for a swab to be taken from the woman in order to obtain a sample of the assailant's semen.

In March, the police received a call saying that a prowler had been seen in a particular part of the city; a police car that went to the area in response to the call saw a car speeding away. The police car followed it, until their quarry turned round a sharp corner and crashed his car. The driver was arrested and identified as one Tommie Lee Andrews. Another woman, the victim of an earlier

rape, identified Andrews as her attacker. He was put on trial for rape, battery and armed burglary. The fingerprints from the window-sill proved to be those of Andrews. Further tests were conducted and it was shown that the semen belonged to a person with blood-group O; Andrews was blood-group O. Finally, DNA tests on the semen, Andrews' blood and the victim's blood were compared. The results showed clearly that the semen came from Andrews. DNA from semen recovered from the victim of the earlier assault also showed it to be the same as Andrews' DNA. Tommie Lee Andrews was found guilty as charged and sentenced to 100 years in prison.

In the Blood

BLOOD, OF COURSE, is one of the commonest things to be found at the scene of a violent crime. Almost everybody will have heard about blood-grouping as a method of narrowing down the number of suspects; however what is not generally understood is that the famous ABO system is only one of 14 possible methods of blood-typing. That being said, ABO is probably the most commonly used system. All systems are based on the types of antigen (a protein molecule capable of binding on to an antibody) on the red blood cell's membrane.

In the ABO system the two antigens are known as A and B; and four blood-groups are determined according to this system – A, B, AB and O. People having the blood-group A have the A antigen; those belonging to the B group have the B antigen; those belonging to the AB category have both antigens; while those classified as belonging to the O group have neither antigen.

The antibodies present in a person's blood correspond to the opposite group, thus A-group people have b antibodies; those having B antigens have a antibodies; AB people have neither a nor b antibodies; and, finally, O-group people have both a and b antibodies. If, say, b antibodies are introduced in to the blood of a B-group person, the reaction will make the red cells clump together, resulting in death.

The test employed for determining the blood-group of a person thus depends on the addition of antibodies to a sample of blood and taking a note of the reaction. It can easily be seen that blood-group O can only give a negative result, although other, more specialized methods are used to determine blood-group positively. Contrary to popular belief, the antigens used in ABO testing are to be found, in most people, in other body fluids, such as saliva and sweat. This means that even traces of saliva found on a piece of cloth may reveal a person's blood-group.

Below: *Detecting biological stains. Biological stains (blood, sweat, semen, fingerprints etc) often fluoresce (glow) under ultraviolet light. Red lighting makes the fluorescence even more visible.*

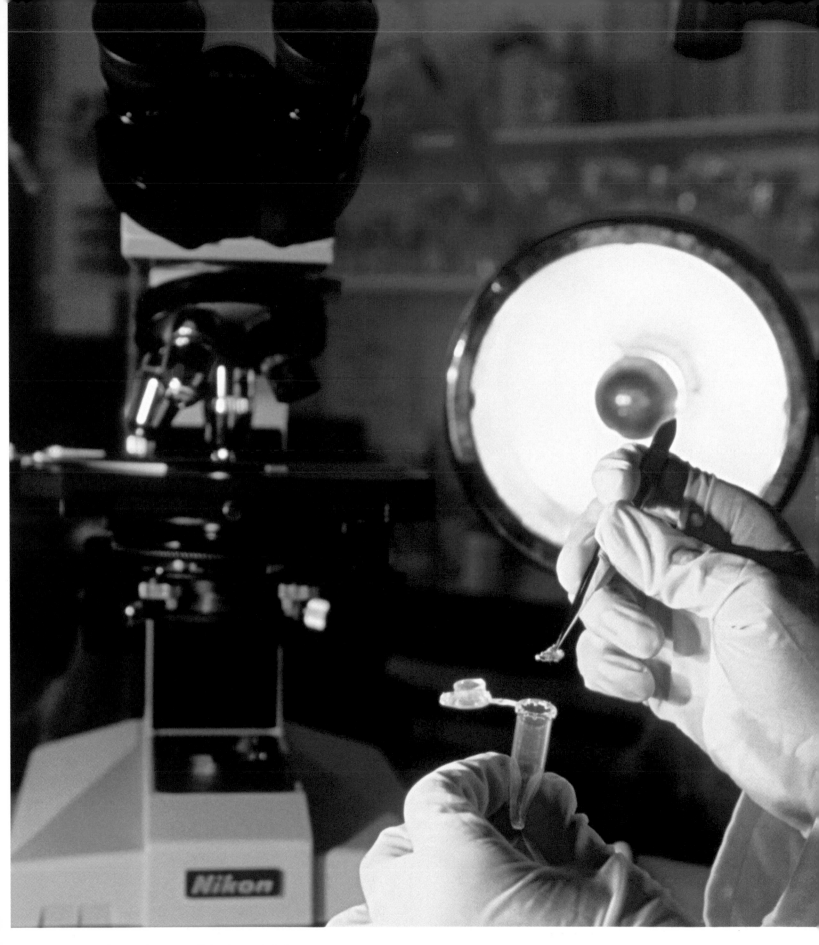

Above: *Blood sampling. A fragment of bloodstained clothing from a crime scene can be used to extract a blood sample for blood typing and DNA fingerprinting analysis.*

* This remark does not apply to examiners in the United States, where there is more concern with profressional standards than there is with the counting of matching points.

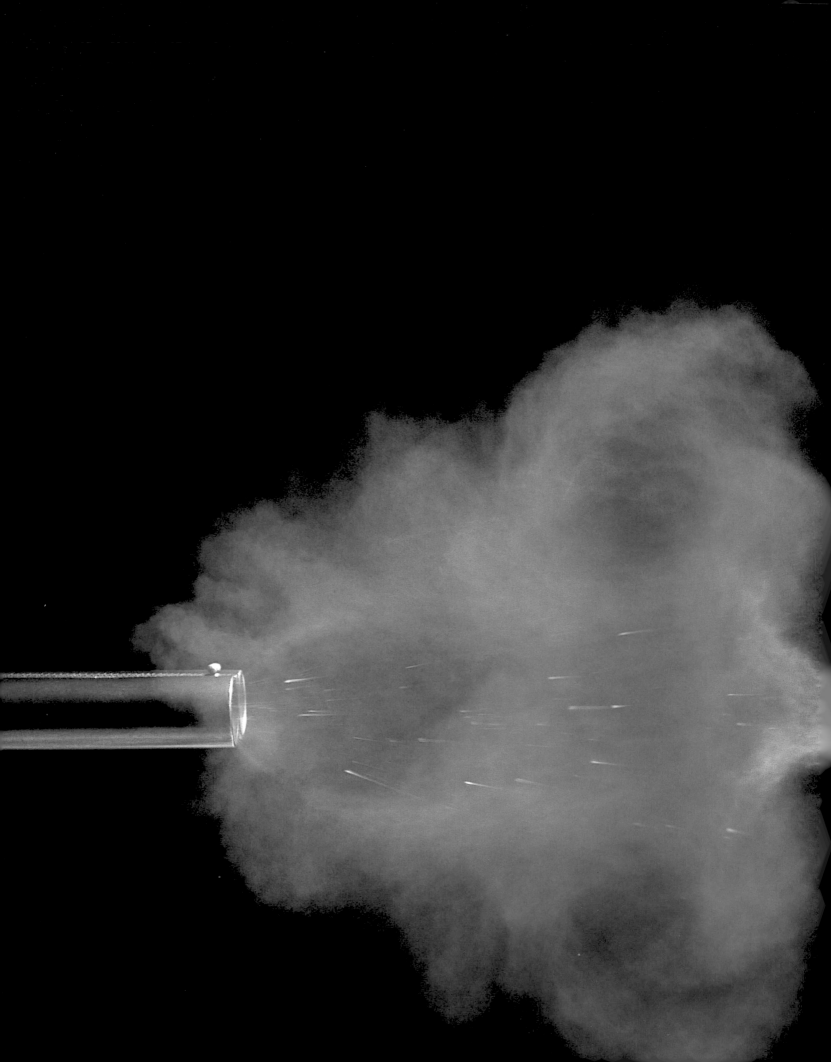

CAUSES

We enter now into the realm of causes – the "How?" of forensic science. Forensic pathologists distinguish between the *cause* of death and the *manner* of death.

The cause of death can be something like heart failure, but the manner of death may be a stabbing through the heart. In other words, the manner of death is the cause of the cause. Another expression used in describing violent death is the mode of death. This is the way the person died – was it a "natural" death, was it suicide, or was it homicide. A "natural" death in the context of violence may mean, to use the classic phrase, that someone jumped and was not pushed. "Homicide" is a general term, used for the killing of one person by another: it could be murder – a legal term carrying with it implications of intent (malice aforethought) – but it could also be manslaughter, the unlawful killing of one person without malice aforethought, or even excusable killing (e.g. self defence).

Stab Wounds

Stabbing someone to death with a sharp-tipped weapon has a long history and is still a very common means of murder. The injuries caused by stabbing often appear so trivial, since a powerful stab with a sharp knife will enter the body with minimal damage to the skin. Moreover, a thrown knife will enter a body with greater force than will a knife held in the hand and stabbed into the victim.

A case in point concerned a young woman, who was cutting bread at a table. Her sister, sitting on a settee with her fiancé, was teasing her about her lack of success with boyfriends. Annoyed, the woman threw the knife at her sister, who turned away. The knife entered her head behind her left ear. Although her fiancé immediately pulled the knife out, she fainted and died about 40 minutes later.

The post-mortem examination showed such a trivial external wound that it was difficult to see how this could have caused death. In fact, the knife had penetrated under the base of the skull, passed through the jugular vein, through the neck muscles between the first and second cervical vertebrae, the tip coming to rest at the very centre of the lower medulla, or brain stem.

Stab wounds, by definition, are deep wounds. Not all stabbings are carried out with a very sharp instrument; many blunter implements, such as closed scissors or a poker, are sometimes used. Generally speaking, the blunter the instrument, the more ragged the entry hole is and the more bruised the surrounding skin becomes. When a sharp knife is used, the entry hole can be no more than a slit, particularly if the weapon is double-edged, like a dagger. A single-edged knife, such as a kitchen knife, will often leave a slit that tapers toward one end, as may be expected. However, the expected shapes of the holes or slits may be modified by the circumstances of the stabbing. If, for example, the victim twists, or the perpetrator turns the knife in the wound, the resulting entry hole will look very different. Therefore, it is not always easy to decide during the post-mortem what the width of the blade was. As regards the length of the blade, one is on firmer ground, for the depth of the cut (or the deepest cut, if there are several) will give a measure of the minimum length of the blade – minimum, because the blade may not have gone in right to the hilt. Similar reasoning applies to the estimation of the width of the blade; if wounds of various widths are present, then clearly the one with the narrowest width will give the surest indication of width. Again, one must interpret narrow wounds with care, since they may have been inflicted very shallowly, with only the blade's tip entering and cutting the skin. Such surface wounds are no guide to width of blade.

The way a stab is inflicted, or, more generally, the way an edged weapon is used, may give an indication as to whether the wound was self-inflicted or not. Cutting of the throat and stabbing through the heart are often a means of suicide, although this happens less frequently these days, due to the ease with which various poisonous substances are available. It is obvious that stabs in the back are unlikely to be suicidal.

In cases in which the victim's throat is cut, there are several

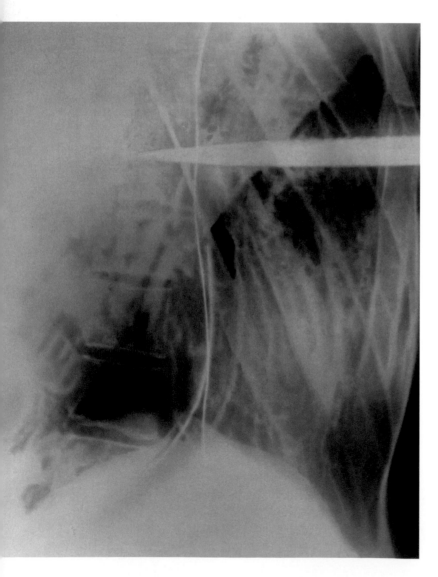

Left: *Coloured X-ray of knife in chest cavity. The ribs and spine (vertical blocks, left) are pale orange. A thorough examination of a stab wound is always necessary to check that the weapon can be removed safely.*

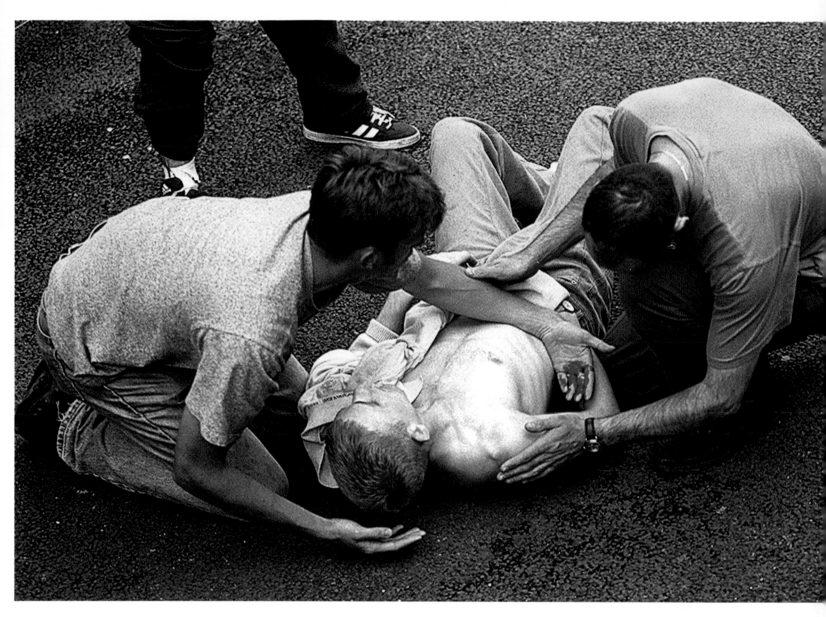

signs that point to the death as being suicidal or homicidal. Suicides never kill themselves with one clean cut of the throat. There are always several "experimental" cuts before the final, fatal cut or cuts are made. Dozens of cuts may be made experimentally, and some suicides have been known to give up the attempt after several trials, resorting to poison in the end.

In a suicide the cuts on the throat are shallow at first; and they are close together and more or less parallel to one another on that side of the throat opposite to the hand that is normally used for writing. The fatal wound or wounds are deeply cut downwards, then across the throat, then upwards again toward the other ear. These wounds can be very deep indeed, with knife-strokes cutting through to the spine; cases are known in which the head was almost completely severed.

Interestingly, people committing suicide in this manner often make it harder for themselves by tilting the head back, which causes the carotid arteries to slide back on either side of the

Above: *Riots in Bradford, England. This youth suffered stab wounds in the back during riots in 2001. By examining the wound it may be possible to tell what kind of weapon was used.*

spine. This means that most of the blood lost is venous, not arterial, which, in turn, means that the subject remains conscious for longer and that the agony is prolonged.

In homicidal throat-cutting the cuts are fewer and more cleanly incised; and the hesitant, experimental cuts are absent. Also, the cuts usually occur either higher or lower than the cuts made by suicides. Often, the victim's hands will be injured, as a result of the defensive action taken to fend off the attack.

If it seems odd that suicides can continue hacking at their throats for a long time without killing themselves instantly, it is worth making the point that many injuries usually regarded as being instantly fatal are, in fact, not always so. One such kind of injury is the stab to the heart; in one case a man stabbed in the heart was able to run to a window and jump out.

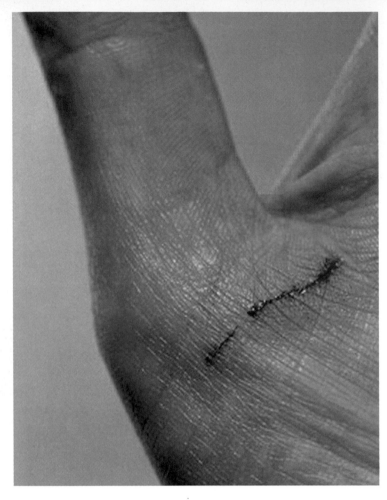

Above: *Cuts and grazes. These can be useful clues as to whether injuries are accidental, self-inflicted or due to an attack.*

So far, we have considered what are called incised wounds, but there are, of course, many other kinds of injury. It is sometimes assumed that deep, complex injuries provide more clues to the forensic specialist, but, in fact, it is the simpler, non-fatal wounds that usually yield most information. Grazes of the skin, or abrasions, are considered to be the most informative of all wounds.

The reason that slight surface injuries often yield so much information is that they can show the marks of an attack, including a self-inflicted one, very clearly. For example, the marks left by the fingernails of a strangler on the neck of his victim may be mild and would certainly not have caused death, but can be recognised very easily. Finding such impressions could suggest that the examination of material from under the nails of a suspect is indicated, since blood or tissues from the victim may still be found there. Such material may be identifiable as belonging to the

victim. Fingernail marks may sometimes be long and drawn, which may be caused by the victim's attempts at escape or at forcing the strangling hands away. We have already seen how bite-marks may be important clues in identification.

Bruises are another kind of injury; they are caused by the diffusion of blood from broken blood vessels into the surrounding tissues, where it clots. Bruises, or contusions as medics call them, are very often not accompanied by any injury or break of the surface skin, although this is not always the case. A stab from a blunt instrument may result in an incision and a bruise around the edges of the cut itself. Unfortunately, the size and shape of a bruise is not a reliable guide to its cause, since much depends on the force of the blow, the kind of tissues that received the blow, the age and medical condition of the victim and so on. However, it is worth disposing of one particular myth, namely, that bruises cannot be inflicted on a dead body. They certainly can be, since a bruise results from the seepage of blood from broken capillaries into the tissues. After death there is no heart pressure, so the blood seeps out to a lesser extent. Microscopic examination of the bruised tissues can reveal whether bruising took place before or after death. A bruise inflicted during life will contain a higher than usual count of white blood cells, which move to the injured site to start the healing process. Such a reaction does not take place if the bruise is inflicted after death.

Below: *Bruising patterns can help in reconstructing events (see case history). This rib bruise was caused by an iron bar.*

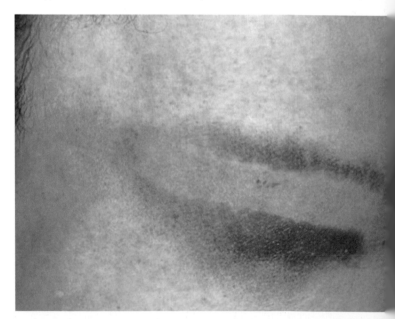

The Tell-Tale Hand

Late in November, 1943, a woman named Rose Ada Robinson was found dead in her bedroom in Portsmouth. She was the licensee of a public house and was in the habit of taking the day's earnings up to her room in two bags every evening and, ill-advisedly, of telling everyone that she did this. When the police entered her room they found the bags empty; they had contained £450. The time of death was estimated as being at about 2.00 am or 3.00 am. The window was broken, but the door was unbolted and unlocked, which clearly meant that the murderer came in through the window and left through the door.

Mrs Robinson was strangled to death. Bruises showed that she had struck her head against the window-sill, before being dragged to the floor and killed. Yet the marks on her neck were rather unusual. There was one large bruise over the voice-box and three smaller ones to the left as one looked down at the neck. Oddly, there were no fingernail impressions where one would have expected them to be; but there were scratches that had clearly been caused by Mrs Robinson herself as she struggled to free herself. Odd, too, was the small span of the hand that strangled her – four inches.

What could it mean? Suspects were questioned and cleared. Some time later, the police arrested a man who was trying to sell some stolen shoes. His name, he said, was Harold Loughans. No doubt to the officers' surprise, he began to confess to other crimes. Weeping, he said that he had killed Mrs Robinson a month earlier. Interestingly, the tips of all the fingers of his right hand, except the thumb, were missing. This fitted in with the marks, suggesting a small hand, on Mrs Robinson's neck.

When the case came to trial, Loughans denied his confessions and said that they had been made up by the police. An important part of the evidence concerned the question of whether Loughans had enough strength in his right hand to strangle someone to death. The prosecution's pathologist, Professor Keith Simpson, believed that he had, but the defence pathologist, the great Sir Bernard Spilsbury, did not. Spilsbury had asked Loughans to grip his hand as hard as possible and, on the basis of this, concluded that his hand was too weak to strangle anyone. Both pathologists gave evidence, but, such was the awe in which Spilsbury was held, the jury found Loughans not guilty.

When Loughans left the court-room, he was immediately arrested by the police for another crime, for which he was convicted. In prison he became known as "Handy", because of the dexterity of his right hand. Years later, the newspaper, The People, published an article, saying that Loughans was, in all probability, guilty of Mrs Robinson's murder. Loughans took the newspaper to court for libel, an action he lost. A few months later, knowing he was dying of cancer, Loughans walked into the offices of The People and made a written confession: "I want to say I done that job. I did kill the woman in the public house in Portsmouth". He wrote the confession with his right hand.

Below: *Sir Bernard Henry Spilsbury (1877–1947). His career as a forensic pathologist began with the trial of Dr Crippen in 1910.*

Above: *Death by drowning. This specialized underwater brigade from Paris is recovering a body from the Seine. A post-mortem will establish whether death was due to drowning or another cause.*

Death by strangling is due to asphyxia – the inability to breathe because of obstruction of the respiratory apparatus. The biochemical changes that occur include a decrease of oxygen in the blood and tissues, together with an increase of carbon dioxide, and the development of a suffused, purplish colour – cyanosis – in the skin. Blood-staining may appear around the nose and mouth. Petechiae, or spots of haemorrhage, appear, due to the bursting of small capillary blood vessels. These petechial haemorrhages are particularly good signs of asphyxia. However, sometimes the inhibition of the vagus

nerve (because of the pressure applied to it) during strangulation may cause death suddenly and quickly, before the usual symptoms of asphyxia appear. In such cases the natural tendency to struggle to breathe does not happen.

People being strangled often vomit, increasing the probability of asphyxia, since the vomited matter may clog up the air passages further. However, in cases in which vomiting has occurred, it is important to consider the possibility that the vomiting may not have been caused by strangulation, but that the act of vomiting itself caused the asphyxiation of the victim. In other words, vomiting could be the cause, rather than the consequence.

Clearly, asphyxia can be caused in a number of ways, such as by choking on food, suffocation (in which the victim's mouth and nose are covered), or by what is known as overlaying, as when a mother rolls over in bed and accidentally comes to lie on top of her baby. Many such cases are clearly accidental, but overlaying is sometimes treated as a criminal matter, even if it is accidental. This is the case when someone has been drinking and then gets into a bed where a baby is sleeping. Overlaying in such a case is a criminal offence.

A particularly common form of death caused by asphyxia is, of course, drowning. When someone drowns, the air passages, as well as the stomach are filled with water. However, due to the pressure of water in the lungs, the blood vessels tend not to burst and rarely do petechiae appear. Also, people who drown in natural bodies of water will often have large numbers of diatoms – microscopic algae with silicon shells – in their blood, bone marrow and brain. Debris from the water, such as soil or small water organisms, will be found in the stomach. Drowned persons will show froth emanating from the mouth and nose.

Not all water deaths are, strictly speaking, drownings. Vagal inhibition, caused by a sudden change in temperature, such as falling into icy water, may cause death before drowning takes place. It is often said that those who died when the *Titanic* sank were drowned; in fact, they died of the cold.

Our bodies have a particular osmotic balance, which it is harmful to alter to any great extent. The inhalation and swallowing of water during drowning, therefore, results in great disturbance to this osmotic state, with severely damaging consequences. Interestingly, drowning in fresh water is usually very rapid, since the blood is diluted to such an extent that water will enter the blood cells, causing them to burst. In sea water, drowning is much slower, since the increase in osmotic pressure in the blood will cause water to flow out of the blood cell into the plasma, a state with which the body can cope much better.

Drowned people found unclothed or wearing a swimming costume are likely to have drowned by accident, although this is not necessarily always the case. People found drowned while fully-clothed are more likely to have drowned by intent, usually murderous intent. Suicides tend to remove some of their clothes before taking the plunge.

People can sometimes drown in very shallow water, although foul play may not necessarily be the cause. Injured or sick people may collapse and die in situations that look suspicious, and it is not unknown for such people to fall into, say, the edge of a lake or river and drown in a foot or two of water.

Whenever I have lectured about forensic science to students or general audiences, I have noticed that there is a general assumption that the more scientifically complex a forensic investigation is, the more impressive is the evidential value of the results. In fact, the opposite is often true; a simple, straightforward clue, correctly interpreted, may shed a good deal more light on a case than can a clue that requires investigation using sophisticated and expensive equipment. The historic drowning incident in the following case study is a good example.

Below: The Titanic. *During its maiden voyage in 1912, the unsinkable* Titanic *struck an iceberg in the North Atlantic and sank. Of the 2,200 plus passengers and crew, nearly 1,500 died, mostly from the cold.*

The Mysterious Death of King Ludwig II of Bavaria

On the afternoon of June 13, 1886, Ludwig II, King of Bavaria, left his castle, Schloss Berg, and went for a walk with his physician, Dr Gudden, by the shores of Lake Starnberg. They were expected back at the castle by eight o'clock in the evening but, when that hour arrived, they had still not returned.

An hour later, a search was started. Before long, the searchers found ominous signs that a dreadful thing had happened, for on the path that went round the lake the king's umbrella and his jacket and overcoat were found. It had been raining heavily and the clothes were drenched. The jacket and overcoat must have been removed in a hurry, since they were both turned inside out, with the sleeves of the jacket still inside those of the overcoat.

Close to the spot where the clothes were found were several bushes and trees. Some branches were broken, suggesting that someone had moved quickly, or been pushed, through the vegetation. Beyond the bushes was the lake. Soon, the search party found what it was looking for; the dead body of the king was found floating face-downwards, with his arms stretched out toward the shore. The water was less than four feet deep at that spot. Not far from the king, Dr Gudden's corpse was found floating; although he too was face-down, he was in an odd half-kneeling, half-sitting position.

What had happened? Was it accident, suicide or murder? The first possibility can be ruled out; strong men who are also strong swimmers do not drown in four feet of water; and the king was an exceptionally strong swimmer. The full story of King Ludwig is too complex to recount here; suffice to say that he was surrounded by political intrigue and that he was a very unstable character. In short, both murder and suicide were possible under the circumstances.

The accounts of who saw what and when are all so confusing and unclear that it is difficult to arrive at the truth. But there is one piece of evidence that is quite undisputed and which has been overlooked as a clue in all the debates about the way King Ludwig met his death.

It is simply this: his bowler hat was found floating on the water. So, too, was Dr Gudden's silk top hat. Now it is an interesting fact that people who commit suicide invariably remove their hats before they throw themselves into the water. Also, deep water is chosen for suicidal purposes, as well as a high jump. Choosing less than four feet of water in which to drown oneself is absurd.

But what of the jacket and overcoat, how can their removal be explained? We have seen that they were removed in a hurry and turned inside out; this suggests that they might have been removed to escape the clutches of someone gripping the king by his clothes. The king may then have reached the lake, with his bowler still on his head, was then pursued into the water by his attacker and drowned or shot. It is the only scenario that covers all the undisputed facts. Accident can be ruled out; suicide is extremely unlikely – what is left is murder.

Below: *King Ludwig II of Bavaria (1845–1886). His death is surrounded by mystery, but there is some evidence that he was shot not drowned.*

Death by Hanging

HANGING IS A PARTICULAR manner of death, of which asphyxia is only part. It is important to remember that the word "hanging" is used to describe two somewhat different manners of death. A judicial hanging, or execution, involves a long drop that breaks the neck. This seldom happens in non-judicial hangings, most of which by far are suicides. A suicide hanging causes death in three ways: first, the pressure on the jugular veins and carotid arteries results in a lack of oxygen reaching the brain; secondly, the pressure on the vagus nerve causes breathing inhibition; and, finally, asphyxia results, because the breathing passageways are obstructed by the tongue and glottis, which are pushed into the pharynx.

Victims of hanging show much the same post-mortem signs as do victims of strangulation, notably cyanosis and petechiae. In addition, the tongue is often found protruding through the mouth, the eyes may bulge out and ligature marks will, of course, be present.

Although very few hangings indeed are homicidal, some occur by accident. I know a case of a 12-year-old boy who hanged himself accidentally while playing with a rope on the stairs, tying one end of the rope round the bannister and the other end round his neck. He slipped, the noose tightening around his neck, probably inducing him to lose consciousness very quickly before dying. However, most accidental hangings take place when young men indulge in certain masochistic practices. It seems that these practices and their consequent deaths are much commoner among men than women.

Death by hanging is not always caused by the three factors listed above. When, on March 7, 1975, the body of Lesley Whittle, the victim of Donald Neilson, better known as the Black Panther, was found hanging 60 feet below ground level in a concrete shaft, it was first concluded that she had died of asphyxia. Later, it was found that vagal inhibition was the true cause, her heart stopping through sheer terror.

Blunt Instruments

We come now to the use of the blunt instrument as a murder weapon. Murders committed this way are usually unpremeditated killings and may not be murders in the strict sense at all, but such things as crimes of passion or assaults committed under provocation. However, premeditated murders are committed with blunt instruments, and can be among the most horrific of all kinds of murder.

To begin with, an assault with a blunt weapon is usually made at the head, not at other parts of the body. Death is often caused by brain injury and the scene of the crime is almost always very bloody, since head injuries bleed copiously.

The "effectiveness" of a blunt instrument depends on two attributes: its weight and the speed with which it is wielded. The resulting force of the blow – its kinetic energy – can be expressed as follows:

$$E = \frac{m \times v2}{2}$$

Where E = kinetic energy, m = mass and v = velocity.

It is clear from this equation that the speed with which the weapon is travelling at the time contact is made has the greater effect, since its value is squared. In other words, a strong blow with a piece of wood will cause more damage than a feeble blow with a sledgehammer, speaking in very general terms. Among the commonest blunt instruments are hammers, pokers and other household implements.

Although blunt instruments may be seen as being the least "professional" of murder weapons, to my mind they are among the most unpleasant. This is not only because of the large amount of blood that is splashed about the scene, but because several well-aimed, powerful blows are required to kill the victim. A stab from a knife or a bullet from a rifle will, usually, kill instantly, whereas the wielder of the blunt instrument displays a kind of brutal tenacity that is particularly dreadful.

Once the skull is cracked or smashed by a blow, damage to the brain and its membranes will occur. In fact, damage to the membranes can occur even if the skull is not fractured by the blow. Epidural haemorrhaging (bleeding outside the dura mater, the tough membrane that lines the skull) can occur due to the tearing of the blood vessels supplying the brain. This type of injury is most commonly seen in teenagers. The blood

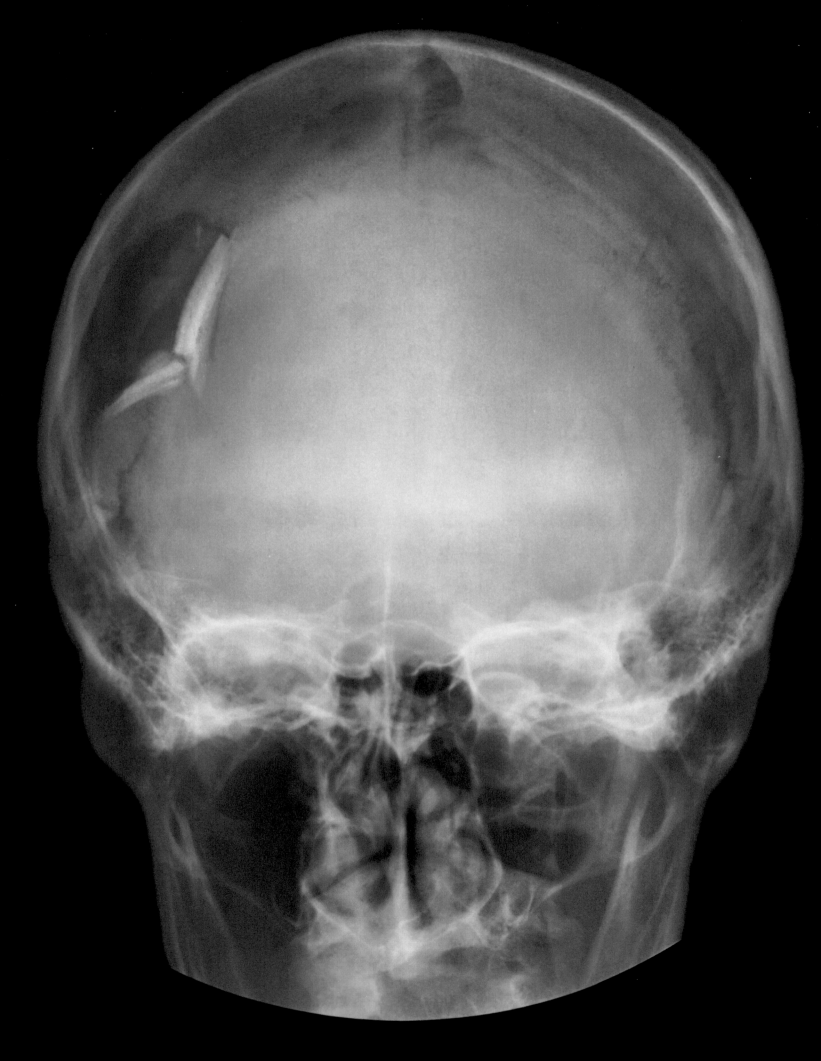

accumulates between the dura and the bone of the skull. Often, no injury, apart from bruising of the skin, is apparent, whereas, in fact, the blood is accumulating in the space between membrane and skull, putting pressure on the brain. Death may follow a few hours later; post-mortem examination will show a blood clot at the site of bleeding.

Subdural haemorrhages (bleeding between the dura and the brain itself) often result in a blood cyst. As blood leaks very

Left: *Fractured skull. Coloured X-ray of a depressed fracture (red) caused by a blow from a blunt instrument. In severe cases, the bone fragments may need to be surgically restored to their correct position.*

Below: *Coloured computed tomography scan of an axial section of the head shows a subdural haematoma (red). An impact to the head caused bleeding between the membranes surrounding the brain.*

slowly in this type of injury, it is rarely fatal and may go unnoticed for years. What are known as subarachnoid haemorrhages (bleeding below the arachnoid membrane of the brain) are as often caused by natural causes as by blows to the head and are often associated with aneurysms (dilations of the arteries, due to the weakness of the arterial wall). Sometimes a relatively light blow may cause haemorrhaging. In one case a father, sparring with his grown son, was horrified to see the young man collapse and die after he had struck him a few light blows. The post-mortem showed that the son had an aneurysm and the father was discharged. Subarachnoid bleeding in the absence of an aneurysm gives grounds for suspicion of foul play.

Blows to the head, even with the fist, can cause damage to the brain as a result of the movement of the brain within the

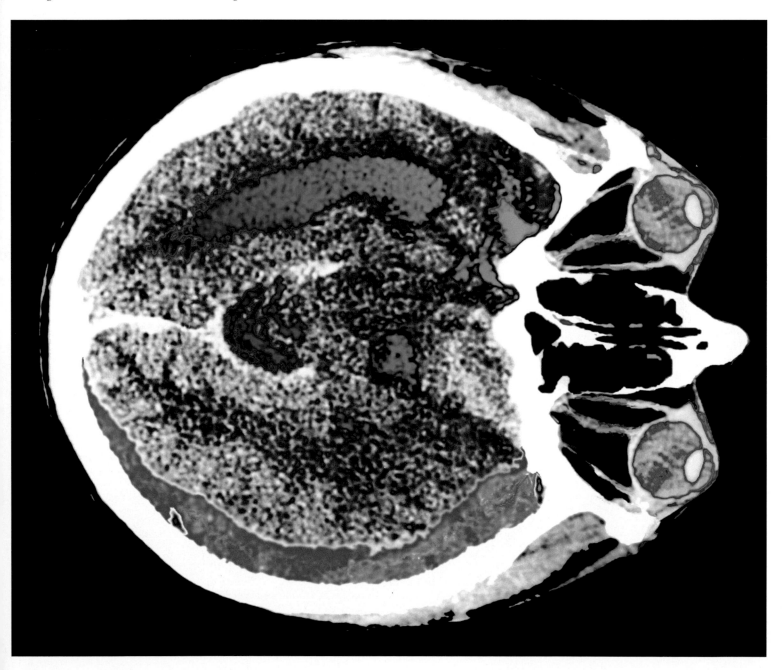

Above: *Lithograph of General George Armstrong Custer at the Battle of the Little Big Horn, Montana, USA, 25 June 1876. After the battle the victorious Sioux and Cheyenne Indians mutilated the dead.*

cranium. A blow in itself may not cause much damage, but if the head twists round at some speed as a result of the blow, the brain will be chafed against the inside of the skull, since the latter will be travelling faster than the former. In this context, I have often been puzzled by the fist-fights that are commonly shown on film, typically in cowboy westerns. The blows inflicted by these people on one another would, in reality, cause severe external and internal damage, although in the films they hardly ever sustain even a minor bruise! This would be merely amusing, were it not for the possibility that youngsters, emulating their film heroes, may injure themselves quite seriously.

Another type of head injury, known as contre-coup, results when the head strikes the ground after a fall. Here the injury takes place at a spot opposite that at which the head was struck. If a man falls backwards, striking the back of his head on the

floor, injury to the front of the brain may occur. This is because the skull is travelling much faster than the brain, which will receive chafing injuries, as well as "piling up" injuries to the front of the brain.

It is quite remarkable how injuries to the brain can sometimes fail to result in death. One case on record involved a man who drove a four-inch nail into his brain through his forehead in a suicide attempt. The nail was removed and the man survived!

Injuries inflicted after death are usually easily recognisable as such, since there is no cellular reaction, as we have seen in the case of post-mortem bruises. Injuries inflicted by blunt weapons are no exception, as was shown very clearly when the battlefield of the Little Bighorn River in Montana, was excavated by archaeologists. This battle – in which General Custer, at his last stand, was killed, together with all his men – was followed by some horrific cruelties. The Sioux and Cheyenne Indians were apt to mutilate the dead and the nearly dead after a victory. Black Elk, the warrior chief, described how his warriors used clubs and hatchets to mutilate the dead and finish off the injured survivors. Interestingly, the anthropologists working on the archaeological dig were able to confirm his story and showed how the bones of so many of the bodies had been broken while the bone was still "green". Such injuries, inflicted at or about the time of death, have been termed perimortem injuries.

It is fortunate that it is possible to distinguish between injuries inflicted after death and those inflicted before death, since much can turn on such matters. Injuries are sometimes inflicted after death in order to suggest that death was due to suicide, not murder. A case in point concerns the death of Sir Edmund Berry Godfrey, who was found impaled on his sword in 1678. Initially, it was believed that he had killed himself, until the post-mortem examination revealed that he had been strangled to death, the sword having been thrust through him after death.

Right: *This woodcut depicting the murder of Sir Edmund Berry Godfrey (1621–1678) was used in a pack of playing cards.*

CASE HISTORY

The Case Of William Podmore

Vivian Messiter's body was discovered in a garage in Southampton in January, 1929. At first, it was thought that he had been shot; then it was believed he had died of a haemorrhage. In fact, he was battered to death with a hammer.

It is worth pointing out at this juncture that, contrary to popular belief, most uniformed police officers never see a case of murder and their initial description of the scene may leave a great deal to be desired. Despite the fact that Messiter's head had been severely battered, the above conclusions about manner of death were suggested.

The full story of this case is a very involved one, but the essential point is that Messiter, who was an agent of the Wolf's Head Oil Company, discovered that Podmore was embezzling company funds. When Messiter confronted Podmore with this, there followed an argument, which ended in murder.

The interesting findings of Sir Bernard Spilsbury, who examined the body, were as follows: there were several blows to the head with a blunt instrument like a hammer; one of the injuries was inflicted on the forehead, just above the eye, by the pointed, back end of the

hammer, the others by the flatter, heavier end; the hammer had to have been of the type that had a pointed end, not the usual kind of hammer with two curved prongs for the extraction of nails; one injury was to the back of the head, suggesting that the victim had been either bending over or was struck from behind.

It was the hole-like puncture above the eye that gave rise to the idea that Messiter had been shot. Whatever suggested a haemorrhage remains a mystery, but, as we shall see later, such bizarre conclusions are not unknown.

A blood-stained hammer, of the type Spilsbury described, was found in the garage not far from the spot at which Messiter fell. But the most damning of Spilsbury's conclusions was that two of the injuries were inflicted when the man was down, with his head resting on a hard surface. This weighed heavily against Podmore in court, suggesting as it did a callous vindictiveness. Another clue was the final nail in Podmore's coffin. Two hairs were found by Spilsbury adhering to the hammer. These were compared with the victim's eyebrows and were found to be identical. Podmore was found guilty and was hanged.

Death by Shooting

irearm killings are commoner in the United States than in Britain and western Europe, although they are increasing on this side of the Atlantic. Essentially, there are two types of firearm: smooth-bored and rifled.

Smooth-bored weapons, better known as shotguns, have barrels that are smooth on the inside; and they fire shot pellets rather than bullets. The barrel is usually narrower toward the muzzle end, which helps to keep the pellets together.

Rifled weapons are not smooth on the inside of the barrel, which is spirally scored or "rifled". This ensures that the bullet rotates on its axis as it travels through the barrel and outside it; this helps to stabilize the bullet in flight and prevent it from wobbling, enabling it to travel on a straight course for up to 1,000 metres. The inside of the barrel will, therefore, be made up of raised spiral bands (the lands) and indented spiral bands (the grooves). Rifles, revolvers and pistols are all rifled weapons and they fire bullets, which are solid lead hardened with tin, or have a lead core coated with steel, which is itself coated with cupro-nickel. A number of other kinds of bullet exist, but they need not

Below: *This French firearm collection from around the world is used to compare the damage caused by a criminal's weapon to that caused by these reference guns. The weapon type can thus be identified.*

concern us further here. The calibre of a gun is its diameter from land to land (not groove to groove) in inches. The types .303, .45 and so on refer to this diameter. It is clear that the calibre should not be measured from groove to groove, since this will give a diameter greater than that of the bullet, which fits between the lands, not the grooves.

One of the standard acts so often seen in whodunit films is when the police inspector finds a handgun at the scene and picks it up gingerly by putting a pencil inside the barrel and lifting the weapon. This is meant to show that the inspector is trying not to destroy evidence by holding the gun with his hands, in case he smudges any fingerprints on it. In fact, picking up a gun in this way is the very last thing one should do, because anything inserted into the barrel will almost certainly leave its mark on the "lands" of the rifling. This is important, since bullets fired from a particular gun will show markings corresponding to the rifling of the weapon from which it was fired. No two guns being identical, even those made by the same manufacturer in succession, it is possible to compare a bullet discovered at the scene or inside a victim, with a bullet experimentally fired from a suspect gun. This can reveal whether a bullet was or was not fired from that gun. For this reason, guns must be handled carefully – by someone wearing gloves – and placed in a bag for subsequent examination.

Sometimes it is necessary to restore the serial number that manufacturers stamp on a gun, since this may help to trace the history of the weapon. Even if the original stamped number is obliterated by rubbing or the rifling of the weapon, it is often possible to restore the number by the use of etching agents. This is possible because the die that stamped the number will have given rise to stresses in the metal beneath the indentation it caused. These stressed areas will dissolve much faster than the surrounding unstressed areas, showing up the number once again.

Much has been written about the wounds inflicted by bullets. Generally speaking, most textbooks say that the exit wound of a bullet is much larger and more ragged than the entry wound. Other books – a small minority – assert, equally authoritatively, that entry wounds are

larger and more ragged than exit ones. Who is right?

Both and neither. Much depends on the circumstances of the case and the nature of both the bullet and the part of the body it went through. In principle, when a bullet enters the body and emerges from it, the entry wound is larger than the exit one, *if it is a normal bullet and if it is moving through flesh*. In fact, this rarely happens, since most bullets hit bone at some point during their "journey". When this happens, the exit wound is larger and more ragged than the entry wound.

An entry wound is often easily recognisable as such by the discoloration around it. Bullets are not the only things that

Right: *Unfired bullets from a handgun found at a scene. Latent fingerprints can be developed using cyanoacrylate in a fume cupboard.*

Below: *Shotgun injuries. A coloured X-ray shows shotgun pellets (white) around the teeth and at the back of the skull and neck.*

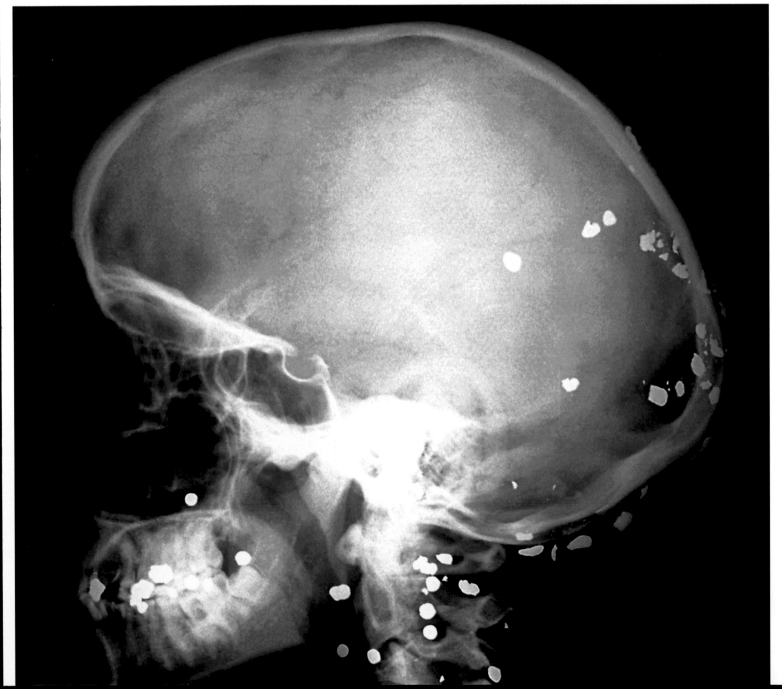

emerge from the muzzles of guns; soot and primer residues are produced and, in contact shootings in which the muzzle is held against the body, the skin around the entry hole is blackened and may be pinkish in colour due to the emission of carbon monoxide. The hole itself will have a splintered or star-shaped appearance, since, despite the rifling, a bullet that has just emerged from the barrel will show some degree of wobbling, or tail wag, before it stabilizes. This tail wag tears the skin and produces the ragged-edge effect.

A shot fired from about a yard away will also show these characteristics, but to a much lesser extent, the hole being smaller and the "tattooing" of the skin much slighter. From a greater

Below: *Dual laser system for determining a bullet's trajectory. The main laser beam (red) is aligned with the bullet's impact point. Tracing the weaker beam (top left) back gives an estimate of the gunman's position.*

distance there will be little or no blackening and the exit hole will be roughly the same size as the entry wound. However, the margin of the wound will be soiled; this is because the bullet, spinning at a rate of 2,000 and 3,000 revolutions a second, will wipe off any material coating it on to the skin.

In cases in which the bullet strikes bone, the flattening of the bullet and the bone material it carries with it through the body will result in an exit wound that is much larger and more messy than the entrance wound.

The angle at which the bullet entered the body can sometimes be important evidentially. It is possible to gain some idea of the kind of angle involved by examining the blackening of the skin around the entry wound. For example, if the gun is held at an upward angle, the blackening will be more intense on the skin above the wound.

In the Libyan Embassy siege in London, during which a policewoman standing in the square outside was killed by a bullet, it was important to determine the direction from which the bullet came. The post-mortem findings revealed that the bullet entered the chest at an angle of between 60 and 70 degrees to the horizontal. Examination of the pavement revealed bullet impact marks that further supported the autopsy conclusion about the angle of the shot. The general conclusions showed that the bullet was fired from the first floor of the embassy. Later, an examination of one of the first floor rooms facing the square revealed a fired cartridge case of the right calibre, it having been missed by the perpetrators when they attempted to clear up the room.

Above: X-ray beam dispersive analysis of gunshot residue (GSR) yields a graph showing which elements are present. In this example there is lead (Pb), antimony (Sb), and barium (Ba).

The superficial appearance of gunshot wounds is, in certain respects, the exact opposite of those of bullet wounds. Contact or near-contact shots will result in the shot-pellets not spreading, but entering the body as a single mass. From greater distances, the pellets will spread and cover a greater area of the body surface; so, generally speaking, the greater the area of spread, the farther away the shotgun was fired.

Primer residues will also be left on the clothes of both victim and murderer, as well as on the murderer's hands, in the latter case especially from handguns. Chemical tests can be used to determine whether gunpowder residues are present on skin or clothes. These tests are now highly specific, but for a long time the dermal nitrate test was widely used. Unfortunately, this test was eventually shown to be very undiscriminating and positive results could be obtained from skin or clothes that had been contaminated with tobacco, fertilizers, cosmetics or urine. The test is no longer used, but it is salutary to reflect that forensic science is constantly developing and any current tests must be looked upon as potentially fallible, a fact many forensic scientists, lawyers and police officers have difficulty in accepting.

It is often the case that doubt exists as to whether a fatal shooting is murder or suicide. Clearly, if the distance from which a bullet was shot was greater than arms length, as can be shown from the presence or absence of skin discoloration, then foul play must be suspected. Other cases are more complicated and require a more searching investigation. The following case makes the point.

A young woman was found dead indoors, with a wound in her neck. Beside her was a .22 semi-automatic rifle. Her two children, as well as her mother and father, were also found dead. It seemed that the woman had murdered her family, then shot herself. However, a search of the premises resulted in the discovery of a silencer from the gun cupboard; it was wiped clean on the outside, but still had blood on the inside. If the silencer had been used in the murder, then it is obvious that the woman could not have shot herself, then have gone to the cupboard, placed the silencer in it and, finally, returned to die beside the rifle. The woman's brother was the only surviving member of the family; he was arrested and convicted of murdering the five members of his family.

CASE HISTORY

The Bullet that Killed JFK

A particularly interesting case of bullet identification took place when President John F. Kennedy was assassinated. Ever since that time many people believed that the crime was the result of a conspiracy and that the assassin, Lee Harvey Oswald, could not have acted alone. Others ridiculed the notion. Over the years something of the order of 10,000 books on Kennedy's assassination were published, some arguing the case for conspiracy, others arguing the case against it. The usual accusations and counter-accusations were made: "cover-up" on the one hand, "conspiracy theorists" on the other. What does the forensic evidence have to say about this?

The Warren Commission examined all the evidence, scientific and otherwise, and concluded that there had been no conspiracy.

Of course, there is always a small group of paranoid people who will always shout "conspiracy" on every occasion. In the case of President Kennedy, it must be said that there is a *prima facie* case for conspiracy. The idea is not an absurd one. Kennedy had many enemies at every level in society, including powerful political circles. The murder of Oswald himself has not been adequately explained. Eyewitness and other evidence also supported the idea of conspiracy. Some people who expressed their belief in the conspiracy theory did not survive for very long, although this line of "evidence" has been greatly exaggerated.

None of this means that Kennedy was murdered, but it shows that it is a valid suspicion. What I find particularly interesting is that the forensic evidence from the case has been held to reveal that there is no rational basis for supposing there to have been a conspiracy. The Warren Commission held that Oswald acted alone. I have reviewed the forensic evidence and find that I cannot agree with that conclusion.

This is not the place to go into a detailed examination of this evidence. The relevant facts are these: Oswald was said to have fired three shots, one of which totally missed the car; one struck Kennedy in the back, emerging from his throat to strike Governor Connally, who was sitting in front of him, in the back; the bullet left through Connally's chest striking first his right wrist, then his left thigh. The last, fatal, bullet struck the president in the head.

The recovered fragments of these bullets were examined for the trace elements of silver and antimony. The amounts of these elements found in a bullet vary in such a way that their proportions in the fragments can suggest the number of bullets from which they came. The results of the study of the fragments were held by the Warren Commission to show that only two bullets struck the occupants of the car. This is puzzling, since it is clear that the trace element evidence shows that more than two bullets were fired.

The results for traces of silver, in parts per million, were as follows (the ranges of the results are given in brackets):

1. Bullet from Connally's stretcher   8.8 ± 0.5 (8.3–9.3)
2. Fragments from Connally's wrist   9.8 ± 0.5 (9.3–10.3)
3. One large fragment from the car   8.1 ± 0.6 (7.5–8.7)
4. Fragment from Kennedy's brain   7.9 ± 0.3 7.6–8.2)
5. Small fragments from the car   8.2 ± 0.4 (7.8–8.6)

The range of trace silver in (1) and (2) just meet, which is inconclusive, since they could represent either one or two bullets. The ranges for the remaining three specimens overlap considerably and suggest that the fragments came from one bullet.

The results of the antimony analysis showed the following results:

1. Bullet from Connally's stretcher   833 + 9 (824–842)
2. Fragments from Connally's wrist   797 + 7 (790–804)
3. One large fragment from the car   602 + 4 (598–606)
4. Fragment from Kennedy's brain   621 + 4 (617–625)
5. Small fragments from the car   642 + 6 (636–648)

None of the ranges of trace antimony in the bullets or fragments overlap, yet these results were used to demonstrate that only two bullets were fired, which is an impossible conclusion. Of particular interest is the fact that the two Connally bullets show very different ranges. What all this means is another matter. It certainly does not prove conspiracy. But this is not the point. The point is that, in spite of the fact that some of the evidence suggests that the accepted version of events is incorrect, that very evidence was used to "demonstrate" the opposite. Such things do happen in forensic science.

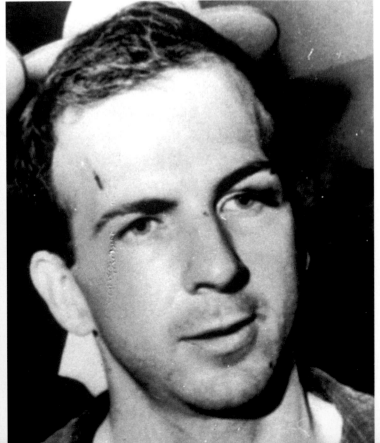

Above: *Assassination of President John F. Kennedy. On 22 November 1963, Kennedy was shot and killed in Dallas, Texas. Governor John Connally of Texas, seen sitting in front of Kennedy, was wounded.*

Left: *Lee Harvey Oswald (1939–1963). He allegedly assassinated President Kennedy on 22 November 1963. Having been captured that same day, he was himself shot two days later by nightclub owner Jack Ruby.*

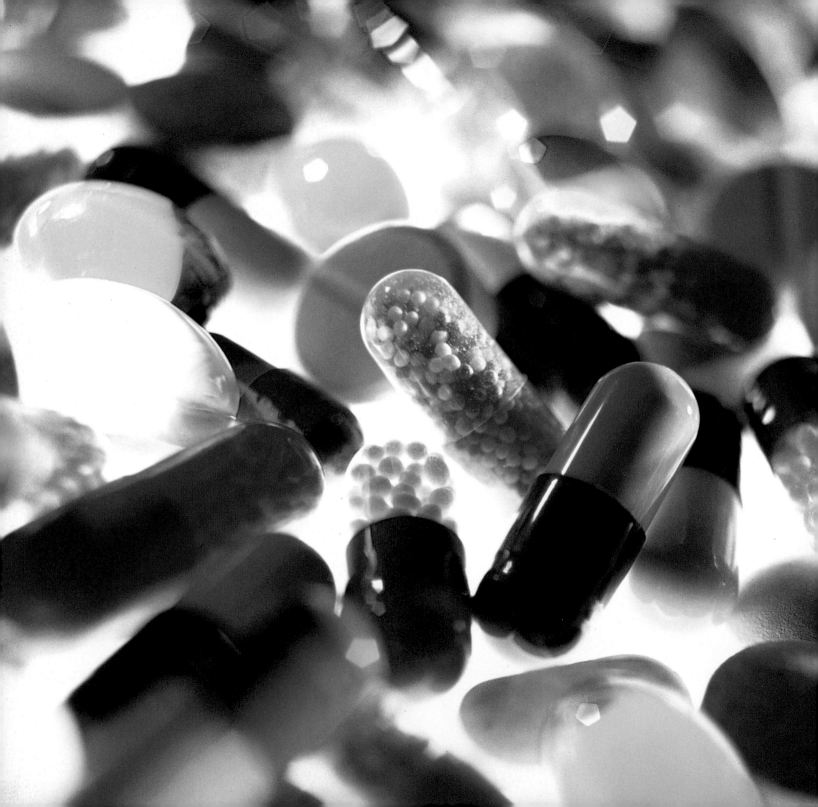

For some reason, poison has an enduring fascination. Most people seem to be both repelled and attracted by it, possibly because it is deadly and, at the same time, discreet.

Its effects, unlike those of more obvious weapons, are not messy and unpleasant. And yet, for all its fascination and despite all we know about poison, we have no adequate definition for the word. I remember reading a newspaper article about a man who drank six pints of water in 20 minutes, then fell down in fits and died. Imagine what one would have thought, had the substance been anything other than water. Most people, including most scientists, would probably have wondered whether a substance that could kill at such a high dose would be safe to take at all. "If six pints of that stuff can kill instantaneously, just think what the cumulative effect of swallowing a few drops every day would be," people might have said.

Toxicological Investigation

In forensic work, the questions that usually arise are: "Was the victim poisoned?"; "What was the poison used?"; and "Was it accident, suicide or murder?" Once poisoning is suspected, scientific techniques can be brought to bear, but the precise technique will depend on the circumstances. Sometimes suspicion of poisoning can arise without one having any idea what the poison may have been and, in such cases, screening for a wide range of possible poisons must be done.

More often, a particular poison is suspected. The first step in a toxicological investigation is, of course, the taking of a sample from the deceased, or, in a case of non-fatal poisoning, from the living victim. Samples from the latter are usually much easier to analyze, since the complicating factor of new decomposition products is absent. Before any actual analysis can be made, the sample must be treated in various ways in order to extract and purify the poison in it. The amounts of poison present in a sample are usually very small, since what we usually call a poison is something that kills at very low doses. Depending on their nature, poisons can be extracted using organic solvents, such as ether or chloroform, or by the use of solid silica absorbents.

Chromatography, a technique that separates the various compounds in a sample, is used as a means of identification. There are several kinds of chromatography, each of which is used for a special purpose. However, all types are based on the fact that different compounds will pass through an absorbent medium at different rates, which depend on their different chemical compositions. In gas chromatography, in which the test substance is made volatile by heating, the molecules from the various compounds will move through a long narrow tube of glass or steel, toward a detection device that "recognizes" the specific electrical impulses emanating from each compound. A recorder will then produce a chart plotting the concentration of each compound as a peak, against time. The time at which a compound appears – the so-called retention time – is an attribute of that compound; the height of the peak will

Below: *Poison detection. A gas chromatograph can be used to analyse samples from body fluids or tissues in cases where poison is suspected. The resulting chart gives a guide as to what compounds are present.*

demonstrate how much of it is present.

Nowadays, chromatography is coupled with a technique known as mass spectrometry. The mass spectrometer is a machine that bombards the molecules emerging from the chromatograph with electrons. This treatment ionises the compound (i.e. breaks them up into electrically charged ions); and produces a spectrum, which is essentially an identification of each ion according to its atomic mass. The reason chromatography and mass spectrometry are used together in this way is that chromatography is not a certain method for identifying compounds. This is because the retention time, while an attribute of that compound, may be shared by other compounds as well. Essentially, it is a crude sorting process, after which the fine-tuning of the mass spectrometer can be brought into play. Actual identification is made by comparing the results obtained with control results from samples of known chemical composition.

Another identification technique is immunoassay, in which the fact that a foreign compound (an antigen) entering the blood will cause the body to produce a defensive antibody can be exploited to good effect. Antibodies will bind on to antigens; the resultant "clumps" are then consumed by the white blood cells. In many cases, the antibody-antigen complex (the antigen here being a particular poison) can be identified. This technique is still being developed and is not as widely used as the methods described above.

While the sophisticated techniques used in forensic science are very effective in identifying the many known poisons, the chemical make-up of most poisons is unknown. So many poisons occur naturally in plants and fungi, and even in animals, that cases of poisoning can occur, but cannot be identified as such.

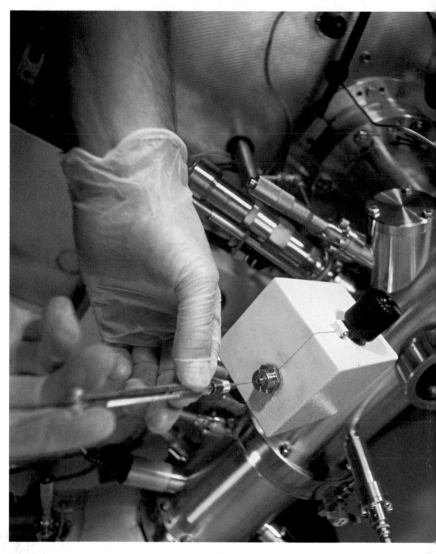

Above: *Poison detection. Sample being injected into a mass spectrometer, which will identify the elements in the compound. This technique can also be used for very low concentrations of chemicals.*

What is a Poison?

ALMOST ANY SUBSTANCE could be a poison – almost any substance can harm or kill, depending on the exact circumstances. Essentially, the toxicity of a substance depends on how much of it is ingested and over what period of time. Also, the age and weight of a person, as well as their state of health, would determine whether or not a swallowed substance would cause death or injury. What we usually mean when we say that something is a poison is that a very small quantity of it can kill. But what is a small quantity? Cyanide, normally considered a deadly poison, can be taken in small doses – less than 300 milligrams – with impunity. Indeed, small amounts of cyanide are essential for good

health, since without it the body cannot synthesize vitamin B12. The "poison" is present in the seeds of many fruits, notably apples, peaches, cherries, plums and, famously, in almonds.

None of this means that cyanide is not a deadly poison; my point here is to illustrate the fact that even the deadliest poisons are deadly only above a certain dose. What must be remembered is that anything can be a poison. A man obsessed with his health lived for three years on nothing but carrot juice. One day he was found dead, his skin a bright orange colour. Carrots are certainly good for you, but not in superabundance and to the exclusion of all else.

The problem of how the poison was administered is often of some importance, since it may be relevant to the question of whether one is dealing with a case of accident, suicide or murder. Particular poisons are associated with particular forms of administration. For example, cyanide and arsenic are usually ingested through the mouth, while substances like heroin are often injected into the blood. Some poisons, such as snake venoms, are not poisonous unless they enter the body through the bloodstream. These venoms, being proteins, are simply digested in the stomach, if taken by mouth.

However, things may not be as simple as they seem, since any cut or graze inside the mouth would allow the poison to work if swallowed and we know that the spitting cobra's venom enters the body through the mucous membranes of the eyes.

Drugs such as cocaine and nicotine – the latter as snuff – are often "snorted" into the nose, where they enter the body through the nasal membranes. Amphetamines are sometimes taken in the same way. More familiarly, eye and nose drops function in the same manner. Related to this route of entry into the body is the inhalation of substances, which reach the lungs and pass from there into the blood vessels.

Injecting drugs, such as heroin, directly into the bloodstream is a very effective means of introducing the poison into the system. Toxicologists use the term "bioavailability" to describe the percentage of the drug taken that will cause a physiological effect. Thus, the bioavailability of cannabis resin is very low if swallowed, since it is not easily absorbed at any point of the digestive tract. On the other hand, the bioavailability of injected heroin is effectively 100 per cent, as are effectively all substances taken intravenously. Heroin taken orally, however, has a bioavailability of zero, to all intents and purposes.

Most poisons are, of course, taken by mouth. A major factor controlling the bioavailability of poisons taken orally is the metabolic action of the liver. When drugs are absorbed in the intestine, they pass into the blood vessels that carry blood to the liver, where they, like all other food, are metabolised for energy. It is in the liver that many potentially poisonous compounds are deactivated. So, although drugs may be absorbed in the digestive tract, their bioavailability is often drastically reduced by the liver.

Before the formidable barrier of the liver is reached, however, the first barrier – the poison's capability of being absorbed into the bloodstream in the first place – must be overcome. This readiness to be absorbed may be high or low. Much depends

Left: *A Spectacled or Indian cobra (*Naja naja) *in its threat posture, ready to strike. Its venom is a potent neurotoxin, causing paralysis then death to thousands of people in Asia each year.*

Below: *A drug user snorts a line of cocaine into the nose where it is quickly absorbed into the bloodstream.*

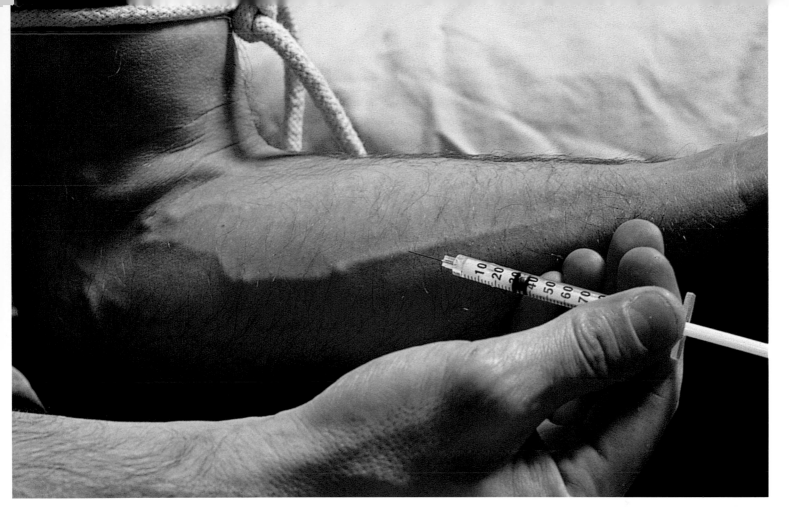

on the chemical composition and structure of the substance; we have already seen that an oily substance like cannabis resin is but poorly absorbed. It is for reasons such as these that different poisons are introduced into the body in different ways – the way chosen being the one that gives the substance its greatest bioavailability.

It is clear that the bioavailability of a drug or poison can be an important legal matter. If the substance ingested was of such a dose and taken in such a manner that it caused hardly any harm to the person to whom it was administered, then these points would be significant in a court of law. As we have seen in our discussion of techniques above, the forensic toxicologist can determine not only the type of poison used, but its dosage as well.

Metabolic activity usually results in the deactivation of poisons and their excretion. The excreted products are metabolites – substances produced by the breakdown or transformation of the ingested compounds – and are passed out of the body, usually in the urine. Some substances – heroin is a good example – are metabolised so quickly that the toxicologist in most cases has to detect the metabolites, rather than the drug itself. Therefore, a knowledge of the biotransformation (as it is called) of drugs is essential when attempting to determine the type and dosage of the poison. Sometimes, a drug is metabolised and its

Above: *A drug user injecting heroin directly into his bloodstream. The rope around his arm acts as a tourniquet to make the veins stand out.*

metabolites excreted so quickly that toxicological investigation may not succeed.

However, some compounds and their metabolites are retained in the body for an unusually long time, as compared with most drugs. Cannabis metabolites are an example of compounds that can be retained within the body for a long time – sometimes up to several weeks – facilitating the work of the toxicologist, or at least prolonging the time after ingestion and during which the search for signs of the drug is still likely to be fruitful. Some poisons are "excreted" simply by removing them into the hair or fingernails, where they can do little damage.

The toxicological facts and methods discussed above allow toxicologists to present much useful information on the course of events in a case of suspected murder or suicide. As we saw in the last chapter, people committing suicide behave in a fairly predictable way. In the case of suicide by poison, the "victim" usually removes his spectacles before swallowing the fatal draught. Murderers may not be aware of this and will fail to remove their victims' spectacles. Although this matter of behaviour may not be a scientific fact of toxicology, it suggests that a case may be one of murder, not suicide and so should be followed up with a toxicological investigation.

Interpreting the Evidence

The toxicological techniques at the disposal of the forensic scientist may be very refined, but, in the end, it is the interpretation that matters. Let us say that the results show that such-and-such a poison at such-and-such a dose was used. What does it all mean? Perhaps it can be concluded that the kind and dosage of drug were such as to cause death. But what is the dosage that causes death? In fact, there are no hard-and-fast facts or figures. Some people are able to tolerate much higher levels of certain poisons, depending on their general medical condition, their size and weight and even their mental state. A sick person of slight build will succumb to much lower doses of a drug that would have little or no effect on a larger and healthier person.

Nor are such things the only potentially misleading factors. The concentration of a poison or a metabolite will vary according to where in the circulatory system a blood sample was taken. More confusing still may be samples from the urine, which can vary widely from person to person and, in the same person, according to their state of hydration. The amount of urine excreted is affected by how much water a person may have drunk, affecting the concentration of the drug in it. Coffee and tea are diuretics, which will result in larger volumes of urine. Some metabolites that could have arisen from poisonous compounds may equally well have had another, more innocent, origin. Decomposition products of a dead body may include compounds that confuse the issue.

This point was made during the trial of Dr Harold Shipman, described as Britain's most prolific serial killer. Shipman was put on trial for the murder of 15 elderly women, whom he injected with overdoses of morphine and diamorphine, the main active component of heroin. Traces of the drugs were found in the bodies of the women, but the defence lawyers claimed that the drug levels could not be accurately ascertained, since the bodies were decomposed and, therefore, the results could easily have been misleading. However, morphine is a stable compound, which does not decompose very quickly after the death of the victim, although it is true to say that it is not known for certain how soon such decomposition will occur and to what extent and under what conditions. Although Dr Shipman's guilt appears to have been established on the basis of other evidence, including the forgery of the will of one of his victims, the point raised by the defence was, toxicologically, a valid one.

In view of all these sources of error, the interpretation of toxicological results must be made with extreme care. The toxicologist may need to be supplied with information about a victim's state of health, or the nature of his last meal. The place from which a blood sample was taken must be chosen carefully and notice of it taken when interpreting the results. If a dead body is infested with maggots, it is safer to conduct tests on the tissues of the maggots, since such living tissues would yield more reliable results; however, it must be borne in mind that maggots will concentrate certain substances in their tissues at higher levels than those obtained in the human tissues and this relationship should be understood and taken into account.

Toxicity curves – graphs plotting the dosage against the effect on the person – have been drawn up and may be used as a general guide. In principle, such a curve will rise as a shallow incline, then become much steeper, then, finally, level off. At the lower dosages, where the incline is shallow, the poison may have little or no effect. At the lower parts of the steep incline symptoms of mild toxicity will appear; whereas at the higher parts, symptoms of severe poisoning will appear. Finally, death will take place at the levelling-off phase, where, naturally, no further symptoms of ill-health will appear!

Poisoning as a means of suicide appears to be much commoner than it is as a means of murder. At least, that is what the figures appear to suggest. However, one must not forget that those poison murders that have been discovered are, by definition, the only ones that have come to light, if that is not a tautology. The fact that some poison murders are discovered only by sheer luck or accident suggests that many more such murders are committed than is generally supposed.

Accidents at work and at home, or medical error or malpractice, are other causes, the latter being, thankfully, very rare.

We will now look at the various common poisons and their effects on people. Chemists classify poisons according to their chemical composition, but here we will group them together on a functional basis, i.e. on the basis of the way they act on the human body.

Right: *Dr Harold Shipman (1946–2004) is thought to have taken the lives of at least 215 of his patients, mostly middle-aged and elderly women, by giving them overdoses of diamorphine and morphine.*

Cyanide

Above: *The Jonestown Massacre. In the Jonestown commune in Guyana, over 900 members of the People's Temple cult, led by Jim Jones, committed suicide on November 18, 1978 by drinking cyanide-laced punch.*

Most poisons act systemically; in other words, they act by adversely affecting the biochemical processes of the cells. Other poisons act in other ways, and we will consider these at the end of the chapter.

Some of the commonest poisons are called gaseous, or volatile, poisons, although they are not always taken in that form. We have already met one of these – cyanide.

What is called cyanide in the vernacular can be one of two chemical compounds: hydrocyanic, or Prussic, acid (HCN); and one of its salts, usually potassium cyanide (KCN). The acid is by far the more fast-acting of the two. In one case a laboratory technician was seen by one of his colleagues to raise a bottle of 25 per cent Prussic acid and literally drop dead before he could place the bottle down. By contrast, potassium cyanide may take up to 20 minutes to kill and, judging by the accounts of those who have witnessed such deaths, it is a horribly painful way to die.

Both the acid and the salt kill by blocking the mechanism that enables the cells to take up oxygen from the blood. A consequence of this is the flushed appearance of the victims, since the haemoglobin in the red blood cells remains saturated with oxygen, forming the normally unstable oxyhaemoglobin. (Its normal instability is what allows it to release the oxygen into the cells.) Oxyhaemoglobin has a bright scarlet colour, hence the red blotches on the skin of those who die of cyanide poisoning.

Was Rasputin Given Cyanide?

It is generally believed that Rasputin, who exerted such a strong influence over the Russian Imperial Family through his alleged ability to cure the Czarevitch, was given large amounts of cyanide, but refused to die, until he was shot several times, brutally beaten and thrown into the River Neva to drown. The dosage of cyanide given to Rasputin was said to have been one ounce – 95 times the lethal dose. It is said that Rasputin may have suffered from gastritis – in fact, this is an unsubstantiated rumour – a condition that slows down absorption of the poison somewhat, but this cannot possibly have prevented his death from an ounce of cyanide.

As we have seen, cyanide poisoning causes a livid colour to develop in the skin, and a smell of bitter almonds emanates from the mouth and from the body when it is opened during the post-mortem. Yet when Rasputin's daughter, Maria, saw his body after it had been recovered from the river, she wrote a description of it, but made no comment on the lividity of her father's appearance or the tell-tale odour, neither of which she could have failed to perceive had they been present. Yet the belief persists that Rasputin could resist the toxicity of cyanide, unlike all other human beings and animals. It is simply not credible that Rasputin was given cyanide; he died of his bullet wounds.

Two of Rasputin's murderers, Prince Felix Yusupov and Vladimir Purishkevitch, wrote accounts of what happened. Both agreed that the drinks and cakes at the party in Felix's home, the Moika Palace, contained cyanide. In view of what we know about cyanide, they must have been either lying or mistaken. The latter is the more charitable view, and there is some evidence to support it. Dr Lazovert was the conspirator who was said to have brought the poison and laced the drinks and cakes, but the doctor may have bungled the job. Felix wrote that he gave Dr Lazovert "a box" containing the poison. This implies that the cyanide was not in an airtight container, which is how it should be kept, otherwise it begins to decompose into a carbonate. When partially decomposed cyanide is swallowed, the carbonate, which has a corrosive and irritating effect on the stomach, usually induces vomiting in the victim, yet Rasputin showed no such symptoms. However, gastritis might have prevented the appearance of such symptoms in the relatively short period of time before he was shot.

It is interesting that Maria Rasputina believed that Dr Lazovert did not administer cyanide, but an opiate. This would explain Rasputin's drowsiness, as reported by Felix. Even more interesting is the rumour that circulated after Dr Lazovert's death, that the doctor made a death-bed confession, saying that he lost his nerve at the last minute and substituted a harmless powder. No-one has been able to trace this statement to its source, although on one occasion I thought the truth was about to be revealed. A letter appeared in *The Daily Telegraph*, saying that Dr Lazovert had told the actor, Christopher Lee, who played Rasputin in a film, that he never put cyanide in the cakes, and that Mr Lee had told the author of the letter this story. Intrigued, I wrote to Mr Lee, asking him to confirm this, but he telephoned back, saying that he had never met Dr Lazovert and had not even heard of the writer of the letter. Documentary evidence can be very misleading, as we shall see in the chapter on "Words and Images".

Below: *Grigory Efimovich Rasputin (1869–1916) was allegedly poisoned with cyanide before being shot, beaten and finally drowned.*

РАСПУТИН

Carbon dioxide (CO_2) is a natural gas, present at a concentration of about 0.03 per cent in the atmosphere. It is often present in industrial sites and in places where explosions or fires have just occurred. Its concentration in the lungs prevents the expulsion of CO_2 from the body, so that respiration is hindered. Concentrations as low as three per cent in the atmosphere will cause symptoms to appear – dizziness headaches and general weakness. Concentrations of over 25 per cent are fatal.

A case from the Sudan demonstrates how easily lethal concentrations can build up. In 1954, in the town of Kosti, 300 cotton growers were locked in a room at 9.30 pm after some riots. The room measured about 60 feet by 20 feet and there was no room for anyone to lie down. The windows and doors were closed to prevent the men from escaping. By the time the room was opened at 5.30 am the following morning, 189 men had died as a result of the accumulation of CO_2, as well as from heat and exhaustion.

Carbon monoxide (CO) is even more deadly, since it will bind on to haemoglobin to form the very stable compound, carboxyhaemoglobin. This means that oxygen can no longer be carried by the blood, since the site on the haemoglobin molecule at which the oxygen is normally bound is now permanently occupied by the CO.

Death by CO poisoning is a common form of suicide. The victim usually places his head in an oven or connects a tube from the car exhaust to the inside of the car and lies back. Death will follow soon afterward. Interestingly, people who commit suicide in this way take some trouble to lie comfortably, often arranging cushions and blankets before lying upon them to die. These facts

Left: *CO_2 poisoning. A forensic scientist photographs the customs bay at Dover docks where, in June 2000, 58 illegal Chinese immigrants hidden in the back of a lorry were found dead from suffocation.*

are often useful in cases in which a death looks like suicide, but which it is suspected may be murder. In one case, a woman was found dead with her head lying in a greasy tray inside an oven. This was a highly uncomfortable and atypical position for a suicide and so murder was suspected. Tests showed that no carboxyhaemoglobin had formed in the blood; also, a mark on the woman's neck suggested death by strangulation, a suspicion that was later confirmed by the husband's confession that he killed her.

The symptoms of CO poisoning during life are surprisingly similar to alcoholic drunkenness and it is not unknown for drivers to be overcome by CO if the gas is leaking into the interior of the car because of a faulty car-floor. People accused of drunkenness will sometimes plead CO-poisoning as a cause of their condition, but testing for the presence of carboxyhaemoglobin in the blood soon reveals the truth. One of the post-mortem signs is the development of a bright red tinting, which is remarkably similar to the colour changes due to cyanide poisoning. The absence of the distinctive bitter almonds smell, however, easily distinguishes the two.

The gross changes or odours that suggest that a particular poison was used are not the only indications; specific chemical tests are conducted on the tissues to confirm the original identification. For example, suspicion of cyanide poisoning can be confirmed by treating the tissues with silver nitrate, which produces a white precipitate of silver cyanide, which is insoluble in nitric acid. Further treatment of the precipitate with ammonium sulphide and ferric chloride will result in the production of a scarlet solution. Similar simple chemical tests are available for other poisons and chromatography or mass spectrometry need not always be used.

Chloroform

A VERY WELL KNOWN, but largely misunderstood, volatile substance is chloroform. Although it is not often used as a poison, it is a very dangerous substance indeed, especially in view of the way it seems to be treated in whodunit films. Chloroform, far from inducing a person to sleep as soon as a chloroform-soaked handkerchief is placed over the nose and mouth, will actually make the victim struggle and, if asleep to begin with, to wake up. The convulsions caused by chloroform inhalation seem

never to be shown in such films; it is usually the case that the victim goes limp almost as soon as the handkerchief is clamped over his mouth.

Although the poison will certainly take effect in due course, it takes many minutes for this to occur. The typical picture of the victim succumbing immediately is not only misleading, but can also be dangerous. This is because the point at which the victim relaxes is not far from the point of death, due to paralysis of the heart muscles.

Alcohol

Left: *Social drinking can lead to drunkenness: an offence if the drunk is in charge of a vehicle or a child. Chronic intake of high levels of alcohol can lead to liver failure and eventually death.*

Probably the most easily available of all poisons is alcohol. To call alcohol a "poison" is not an exaggeration, since high doses can cause death within a few a hours, or less. It is humanity's familiarity with, and use of, alcohol for most of its recorded history that allows us to think of it as a much more innocuous substance that it really is. Alcohol blood levels of over 400mg% (400 milligrams per 100 millilitres of blood) are usually fatal, but much lower doses can also be fatal, especially in young people. There is an entire class of chemical compounds called alcohols, but in the vernacular sense, alcohol means ethyl alcohol, or ethanol (C_2H_5OH).

Alcohol is a depressant, adversely affecting the function of the central nervous system. It is a substance that is absorbed very quickly into the bloodstream (within minutes), but it has the unfortunate attribute of taking much longer to leave the system. In other words, soon after the drink is swallowed, the blood alcohol level rises sharply to a peak, but the level subsequently declines slowly.

Alcohol consumed on an empty stomach will be absorbed much faster than alcohol taken with or after a meal. A high concentration of alcohol is absorbed more quickly than a similar dose at a lower concentration. Personal differences and medical conditions may also affect the rate of absorption.

Alcohol is removed in two ways: most of it – well over 90 per cent – is metabolised in the liver into acetic acid, which itself is then oxidised into carbon dioxide and water. About two per cent to five per cent is excreted in the urine. Some alcohol is released into the lungs when the blood carrying it reaches the alveoli, or small sacs within the lung. This is why alcohol can be detected in the breath and how it can be detected there by the various "breathalysers" used to establish whether a driver is in charge of a car after having drunk too much alcohol to make it safe for him to drive. Since it is impracticable, as well as being time-consuming and expensive, to take a blood sample from a driver who is suspected of being over the limit, the alcohol in the driver's breath is measured instead. Since there is a relationship between the amount of alcohol in the breath and the amount of alcohol in the blood, the measured breath alcohol makes it possible for the blood alcohol level to be calculated.

The forensic interest in alcohol is not limited to drink/driving offences and outright fatalities. Drunkenness and chronic alcohol poisoning are two other aspects of the problem of alcohol abuse. It is worth mentioning that drunkenness is not necessarily a reflection of the amount of alcohol consumed in a population, but it is related to the way it is consumed and at what times. Thus, more alcohol is consumed per individual per year in France than in Britain, but there is far more drunkenness in Britain than there is in France.

Drunkenness, in itself, is not an offence, but it becomes so when the person in question is in charge of a vehicle – car, or ship or aeroplane – or in charge of children. Causing damage or injury while drunk is no defence under the law, although killing when in such an inebriated condition that the perpetrator did not know what he was doing will usually result in a conviction for manslaughter, rather than murder.

It is not very easy to define the term "drunk". Although establishing the blood alcohol level of a person is quite straightforward, having a certain high concentration in the blood does not necessarily mean that that person is drunk, since some people have a greater tolerance for alcohol than do others. Behavioural criteria, such as the ability to stand on one leg without falling over, the presence or absence of jerky movements of the eye and so forth, are good general guidelines, but they should be interpreted with care, since the person in question, due to ill-health for example, may have the "wrong" behavioural responses, even though he is not drunk.

Chronic alcoholism is a much more common condition than is generally supposed. It is expressed as a general degeneration, both physical and mental, loss of weight and appetite, together with "fatty degeneration" of the muscles, including the heart muscles. The liver, too, degenerates. In some cases, inflammation and degeneration of the peripheral nerves may take place.

Alcohols other than ethyl alcohol can be abused, and people are known to drink methylated spirits, based on methyl alcohol, or methanol (CH_3OH). Even the added purple colouring does not seem to put off some hardened drinkers of this extremely noxious preparation, which includes acetone, bone oil, paraffin and various aldehydes, as well as methanol. It is sometimes filtered through charcoal, or even a very thick slice of bread, to remove the colouring, the resulting clear liquid being added to a cheap red wine and consumed. This concoction is known as "Flaming Lizzie" and is sold, quite illegally, in some pubs. Habitual abuse is often fatal.

Below: *Paramedics and police officers tend victims and investigate a multi-car accident on the RN6 highway in France. Alcohol is often a factor in fatal road accidents.*

Stimulants, Excitants and Hallucinogens

Another dangerous group of systemic poisons are the stimulants, excitants and hallucinogens. Of these, the amphetamines are among the best known. A typical example is "speed", which produces feelings of alertness and confidence and makes the user feel more energetic. Unfortunately, abstinence from the drug results in the opposite effects: fatigue and depression. In some cases, it can cause heart attacks and strokes, leading to death. Continued use of the drug causes dependence and general ill-health, which leaves the sufferer prone to all kinds of illnesses.

"Ecstasy" is another amphetamine, revelling in the name of 3,4-methylene-dioxy-methamphetamine. As its common name implies, it produces euphoria – which may turn into hallucinations. Users of the drug experience sharper sensations – music sounds better and sympathy with others is increased. Unlike speed, ecstasy is not physically addictive, but its pleasant sensations fade after continued use. However, its use is often accompanied by feelings of nausea and the substance is known to cause damage to nerves in laboratory animal experiments and can cause depression in some people. Another problem is that ecstasy is often sold mixed with other drugs, the identity of which may

Below: Ecstasy is a commonly used drug at "Rave" parties. A stimulant, it can keep the user dancing for hours. The composition can vary and impurities increase the risks involved when taking this drug.

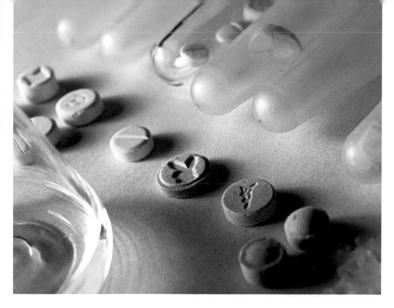

Above: *Branded Ecstasy pills. Chemical analysis can reveal their exact composition, helping link them to specific sources and dealers.*

not be known to the user. Youngsters taking the drug often drink alcohol as well, a habit that increases the probability of adverse reactions.

The infamous LSD (lysergic acid diethylamide) of the 1960s is a very powerful hallucinogen. It is extremely dangerous, often causing mental delusions, such as paranoia and schizophrenia, as well as other psychological disorders like panic attacks and the impairment of judgement. It is not quite as common now as it used to be, but it is still in circulation. It is a synthetic drug, although the lysergic acid used in its manufacture is obtained from ergot, the poisonous fungus.

Many poisons are, of course, derived from plants, sometimes quite common ones. An example is atropine or belladona, which is derived from the Deadly Nightshade, *Atropa belladonna*. The dull purple flowers and shining black berries are well known. Children sometimes eat them, with serious, although usually non-fatal, results. Nevertheless, fatalities are known. The tell-tale berry skins are found in the stomach during the post-mortem. Child deaths due to accidental ingestion of this sort are, of course, extremely distressing; and they have a long history. Lady Anne, the seven-year-old daughter of the fifth Earl (later first Duke) of Bedford, was very fond of fruits and berries; she ate some wild berries from the park at Woburn and, tragically, died. All children are apt to look upon bright, shiny berries as edible things and it is wise for parents to be aware of this. Those children who, like Lady Anne, have a special fondness for fruits are particularly likely to pick and eat wild berries.

The symptoms of atropine poisoning include hoarseness and drying of the skin; as well as a condition akin to mania and rapid breathing, which is followed by coma and respiratory failure in severe cases.

Thorn-apple (*Datura stramonium*) and Henbane

(*Hyoscyamus niger*) are the sources of hyoscine, a drug that is also found in Deadly Nightshade. It causes delirium and renders the user incapable of making reasoned judgements, often blurting out whatever is on their mind. It is this symptom that has led to it being used as a "truth drug", under the more familiar name of scopolamine. The most famous, and possibly one of the first, cases in which hyoscine was used to commit murder, was when the infamous Dr Crippen used it to dispose of his wife.

Cocaine is another plant drug, being derived from the dried leaves of *Erythroxylum coca*, a tropical plant grown in Africa, South America and Southeast Asia. It is a powerful nerve stimulant and overdoses can kill by overstimulation of the heart. It is a most dangerous drug, which, when it does not kill, degrades the addict to such an extent that a description of the symptoms would be indelicate. In this, cocaine is similar to heroin and other narcotics. It is usually taken as a snuff.

More commonly these days, "crack" cocaine is used. This is produced by heating cocaine with baking soda in water. The resulting mixture is dried and is used for smoking. It is much more dangerous than cocaine. It is worth making the point here that one of the difficulties that sometimes arises in toxicological testing is that someone may pick up traces of cocaine and other drugs as a result of passive smoking, having been sitting in a room where someone else had been smoking the drug. This is common enough with tobacco smoking, but it applies to other drugs as well.

Below: *Dr Hawley Harvey Crippen (1862–1910). He poisoned his wife with hyoscine, before dissecting her body into pieces for disposal.*

Above: *Death cap mushrooms* (Amanita phalloides). *If eaten, symptoms begin within 24 hours. Without treatment death follows after a few days.*

A llied to the stimulant drugs are the convulsant poisons, of which strychnine is one. It has an exceptionally bitter taste and is extracted from a number of Indian trees, notably *Strychnos nux-vomica*. It causes powerful convulsions and death follows from the paralysis of the medulla oblongata in the brain. The symptoms are not unlike those of tetanus, with a stiffening and rigidity of the muscles, although the two conditions can be separated by the fact that, in strychnine poisoning, the chest muscles are particularly prone to fixation, whereas in tetanus it is the jaw muscles that stiffen most noticeably. Also, in strychnine poisoning, almost any touch or sound will trigger a

convulsive bout. Although strychnine is not commonly used in murder cases, it is used as a rat and mole poison and is available to people whose profession involves the killing of vermin.

Aconite is another convulsant of plant origin, being extracted from Monk's Hood (*Aconitum napellus*), also known as Wolf's Bane, because the poison was added to dead carcasses in order to kill wolves during Mediaeval times. It is one of the fastest acting poisons known and there is no known antidote; the Ancient Greeks called it the Queen of Poisons. Its symptoms are at first a tingling in the throat, followed by a severe burning sensation. The limbs grow weak, speech becomes confused and respiratory failure takes place.

Other plants containing convulsant poisons include the yew tree (*Taxus baccata*), on which both the leaves and berries are deadly. Laburnum leaves and fruits are also poisonous. Foxgloves (*Digitalis purpurea*) are poisonous, although not as deadly as is sometimes stated. Other common poisonous plants worth mentioning are Marsh Marigolds, Bryony, Holly (berries), Juniper, *Daphne*, Snowberry, Privet, Honeysuckle, Wood Anemones and Greater Celandine. The bulbs of Daffodils and Hyacinths, as well as the roots of Bluebells, are also toxic.

A large number of species of mushrooms produce poisons that range from the stomach-upsetting kind to the instantly fatal. This is not the place for a full discussion of this topic, but it is worth mentioning a few of the most dangerous species, since they are the cause of some quite avoidable deaths. Fly Agaric (*Amanita muscaria*), the well-known red-capped toadstool with white "warts", is very poisonous; worse still is the Death Cap (*Amanita phalloides*), which is the classic poisonous mushroom, causing most mushroom-poisoning deaths. The closely-related *Amanita pantherina*, or Panther Cap, is also extremely poisonous Many of the Boletus mushrooms are good to eat, yet at least one species, Satan's Boletus (*Boletus satanas*), is very poisonous.

Interestingly, there are a number of false beliefs relating to the toxicity of mushrooms. One is that poisonous mushrooms, if boiled, will be rendered harmless; another is that mushrooms that exude "milk" when broken are poisonous. Neither applies to all species. Two completely untrue myths are that all spring mushrooms are safe to eat and that mushrooms that do not cause a silver spoon to change colour while they are being cooked are safe.

One particular mushroom, *Psilocybe semilanceata*, is of some importance in forensic science, since it contains a hallucinogenic poison. In fact, something like 80 species of this genus produce delirium and hallucinations.

Unfortunately, it is also untrue that anything eaten by wild animals is also suitable for human consumption. Snails and slugs will eat Death Caps quite happily; blackbirds will eat the poisonous (to us) berries of Barberry (*Berberis*) and stick insects will eat Privet leaves. It may come as a surprise that ricin, a toxin found in the seed of the castor oil plant, is one of the deadliest poisons. It is present in the hard shell of the seed and the oil itself does not contain any.

CASE HISTORY

The Case Of The Poisoned Umbrella

In September, 1978, Georgi Markov, an expatriate Bulgarian living in London and working for the BBC, was standing at a bus stop on Waterloo Bridge. He felt a sharp sting in his thigh and turned to find a man picking up his umbrella. Later that night, Markov's temperature rose to 104°F and he was having bouts of vomiting. He was admitted to hospital, where a small hole in his thigh was noticed by a doctor. Four days after he became ill, he died.

Georgi Markov was a political dissident and was considered dangerous by the then communist rulers of Bulgaria. He himself spoke of being poisoned by agents of the Bulgarian government, although only his wife, Annabel, took him seriously. After his death, however, a portion of skin around the hole in the thigh was sent to Porton Down, the government microbiological laboratory. A small pellet, capable of holding less than half a milligram of liquid, was found embedded in the skin. If the pellet had contained poison, it would have seeped out through two small holes in the pellet. By a process of elimination, based partly on the poisons that would kill at as low a dosage as half a milligram, the scientists at Porton Down concluded that the poison was possibly ricin. A similar amount of ricin was injected experimentally into a pig, which later died, after showing much the same symptoms as did Markov. After the case was broadcast, reports about another Bulgarian dissident, this time in Paris, began to circulate. He, too, had died after feeling a sting in his leg while waiting for the Metro.

Right: *Georgi Ivanov Markov (1929–1978) a dissident Bulgarian living in London, died three days after being stabbed by a poisoned umbrella.*

A Case of Strychnine Poisoning

On May 26, 1934, Inspector Dodson of the Lincolnshire police received the following letter:

Sir, have you ever heard of a wife poisoning her husband? Look further into the death (by heart failure) of Mr Major of Kirkby-on-Bain. Why did he complain of his food tasting nasty and throw it to a neighbour's dog, which has since died? Why did it stiffen so quickly? Why was he so jerky when dying? I myself have heard her threaten to poison him years ago. In the name of the law I beg you to analyse the contents of his stomach.

signed, Fairplay

The identity of the writer has never been discovered. Arthur Major had, indeed, died two days earlier. The first thing Inspector Dodson did was to ask the doctor who issued the death certificate what was the cause of death. He was told that Major had been taken ill with violent convulsions and spasms and that the cause of death was epilepsy. Dodson then went to see Mrs Major; and he saw Major's body. As he was leaving, Mrs Major asked: "I am not suspicioned? I haven't done anything wrong", which was an odd comment from one who had not been accused of anything.

Major had died on May 24, and on the previous day, May 23, the wire-haired fox terrier of his neighbour, Mr Maltby, died after suffering severe muscular contractions. Maltby buried the dog in the garden. In order to look further into this strange coincidence, the dog's body was exhumed. At the same time the coroner ordered that the funeral of Mr Major be stopped. Post-mortems of both Major and the dog were carried out and organs from both were sent to Dr Roche Lynch, the Home Office toxicologist, for analysis.

Dr Lynch found fatal doses of strychnine in both bodies. Moreover, he concluded that Mr Major received two separate doses – one on May 22 and another on May 24, the day he died. Death could not have been suicide, since once the agony of the first dose had passed, only a lunatic would take a second dose.

Police investigations revealed that the Majors' married life was far from happy. They quarrelled frequently and Mrs Major frequently accused him of drunkenness, idleness and of having affairs with other women. Mrs Major also told the police that her husband had been trying to kill her by "putting something" in her tea. Most significantly, Mrs Major had run up a number of debts and, in exasperation, her husband decided to place a notice in the local newspaper, dissociating himself from her debts. On that day he died; and Mrs Major cancelled the notice submitted to the paper.

The police interviewed the couple's 15-year-old son, Lawrence. He told them that relations between his parents had deteriorated to such an extent that he and his mother slept at her father's house, although she still cooked her husband's meals. When asked about the events of May 24, the boy said that his father was sitting, trembling in his chair and that his mother said that the corned beef in his meal had upset him. Major then began to foam at the mouth, saying that he was going to die, which he did at 10.40 pm.

Interestingly, Mrs Major continued to volunteer information to the police. She said that she had nothing to do with the preparation of his meals. She was also at pains to impress upon the police that she had been staying with her father during the two weeks prior to her husband's death. This interested the police, but in a way that Mrs Major had, perhaps, not intended, for her father was a gamekeeper, who kept poison to kill vermin. When the police asked her whether she was aware of this fact her reply, astonishingly, was: "I did not know where he kept the poison. I never had any poison in my house and I did not know my husband died of strychnine poisoning". When the interviewing officer, Hugh Young, asked her why she mentioned strychnine, since he had never mentioned it, she merely said that she had made a mistake and that she was certain that her husband had died of the corned beef.

Time and again, she returned to the corned beef. She said that she had seen the tin on the pantry shelf, then she made another astonishing statement: "It was quite black. I thought at the time it was bad, but I did not tell my husband". She seemed utterly unaware that she was condemning herself. Further damning evidence followed; Mrs Major told the police officer that she did not send for the doctor when her husband was ill the second time, but gave no explanation.

There was one last interview for Hugh Young to carry out. He went to see Mr Brown, Mrs Major's father, and asked him whether his

Right: *Computer model of a strychnine ($C_{21}H_{22}N_2O_2$) molecule. Its constituent atoms have been colour coded: carbon (C) dark blue, hydrogen (H) white, nitrogen (N) light blue and oxygen (O) red.*

daughter knew that he kept poison. "Yes, mister," was his answer. He kept it in a locked box and kept the key with him at all times. Would his daughter have been able to open the box? "No, mister." There was enough evidence against Mrs Major, who was arrested. But the question of where she obtained the poison was still unanswered. After the arrest, Young searched her bags and found a small key, wrapped in a piece of paper. He went to see Mr Brown again and asked him whether he had another key to his poison box. He said he had had one, but he had lost it some time ago. Young had put the key on his own key ring, which he held up to Mr Brown, asking him to select the one that fitted the box. He chose the one taken from his daughter's bag. It fitted the lock and opened the box. Ethel Major was put on trial for murder, was convicted and hanged.

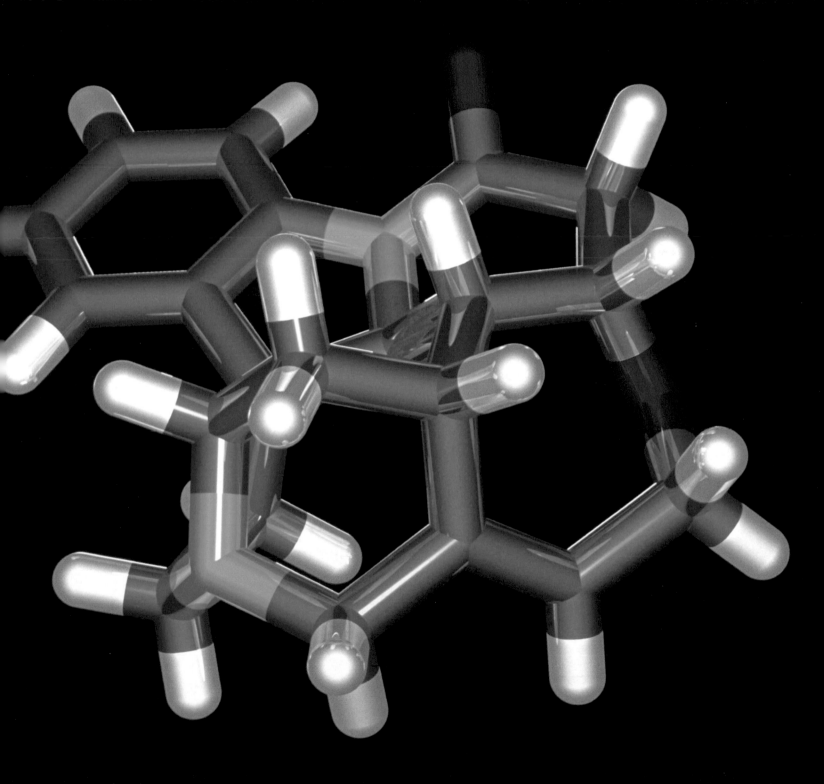

Tranquillizers

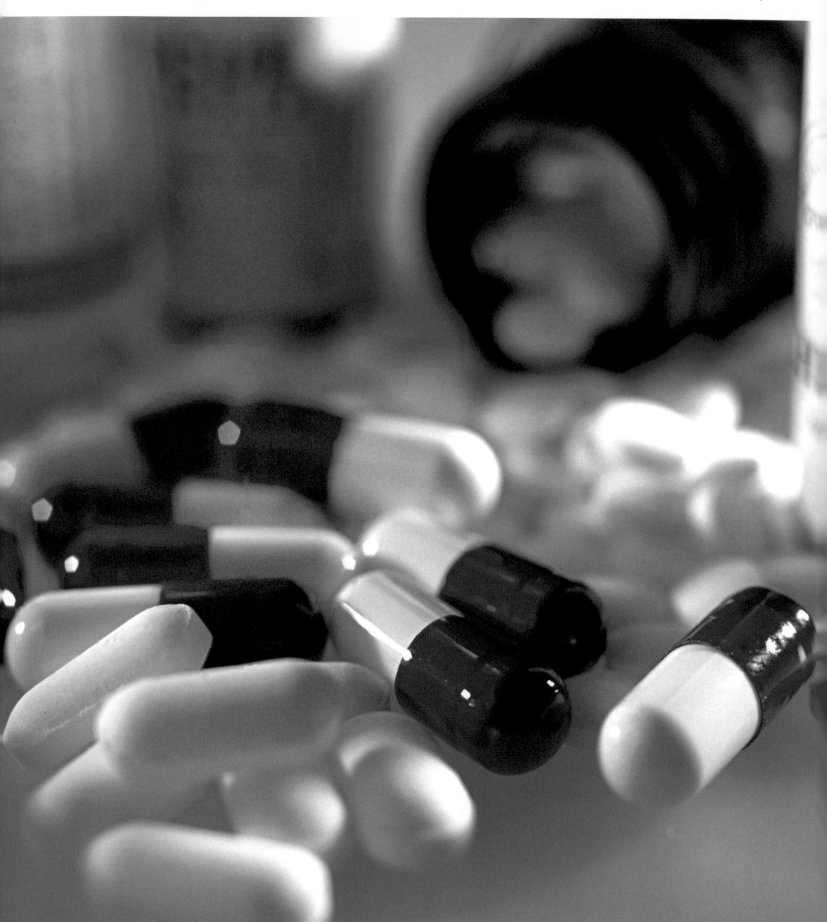

Below: *Aspirin tablets and capsules containing paracetamol. In the UK legislation in 1998 reduced the number of painkillers that could be bought in a single transaction and overdose rates fell.*

The analgesic, hypnotic and narcotic drugs – all of which are "tranquillizers" of one sort or another – are among the commonest poisons used in suicides, simply because many of them are so easily available at home. Paracetamol is one of the commonest drugs to be found at home and people have attempted to commit suicide by taking large overdoses of it. While very high doses will certainly kill – even five grams may be fatal in some cases – what is not generally known is that death is never very rapid. Two or three days of suffering usually elapse before death follows, due to liver failure.

Cases of fatal poisoning can be quite complex, death often being due to a number of combined causes. In one case a woman who had a history of suicide attempts was taken to hospital three and a half hours after she had taken an overdose of paracetamol, together with an antidepressant, prochlorperazine. Three and a half hours later, the level of paracetamol in the blood was found to be 270 milligrams per litre, which is extremely high. In view of this, the doctor administered the antidote drug, acetylcysteine. Inexplicably, however, a 10-fold dose of the usual therapeutic amount was given, despite the fact that both the nurse and the pharmacist expressed reservations. Astonishingly, another 10-fold dose was administered three hours after the first. The woman died two hours later of cardiac arrest.

Unfortunately, the effect of high doses of acetylcysteine is unknown, although the results of experiments on dogs suggest that the drug is safe at high doses. The drug acts by protecting the liver from damage. In the above case, a paracetamol level of 270 milligrams per litre four hours after ingestion suggested that liver function was considerably impaired. At the post-mortem, the level of blood paracetamol was 102 milligrams per litre, indicating a drop of a little less than 170 milligrams per litre in eight hours. This result indicated that the deceased's liver had been severely damaged, since a normal liver would have reduced the blood level of paracetamol to about 70 milligrams per litre in that time.

The amount of prochlorperazine in the blood at post-mortem was 0.07 milligrams per litre. The normal amount to be expected in the blood when the drug is administered at the correct therapeutic doses is between 0.01-0.14 milligrams. The "half-life" of the drug, i.e. the time at which its original concentration will have been halved, is about six hours. This indicated that the highest level in the blood must have been in the region of 0.28 milligrams per litre – a dose well within the dangerous range.

So, what caused the woman's death? In fact, it is not possible to ascribe death to any one toxic cause. It would seem clear that death was caused by a drug overdose, which is what the court inquiry concluded, but it is impossible to be more specific.

Aspirin is another common analgesic; it can be fatal at doses of 25 grams. Aspirin can cause irritation of the stomach and, in some people, can cause bleeding.

Among the hypnotic drugs, the barbiturates must rank as among the most dangerous. Often prescribed for tranquillizing purposes, it is frequently taken with alcoholic drinks, the latter enhancing the effect of the drug while greatly reducing the amount needed for a fatal dose. A dose of one gram of some barbiturates can kill within minutes or even seconds, although most kinds usually take a few hours to take effect. Generally speaking, 10 times the normal medicinal dose is fatal in most barbiturates – a dose that may not seem so high to the patient.

In the case of Terence Armstrong, a six-month-old baby, poison was suspected only when what looked like the red skins of berries were found in the child's throat. Wondering how a baby of that age could have eaten poisonous berries by accident, the investigators decided to examine the "skins" more carefully. They proved to be the gelatine capsules used to contain various medicinal drugs. Toxicological analysis later confirmed this, demonstrating the presence of the barbiturate Seconal in the body.

Both parents were eventually put on trial and the jury found the father guilty; he was condemned to death, but later reprieved. The mother was found not guilty, although she later admitted to having given the child Seconal to make him sleep.

The Misuse of Anti-Depressants

The misuse of anti-depressants can sometimes be the cause of suspicion. In one case, a woman was found lying face down and half-suffocated in her house. The room she was in was in total disarray, with furniture thrown about and curtains drawn, despite the fact it was daytime. Her own clothes were torn off or dragged down and she had a considerable amount of bruising on her body.

Initially, it was thought that the woman had been assaulted by an intruder, but the truth emerged when it was discovered that her body contained an extremely high overdose of the anti-depressant, Tofranil. Such high doses can cause great agitation and hallucinations.

Narcotics

We come now to the narcotic drugs, of which opium and its derivatives are the most familiar. A narcotic is a substance that dulls pain and reduces consciousness. Opium is the dried juice of the opium poppy (*Papaver somniferum*), which is the substance that goes into the pipe of the opium addict. Morphine is a constituent of it and heroin, or diamorphine (also known as diacetyl morphine), is derived from morphine. Other narcotic substances are found in the opium resin extracted from the plant's seeds – thebaine, narcotine, papaverine, and codeine, among others. The legitimate use of opium is the extraction of codeine and morphine, which are used medicinally. Laudanum, beloved of Victorian poisoners, is opium dissolved in alcohol.

The symptoms of opium poisoning are stupor – leading to coma – and heavy sweating. Sometimes the pulse beats very quickly and, as this is a condition caused specifically by thebaine, it indicates that the victim has been using (or has been given) a fairly crude extract, rather than refined heroin. Later, the pulse becomes slower, breathing also slows down and the body becomes cold. Some of these symptoms mimic those of certain kinds of haemorrhage, but the normal or lowered temperatures typical of opium poisoning distinguishes the latter from the former. The most distinctive symptom of opium poisoning is the contraction of the pupils to "pin-points".

Since no two preparations of heroin will have the same percentages of impurities, it is possible for the forensic toxicologist to determine whether two samples came from the same batch or not. Sometimes the difference between two samples may be obvious from the difference in colour alone, although chemical and chromatographic tests can be carried out to confirm that they are different. Also, heroin derived from opium poppies grown in different parts of the world may have different chemical characteristics. What are known as "cutting

Below: *Opium poppies. Their dried juice yields opium, which contains morphine, while resin from the seeds yields codeine, another painkiller used medicinally. Heroin is derived from morphine.*

dried leaves, stems or flowers, as a resin or as an oil. The fresh material smells like spearmint, albeit with a difference. It is often suggested these days that cannabis should be legalised, because it is less addictive than alcohol. This seems to say more about alcohol than about cannabis, although this is probably not a popular point of view!

Paralytic poisons include the toxin coniine found in the leaves of hemlock (*Conium maculatum*), the poison with which Socrates was executed. Like other poisons in this group, it blocks neuromuscular action. Its effect is slow, which is what allowed Socrates to continue his famous discourse for some time after swallowing the fatal draught. Coniine first paralyses the legs, then the rest of the body. Death follows after respiratory failure.

Nicotine, most commonly met with in smoking, is not (smoking apart) a widely used poison, but fatalities occur with more frequency these days, since the purified toxin is used in various insecticides and pesticides. Three or four drops of pure nicotine will kill in a very short time. There are many other paralytic and related poisons, but they are rarely met with in forensic science.

Left: *Cannabis. The hemp or marijuana plant (*Cannabis sativa*) is a fast-growing annual found as a weed in northern India but banned from many other countries because of the intoxicating drug produced from it.*

Below: *Socrates (c.470–399 BC) fostered the development of a critical attitude to established ideas in science. When found guilty of corrupting Athens' youth and neglecting the city's gods he was made to kill himself.*

agents" can also help to distinguish between batches. A cutting agent is simply a substance, like sugar or a barbiturate, used to dilute the drug, or to camouflage it to obscure the fact that it is impure or lacking in a particular ingredient.

I am sometimes asked what is the fatal dose of morphine or heroin. Unfortunately, with these most dangerous of all drugs of abuse, it is not possible to give a simple answer. This is because habitual users may acquire a tolerance to the drug and can withstand much higher doses than can people who are new to it. In general, however, dosages of over 200 milligrams are certainly lethal, although many people will succumb to much lower doses. Children are very susceptible to morphine; in one case a six-year-old child fell into a coma and died five hours after being given 10.8 milligrams of morphine in error.

As with other drugs, the toxicologist must be aware that some source of morphine may be quite innocent. Small quantities of the drug may be found in poppy seeds used in baking and traces of it may appear in the urine. As we saw with cocaine, the detection of a drug on or in a person does not necessarily mean that foul play or abuse has taken place.

One of the commonest and oldest drugs is cannabis, the product of the plant *Cannabis sativa*. It can be met with as the

We have seen that most poisons are toxic as a result of their very precise biochemical effects. Other poisons, including some very well known ones, work by means of a general effect on the tissues as a whole. Nevertheless, some of these poisons have more specific actions, but, generally speaking, their ability to cause death is due to their more general effects.

Strong acids and alkalis, as well as the salts of heavy metals, have a corrosive or "burning" action on the tissues. Phenol (or carbolic acid) and related compounds are commonly used in disinfectant and antiseptic preparations for domestic use and, therefore, are among the most frequently used suicide poisons. Swallowing phenol results in a burning pain in the mouth and the digestive tract. Burn marks on the lips of suicides suggest that phenol or one of its close relatives has been used; the characteristic sweet smell of phenol is also a tell-tale sign. Death

Above: *Rhubarb (*Rheum *sp.). The stalks are a good source of calcium, fibre and vitamin C and are used in sweet desserts, but the leaves contain oxalic acid and are extremely toxic, even after boiling.*

is due to the general destruction of the tissues, as well as the depressing activity the poison has on the central nervous system.

Lysol is another poison in this group. Its effects are similar to those of phenol, although a recorded toxicological case reveals how dangerous these compounds can be. A man who kept a bottle of lysol in his hip pocket fell asleep and the bottle was accidentally broken. The liquid poured out, soaking his entire leg. The man died three-quarters of an hour later, although he had not swallowed any of the poison; the lysol was absorbed through his skin, especially through wounds or scratches, with the consequent effect on the nervous system that caused the man's death.

Oxalic acid is found in many preparations used for cleaning metal and leather and is used extensively in brass-polishing and in the restoration of old book bindings, among other things. It is said that many accidental deaths from oxalic acid poisoning are consequences of the fact that its crystals look very much like those of Epsom salts and are easily mistaken for them. Indeed, there are cases on record in which hospital patients were given oxalic acid in error, the nurse believing the contents of the package to be Epsom salts.

A secondary effect of oxalic acid poisoning is its depression of blood calcium levels. The resulting crystals of calcium oxalate are precipitated in the kidney tubules, a sure post-mortem indication of oxalic acid poisoning.

Oxalic acid is the toxin found in rhubarb leaves. It is not found in the stems, although, unaccountably, the belief has arisen that it is found in the stems, but that boiling neutralises the poison. This has resulted in some people boiling the leaves and eating them as a vegetable, with fatal results.

The other main group of non-systemic poisons comprises those known as irritants. These substances cause great irritation to the stomach lining and, although they are not fast-acting, they include one of the most commonly used poisons in history – the semi-metal arsenic. Arsenic is obtained from its ore, arsenopyrite, which is a greyish-white mineral containing iron and sulphur, as well as arsenic. The white oxide is extracted by placing the ore in a container and heating it to a high temperature, when the vapour produced condenses on the walls of the vessel. In ancient times, extraction was a dangerous process, since the garlic-smelling vapour is extremely poisonous.

Arsenic produces much the same symptoms in whatever form – any of its salts or its vapour – it is administered. Vomiting, often blood-speckled, is one of the earliest symptoms, followed by intense stomach pains, diarrhoea, thirst, nausea, cramps, loss of weight, a feeling of burning and constriction in the throat, and melanosis (darkening) of the skin. These are symptoms of chronic poisoning, but in acute cases in which a large dose was ingested, the pulse grows weak and muscular convulsions may take place before death.

Arsenic was such a popular poison for so long partly because it is effectively tasteless, having only a very faint sweet taste, which can easily be masked by the flavours of the food in which it is administered. Nowadays, at least in developed countries, arsenic is less easily available, as it is no longer used in the manufacture of various dyes, although the 20th century has seen some cases of murder and suicide using arsenic-containing weedkillers. In Africa and India, arsenic continues to be in use as a poison.

Arsenic has the distinction of being the first poison for which a diagnostic test was devised – the Marsh Test. This involves the addition of the suspected fluid (which may be an extract from tissues), mixed with a small quantity of sulphuric acid, to a piece of zinc. The reaction of the zinc and sulphuric acid will produce only hydrogen, but if arsenic is present in the solution, arsine, or arseniuretted hydrogen, will be given off. This gas can be detected by igniting it, then holding a piece of glass above the flame. If arsenic is present, it will be deposited on the glass.

Another useful attribute of arsenic is that it will remain detectable in the body long after death. This is because much of it is "excreted" by the simple expedient of stashing it away in parts of the body, such as the hair and fingernails, in which it can do no harm.

This chapter has only touched upon its subject, there being so many poisons in existence. Whole groups of poisons, such as abortifacient drugs and bacterial toxins are worth mentioning, but a full treatment of these is outside the scope of this book, since they are infrequently encountered in forensic case-work.

Below: *Nannie Doss (1905–1965) confessed at her 1955 trial in Oklahoma to killing four of her five husbands by arsenic poisoning. She was also alleged to have murdered at least seven other relations including her mother.*

DESTRUCTION

The obvious and fundamental difficulty about the forensic investigation of fire is that it destroys even the evidence of its own origin. But fire, destructive though it is, can be investigated, although its investigation must be one of the most difficult in forensic science.

Before we look at the way fire is investigated forensically, it is worth asking why some people deliberately set out fire-raising. The answer, inevitably, is that there are all sorts of reasons, but one of the commonest is the desire to conceal another crime, such as when a murder is committed and the culprit wishes to destroy the evidence, including the body itself or, alternatively, to give the impression that the deceased died as a consequence of what the murderer hopes will be taken as an accidental fire.

Why Fires are Set

Although fires are often set to conceal a murder or other crime, they are rarely started in order to commit murder. It is too hit-and-miss a method for that. Suicide is rarely committed by fire, since it is clearly too painful a way to die. However, some people, most notably political protesters, have set themselves alight in public.

More commonly, however, arson is committed for economic reasons. A robber might burn down a building that had contained stolen goods; the records or actual merchandise of a business may be destroyed by a dishonest employee, who hopes to cover up his fraudulent activities; someone wishing to cheat an insurance company may burn his own belongings.

Evidence that arson is most commonly committed for economic reasons comes from the fact that the incidence of suspicious fires rises during times of economic difficulty. This happened in the USA during the Great Depression of the 1930s; and, in Britain, the recession of the early 1990s saw an increase in suspicious fires, estimated as being a quarter of all fires that happened during that period.

Malice and revenge are other motives for arson. A sacked employee, an insulted or humiliated former friend or a jilted lover may feel sufficiently resentful to exact retribution by means of the destruction of the offending person's property. The burning desire

Below: *Arson. A broken-down and abandoned car has been damaged and then set on fire. Destruction for no gain is a common reason for arson and other acts of vandalism.*

to see justice done may have more literal consequences.

There are other, more complex, motives for arson. Fire has a fascination all its own; most people like to watch a fire burn, even if it is only the fire burning in the hearth. However, the desire to destroy for no actual gain is a much more common reason for arson, the destruction of tombstones, the defacing of monuments and other acts of vandalism than most people suppose. Most forest fires are caused by human activity, although many of these are caused by accident.

Right: *Forest fires rage over millions of acres of land annually. Lightning is the most common natural cause. Whilst some trees are serotinous (their seeds only germinate after fire exposure) most are destroyed.*

CASE HISTORY

A Novel Motive for Arson

Alfred Arthur Rouse was in a social and financial mess and on the brink of disaster when, in 1930, he tried to deceive yet another young woman, Ivy Jenkins. Knowing that Ivy's father and brother were quite capable of dealing firmly with her deceiver, Rouse thought of Agnes Kesson, a woman who had been strangled to death by a rope, but whose murderer was never found. He conceived a brilliant plan of substitution by fire. It was time for him to disappear and rise again in another identity.

In the early hours of November 6, two young cousins saw a car burning with someone sitting in it, clearly dead. The father of one of these young men was the local constable, Hedley Bailey, and he was roused from bed by his son, who told him the news. Both hurried to the scene, where they found that young Bailey's cousin, Alfred Brown, had brought another constable to see the burning car.

At that early stage the police officers did not suspect foul play, but the story the two cousins had to tell raised their suspicions, for they had seen clearly a man acting in a suspicious manner. He had walked past the two men, who had asked him what was happening. He called over his shoulder: "It looks as if somebody has got a bonfire up there".

The fire had not touched the registration plates and the police traced the car and its owner very easily. Rouse was eventually arrested and the two cousins identified him as the man they had seen walking away from the blaze on the night in question. Rouse was accused of murder and put on trial.

In his confession, published after his death, Rouse said he had murdered an innocent victim in the hope that his fire-scorched body would be mistaken for his own. He himself would disappear under an assumed name and would start a new life free of financial and social entanglements. His own story, initially at least, was that he had given a man a lift and, when he (Rouse) needed to leave the car to relieve himself, he asked the man to add more petrol to the car from a can. The man had been smoking cigarettes and Rouse claimed that he must have lit up while holding the can inside the car, starting the fire.

The point that the prosecution had to prove was that Rouse had incapacitated the man in some fashion before he set fire to the car. The only clue to this was the fact that the man lay slumped across the front seats of the car, face-down. This is not a natural posture for someone who was not incapacitated and the prosecution argued that this demonstrated that Rouse had in some fashion prevented the man from escaping. The medical evidence suggested that death was due to shock and burns, which in turn suggested that the man had been alive when the fire started, a view that supported Rouse's own (original) account. In the end, it was not possible to say whether the deceased had been alive or dead when the fire began. The jury found Rouse guilty and he was sentenced to death and hanged. His victim, however, was never identified. According to Rouse's confession, the man was a drifter who "would not be missed".

It usually takes some time before a fire can be investigated. In a metaphorical as well as a literal sense, the evidence, never superabundant to begin with, may have gone cold. Nevertheless, some information may be gleaned, even before the investigators enter the building and even when the fire is still burning. It is not often that arson specialists arrive so early at the scene, but photographs or video recordings taken by others may give some indication of where the fire started – the so-called "seat" of the fire. Observations made of the colour of the fire may sometimes be of use, since some substances burn with distinctively-coloured flames. For example, acetone produces a blue flame. Also, the colour of the smoke differs. It is pale grey when benzene burns, but it is black when it comes from burning rubber. These indications are not fail-safe diagnostic methods, but they may suggest possibilities that can later be investigated.

In an earlier chapter, I described the "scene" as being, usually, a mess. No scene is a greater mess than the site of a fire, as may be imagined. I am sometimes asked how a fire can be investigated at all. It is difficult, and I have to say at the outset and at the risk of offending many fire-investigators that forensic reports on fires

have sometimes struck me as being exceedingly ill-advised, not to say harmful. By this, I do not mean to say that they are fraudulent (although charlatans exist in every profession), but that, in the absence of any other evidence, too much reliance is placed upon them by courts and unwarranted conclusions can be drawn. The available evidence is so scanty, the conclusions so confident, the potential consequences so catastrophic, that it is wise to view the evidence with extreme caution. In fact, experienced fire specialists couch their findings in very guarded terms indeed, but, unfortunately, this does not always happen.

The first thing that must be established during an investigation is where the fire started. When a fire starts to burn in a building, the structural wooden beams will be subjected to high temperatures for a longer time than will such woodwork in other parts of the building, so the extent of charring will be greater in the former than in the latter. Speaking very generally, the lowest point in which the results of intense burning can be observed is

Below: *An incident investigator takes photographs of the scene of a house fire brought under control by the fire brigade. Detailed records may be needed to deduce the cause of the fire.*

probably the point of origin, since fire tends to spread upward. This same characteristic, however, may also complicate the issue, because wood at a higher level may exhibit more charring as a result of the upward progression of fire. It must also be borne in mind that falling, burning woodwork may ignite lower levels where the fire may not have started, although the extent of charring may reveal that the fire did not start at that level.

Other complicating factors may be at work. For example, draughts and wind currents may cause the fire to spread in a way that differs from the norm; the very architecture of a building may encourage the fire to take a certain unpredictable course, and so forth. Experienced investigators are able to note these points and interpret the evidence accordingly.

The intensity of the fire at the point of origin can also be gauged by the extent of damage to other components of the building. For example, glass will distort when subjected to temperatures of over 700°C, while at temperatures above 850°C it will flow and trickle; in this state it has been described as resembling frozen treacle. The steel beams used in modern buildings may also distort at high temperatures and very severe distortion will usually occur at the seat of the fire.

It is sometimes possible to detect the direction in which the fire

Right: *Fire damage. The safety lights will help investigators examine the damage to the wooden door in this badly burned building.*

Hazards of Investigating Arson

IT IS NOT ONLY THE destructive power of fire that makes arson such a difficult crime to investigate, for the investigators themselves are subjected to grave risks. A burnt-out building is in constant danger of collapsing and anyone working at the scene could easily be injured or killed by falling beams or walls. Consequently, the first priority is to secure the building and render it safe, before any investigation into the causes of the fire is made. The methods used to achieve this aim may, of course, result in further destruction of evidence, but it is, clearly, necessary.

Some of the damage may not be outwardly visible. Broken or leaning walls or floorboards are easy to see and, probably, to avoid, but walls may crack internally and collapse suddenly for no apparent reason. The reason this happens is that the fire will have heated the fabric of the walls; after the fire the walls will cool down, generating stresses within the stone- or brick-work, which may then crack, causing a wall to collapse. The fact that ceilings and walls are very likely to be unsupported may not be immediately obvious, but any agitation, such as someone walking over a floor, may result in sudden disaster.

There are other hazards, such as the presence of broken glass, nails, sharp edges of stones and uneven surfaces, or surfaces that may appear solid enough, but which, when stood upon, collapse to expose hot, smouldering material into which the unwary investigator can easily fall.

For these reasons, a structural engineer is often asked to assess the nature of the damage and to make recommendations as to how the building should be secured before investigative works begins. However, there are often more hazards still. Asbestos insulation may have been used in the building and have been exposed during the fire. Noxious fumes and gases, such as carbon dioxide (see preceding chapter) may be present. Measures will have to be taken to ensure that the forensic and police teams are not exposed to the risks posed by such harmful substances. Special protective clothing and masks may have to be worn.

moved by examining certain objects that have suffered greater fire damage on one side than the other. Plaster may break away from the brickwork when subjected to high temperatures and such spalling may give an indication of the intensity of the fire at particular places within the building. Smoke detectors, if present, may record the order in which the detectors were set off and may be recovered and the information taken from them noted.

All sorts of little clues can help to reconstruct the events of a fire. Smoke blackening at the top of a door indicates that the door was open during the fire, otherwise blackening would have occurred over the whole surface. Thin lines of severe burning on the ground, surrounded by areas of less severe burning, indicate that a trail of gasoline was laid by an arsonist. A large mound of combustible materials in one place may also suggest arson, as would the absence of valuables (jewels, documents, money, etc.) from their usual places. Signs of forcible entry, such as evidence of doors forced open; broken windows with glass fragments lying inside the building; broken locks and so forth, will also point to deliberate fire-raising. The number of such details is almost endless and the more experienced the fire investigator is, the more such clues are likely to be noticed.

The search for faulty electrical equipment, which may have been the cause of an accidental fire, must also be a priority. In spite of the destructive nature of fire, it is often possible to find clues in electrical appliances, such as whether regulators were switched on or off. Fuses can also be examined in order to determine whether they had failed. Similarly, gas appliances may

Above: *Two fire officers carefully remove badly-burnt debris from the scene of a fire. This will be carefully searched for clues as to where the fire began and how it spread.*

cause fires if they had been misused, such as when clothes are placed upon them for drying.

From this general review of the kinds of evidence sought by forensic scientists, it can be seen that the investigation of fire is more of an art than a science. To say this is not to demean the subject – quite the contrary – but it does mean that to become an effective fire investigator is not a simple matter of training, but it is a skill that is acquired through years of experience. Hard science certainly comes into it, but in more subtle ways than it does in other areas of forensic work.

Apart from such things as signs of forced entry and the absence of jewellery, what arouses suspicion of foul play in the mind of a fire investigator? The answer, of course, is evidence that the fire was caused deliberately, but what constitutes such evidence? First, it may be concluded that there was more than one origin of the fire. An accidental fire will have only one source – at least, it is extremely unlikely for two accidental fires to start at the same time in the same building – so when the evidence appears to show that the fire began in more than one spot, then it is justified to believe that the fire had been deliberately started. For example, if one should find that two widely separated places within a building show signs of long-term burning and other evidence of the kind discussed above, then it is likely that one is dealing with a case of arson.

Left: *Signs of forced entry, such as a smashed window, point to arson, but if the glass fragments lie outside the building, the window must have been used as an escape route instead.*

Right: *A fire-damaged hairdryer. Faulty electrical appliances can often be the cause of accidental fires.*

The Use of Accelerants

Above: *Fire investigation. Samples taken from the carbonised corpse in this burnt-out flat will be checked for accelerants such as petrol.*

"Sniffing" devices – essentially, hydrocarbon detectors – are often used to test objects at the scene to see whether they contain accelerants. A long nozzle is attached via a cable to a box with a meter. Air around the object in question – say, a piece of floor-boarding – is sucked into the nozzle and into the box, where it passes over a heated filament. If an accelerant is present, it will be oxidised and will raise the temperature of the filament, the increase in temperature being recorded as a deflection of the pointer on the meter. Such a device is used as a preliminary screening method, to show whether more detailed laboratory analysis is worthwhile.

Items, such as pieces of carpet, sections of floorboards or fragments of upholstery, which may contain accelerants and which might benefit from further laboratory examination, are packaged in airtight containers. Small items can be kept in glass jars with tightly-fitting lids, but larger items should not be carried in polythene bags, as these will react with any hydrocarbons present in the item. Usually, large items are broken into smaller pieces so that they can be placed in jars. however, if this is not practicable, specially made bags may be used.

Apart from "suspect" items of evidence, the collection of similar, but unburnt, objects from other parts of the fire scene is useful. This serves several purposes: first, these objects may reveal the presence of larger amounts of accelerants, making laboratory analysis easier. On the other hand, tests on such samples may show a complete absence of accelerants. Such a finding would be useful evidentially, since it could otherwise be argued that the presence of flammable substances was due to the innocent presence of, say, carpet cleaning fluids.

Control samples have yet another function. Intense heat may result in the breakdown of linoleum, glues, plastics and similar materials, releasing hydrocarbons of a kind that could be mistaken for accelerants. It is clear that the interpretation of results from hydrocarbon analysis must be made with great caution.

Arsonists hardly ever simply strike a match to light a fire, using any combustible material to hand, such as a piece of paper or a curtain. Such a course of action is too uncertain, since a fire lit in this way may burn itself out very quickly. Usually, an accelerant is used. A flammable liquid such as kerosene is poured over a wide area of carpets and furnishings, before the match is applied. This ensures that a hot fire will follow and that the building will be ablaze long before any fire-fighters arrive. However, what most arsonists do not know is that traces of such accelerants can be detected, even after the fire has destroyed the building. Small amounts of accelerant will seep into carpets, floorboards, plaster, brickwork and other materials and will not be consumed by the fire. The cooling effect of the water used to quench the fire will slow down the rate of evaporation of the accelerant and enough will usually remain to be detected.

The Waco Seige And Shoot-Out

As so often happens in forensic work, there arises a different kind of evidence rarely encountered in a particular specialism. An example took place when the premises of the Branch Davidians at Mount Carmel, near Waco, Texas, USA, were assaulted by FBI agents on April 19, 1993. The ensuing fire killed 76 members, including women and children.*

The dispute that ended with the assault was concerned with the fact that the Branch Davidians possessed large amounts of firearms and explosives illegally. The attack, consisting of shooting CS "ferret" rounds, as well as the spraying of tear gas, began just before 6.00 am. The FBI said that the firing stopped at 11.40 am; and that at 12.07 pm three or four fires started suddenly. The building was destroyed within a few minutes.

Later, the surviving Branch Davidians claimed that the shooting continued as the building was burning down. An FBI aeroplane film-recording showed flashes of light emanating from the FBI positions, but it was unclear what caused them. An experiment, carried out in 2000 by a British company, Vector Data Systems, simulated what may have happened. Eight shooters, using several different kinds of weapon, were filmed from two circling aeroplanes equipped with special heat-sensing cameras. The images were then compared with those obtained during the attack itself.

The results were said to show that the flashes in the original images lasted much longer than those that were caused by the firing of weapons in the experiment. It was concluded that reflected sunlight from debris was the most likely cause of the flashes and that there was no evidence that gunfire continued during the fire itself. It ought to be said that this result was disputed by the Branch Davidians' lawyers, and the situation at the time of writing seems as confused as ever.

*The acrimonious debate about who was to blame for the fire and deaths continues. The evidence appears to me still to be unclear, so I will not discuss the fire as a whole, restricting myself solely to a discussion of one investigative technique used.

Below: *After a 51-day siege of their Mount Carmel home, a gunbattle between members of the Branch Davidian sect and the surrounding FBI ended just before fires erupted burning the compound to the ground.*

The clothing of arson suspects must also be examined for accelerants, since arsonists hardly ever fail to spill some of the fluid on to themselves. However, the sensitivity of some of the laboratory techniques is such that innocent people may be incriminated, because sweat may react with certain fabrics, producing volatile substances similar to the ones in commonly used accelerants. Clothing can also provide clues of another kind, since synthetic fibres can melt in a distinctive manner in response to heat. Such melting may not always be obvious to the naked eye, but microscopic examination can reveal that it has taken place. Again, it is important to be aware that such damage can have innocent causes, since not only can innocent burning or melting take place, but also the effects of certain fabric cleaners and other chemicals can produce changes that may be confused with heat damage.

Once material suspected of harbouring accelerants arrives in the laboratory, the items are subjected to techniques aimed at isolating the hydrocarbons. The item to be examined is placed in an airtight jar and heated, releasing any volatile hydrocarbons, which are removed with a syringe attached to the apparatus, then introduced into a gas chromatogram, the resulting chromatogram allowing the identification of the chemicals (see preceding chapter). Another isolation technique is to heat the suspect item in the presence of a charcoal-coated Teflon strip, on to which the hydrocarbons will adsorb. This method of concentrating the vapour allows the isolation of a much greater amount of hydrocarbons. The adsorbent strip is then washed in carbon disulphide, which will dissolve the volatiles. The mixture is then injected into the gas chromatogram for identification. The printout for carbon disulphide is known and can be disregarded, the investigator considering only the additional peaks that appear in the chromatograph.

The commonest accelerants used by arsonists are petrol,

Below: *Fire investigators sift through debris. Since, by its very nature, fire destroys most evidence, a painstaking search is often necessary to find any useful clues about how and where the fire may have begun.*

paraffin, methylated spirits, alcohol, turpentine, diesel and other easily available organic solvents. However, the investigator must always be aware that the unexpected may arise.

If an incendiary device had been used in the arson attack, its remains may be found at the scene. The wick and shattered bottle of a Molotov cocktail, for example, can often be found. Even a discarded match may survive the fire unburned, if it is cast aside some distance from the fire. Diatoms (small, single-celled marine algae with silica shells) are found in the so-called diatomaceous earth deposits, which are used in the manufacture of match-heads. The silica shells are abrasive and help with the striking of the match. Different brands of matches contain different mixtures of diatom species, which can be identified from their microscopic shells. Thus, the brand of match can also be identified. In the USA, match "books" are more commonly used than in Britain, and a discarded match torn from such a book can sometimes be matched (no pun intended!) with the book from which it came.

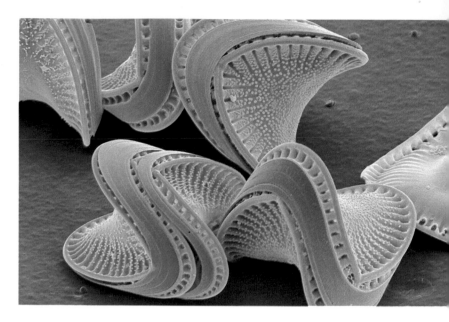

Above: *Scanning electron microscope image (magnification x310) of diatoms* (Campylodiscus sp.). *Fossilized diatoms, used in match-heads, are easily identifiable from their shell patterns.*

Spontaneous Combustion

HORRIFIC CONFLAGRATIONS resulting in many deaths always make the headlines. This is perfectly natural, but such terrible events seems to be associated with a certain kind of mythology unique to them. The Cambridge botanist, Oliver Rackham, coined a very useful word; he referred to "factoids" in science. A factoid is a statement that is so familiar and so often repeated that no one doubts it. It is also totally false. One such factoid is the idea of spontaneous human combustion.

When the story of a mass disaster in the form of a terrible conflagration reaches the newspaper headlines, it is often stated that the surrounding temperatures were so high that some individuals spontaneously ignited and were burnt, even though they had no contact with the flames. On other occasions, when a human body is found displaying severe local burning, but where there is little fire damage in the surrounding area, "spontaneous" human combustion is very often invoked, the "cause" being a supernatural "internal" source of fire. Spontaneous human combustion is sometimes the explanation offered by an arsonist; such a theory coming from such a person, while not excusable, is certainly understandable. What is hard to understand is the fact that some scientists and many journalists, as well as most of the general population, seem wedded to the idea of spontaneous combustion, despite the rebuttals issued by forensic scientists whenever a horrific fire makes the headlines.

There is no scientific evidence whatsoever for spontaneous human combustion. This is not to say that spontaneous combustion – as opposed to spontaneous human combustion – cannot happen, however. For example, a large mass of hay may spontaneously ignite at high temperatures. This happens because redox* reactions are exothermic, producing more heat than they consume. Also, when a large mass of material burns, the amount of reacting components is very large in relation to the surface area of the mass, unlike the situation in small masses. This means that much of the heat released cannot be dissipated quickly through the surface, which is the only area from which dissipation can take place. The result is that the retained heat raises the temperature, causing the reaction to proceed at an even faster rate, which will then release more heat and so on. The conditions required for spontaneous combustion cannot exist in a living human body.

Spontaneous combustion of materials such as decaying vegetation or oil-soaked rags is sometimes the cause of a fire; and a search for a possible source of such ignition should be made. In cases where a person is found dead with localized burning, but where the surroundings are undamaged, the cause is usually the fact that the deceased caught fire near a flame, such as a coal-fire, but then moved away from it and collapsed.

* Redox (reduction-oxidation) reactions are characterized by the loss of electrons from one chemical component of a reaction and the gain of electrons by another component, with the release of energy as heat.

People caught in a fire often behave in an unpredictable fashion. Sometimes it may appear odd that they were unable to escape, when the scene is examined after the fire had been put out. The smoke, which impairs visibility, as well as the sheer terror of the situation may make a person rush toward the fire rather than away from it. The inhalation of carbon monoxide (CO) will reduce the ability of the victim to flee, since the reduced amount of haemoglobin available for the carrying of oxygen will result in muscular weakening, leading to collapse (see preceding chapter).

CO blood concentrations of about 20 to 30 per cent make the sufferer feel unwell, with headaches and dizziness. Forty per cent saturation will result in a lack of muscular coordination and general mental confusion, with the sufferer staggering about, unable to make properly coordinated movements. These effects become more pronounced at 50 per cent, when slurred speech, haphazard, aimless movements, extreme weakness and vomiting take place. By about 60 per cent the victim will lose

Above: *A fireman with breathing apparatus searches through a smoke-filled building. A smoky fire reduces the visibility, makes breathing difficult and can make it hard for victims to find a way out.*

Right: *Foul play or accident? Emile Zola (1840–1902) died in his sleep from carbon monoxide poisoning, the result, officially, of a faulty chimney, although many suspected it was deliberately blocked.*

consciousness. Death follows rapidly at concentrations of around 70 per cent.

These figures represent only rough guides, since responses vary from person to person. On September 28, 1902, the French author Emile Zola died during his sleep as a result of CO poisoning. There had been a fire burning in the grate and I it is said that the chimney had not been swept or was faulty in some respect, although others claimed that it had been deliberately blocked in order to commit murder. (Zola possessed many enemies, especially after his defence of Dreyfus.) Interestingly, Zola's wife was discovered unconscious, but she recovered later.

Absence of CO from the blood in the bodies of people discovered after a fire is very suspicious and points to foul play, since anyone dying in a fire will have a certain amount of CO concentration in the blood.

Another tell-tale sign is the condition of that part of the body (or clothing) that is in contact with the floor. If the clothes or skin in those areas are free from fire damage, the conclusion must be reached that the victim had been in that position before the fire began, or at least fell to the ground during the very early stages of the fire. Such evidence may be useful in cases in which it is uncertain whether the fire was the actual cause of death, although other evidence, such as blood analysis of CO, will be have to be carried out before any definite conclusion can be reached.

CASE HISTORY

Murder and Arson in St Lucia

A case that brought together many aspects of arson and murder investigation took place in St Lucia during the summer of 1971. On June 10 a house on the mountainside near the port of Castries burst into flames. The dilapidated fire engine took a long time to reach the house and, on arrival, the firemen found the house effectively burnt out.

Two charred bodies were found in the bedroom, and were assumed to be those of the owners, James and Marjorie Etherington. At first, no-one suspected foul play and the bodies were taken to nearby Barbados for burial.

As often happens, it was an insurance man who suspected arson. He found soil footprints on the floor of the rear scullery, beneath a window that had been smashed inward. Nosing around further, the man found a green plastic hose running into the house over the sill of another window. He then traced the hose back to the garage, where a car stood with its petrol tank open, the cap lying on the floor. All this amounted to a great deal of evidence that had been overlooked both by the police and the firemen!

When the insurance agent made all this known, Scotland Yard and forensic specialists from Britain were called in to investigate the case. The arson specialist was able to identify at least four, possibly five, seats of fire; and evidence of accelerant hydrocarbons were found in the floorboards.

At this point, the police arrested three suspects – Florius, Faucher and Charles, men who were routinely hauled in whenever a crime was committed, so notorious were their reputations. Florius, the ring-leader, had burn marks on his neck and arm and he and Charles had fingernail scratches on various parts of their bodies. All three men admitted to robbery, but denied killing the couple or burning the house. They just tied them up, they said, then left. Florius challenged the police to prove him false.

They did. Apart from all the evidence already amassed, post-mortem examination of the exhumed bodies revealed that Mr Etherington's skull had been smashed with a blunt instrument; and a clot of blood showed that there had been surface bruising of the brain. Soot particles were found inside the lungs, suggesting death was due to CO poisoning. More ominously, the examination of Mrs Etherington's body revealed the presence of a clothes line running between her teeth, gagging her in life. Laboratory analysis of both blood and muscle samples from the bodies confirmed the presence of CO.

At the trial, the defendants gave the game away, for Faucher said that Florius had told him that they should burn the bodies, "as in England they have a new method to make the dead talk" and that "if we burn them, ashes don't talk". Whatever Florius thought he meant by all this is not clear, but the remains did talk "very eloquently", in the words of the Attorney General, Mr John Renwick. All three men were found guilty and hanged.

We have seen that mixtures of air and petrol, if in the correct proportions, can become explosive when lit. We will now look at substances that are designed to be explosive.

There are two kinds of explosive: low explosives and high explosives. Low explosives are characterised by their ability to burn like any other combustible material under normal circumstances; they only become explosive when they are confined in a small space. The archetypal low explosives are

Above: *Firemen regard the devastation caused to the Alfred P. Murrah Federal Building in Oklahoma. A car bomb exploded outside it on 19 April 1995 killing 168 people, and injuring more than 500 others.*

black powder (commonly called gunpowder) and smokeless powder. All low explosives are essentially mixtures of an oxidising agent and a fuel.

Black powder is a mixture of saltpetre (potassium nitrate), charcoal and sulphur. It can be used as a fuse to ignite a larger amount of powder confined in a container. Smokeless powder is made of nitrocellulose (cotton treated with nitric acid – "nitrated cotton"), or a mixture of nitroglycerine and nitrocellulose. It is a more powerful explosive than black powder.

When a low explosive explodes, it exerts a throwing effect – objects are hurled about, walls are blown asunder and so forth. Mixtures of air and gaseous fuel explode with a similar effect, but they can have an additional burning effect if the flammable mixture is at the high end of the range. In such cases the mixture will explode, but some gas will remain unconsumed and, as air rushes back to the area of the explosion, oxygen will combine with the remaining hot gas and a fire will start to burn. Often, it is this secondary fire that causes most of the damage, not the explosion itself.

It is the sudden generation and expansion of gases within a container that causes the explosion. The gases can rush out at speeds of more than 7,000 miles per hour, which are forces sufficient to make buildings collapse and to throw large objects, like boulders or cars, into the air.

High explosives are far more damaging. They explode at rates of between 1,000 to 8,500 metres per second and their effect is literally a shattering, rather than a throwing, one. In other words, a car exposed to a high explosive will be smashed to pieces, rather than lifted and thrown. High explosives are, in fact, of two kinds, both of which are used in a high explosive system. The first group consists of extremely heat-, shock-, or friction-sensitive compounds, such as mercury fulminate or lead

styphnate. They detonate violently, even when not contained in a confined space. In view of their extreme sensitivity, they are not used in the main charge, but are used to initiate the explosion. In other words, they are detonators, or primers. Most modern detonators are set off by an electric current that passes through a wire filament that ignites the fuse-head, which in turn ignites the priming charge. This latter then ignites the base-charge of secondary explosive, which amplifies the effect, causing the main explosive charge to detonate.

The main charge of a high explosive is usually a substance from the second group which burns rather than explodes, if lit in small quantities in the presence of air. The most famous of these non-initiating explosives include dynamite (nitroglycerine mixed with an absorbent material, such as kieselguhr), TNT (trinitrotoluene), PETN (pentaerythritol tetranitrate) and RDX (cyclotrimethylenetrinitramine).

When fragments of explosive are collected from a scene, the pieces are washed in acetone, which dissolves most of the chemical components. Having isolated the compounds in this way, chromatographic techniques are used to identify the individual compounds. Once this is done, knowledge of the composition of various explosives allows the forensic specialist to identify the particular make of explosive used.

Below: *This disassembled detonator for a bomb was found by Israeli forces during a raid on a suspected bomb factory in the West Bank town of Nablus. The explosives are in sealed packages.*

The Lockerbie Disaster

On the evening of December 21, 1988, a Boeing 747-121 airliner (Pan Am Flight 103), on its way to New York from London at a height of 31,000 feet, suddenly disintegrated above Lockerbie in Scotland. All 259 passengers, as well as the crew and 11 people on the ground, were killed. Although the most likely cause of the disaster was a terrorist's bomb, this was not initially proved and at least one other explanation was possible. (Subtle, yet very strong, pressure can be brought to bear on forensic investigators involved in a tragedy that has international political implications. In highly charged situations like these, pure objectivity is essential.)

The first stage of the investigation was the search for the debris of the plane. This was by no means easy since not only was the wreckage spread over an area of more than 1,000 square miles, but much of that area was woodland. This not only hampered the 1,000 searchers on the ground but also presented difficulties for the large military helicopters. Later, smaller helicopters carrying infra-red camera equipment, which was able to detect debris beneath the canopy, were used and NASA spy satellites photographed the area with excellent results.

The combined operation – ground searchers, aerial photography and satellite images – resulted in the collection of more than 10,000 objects and pieces of debris. Each item was X-rayed and tested for any residues from explosives and relevant details from every item were fed into HOLMES, the Home Office's computer. Pieces of the fabric of the aeroplane were deposited in a hangar, where the airliner was painstakingly reconstructed in order to ascertain how it broke apart – explosive damage would be most pronounced in those parts that were closest to the bomb.

When a bomb explodes on board an aircraft, the metal in the fuselage melts and the hot gases generated punch small holes in the metal. Moreover, the very low temperatures outside an aeroplane travelling at high altitude will lower the temperature of the metal quite suddenly, resulting in a distinctive microscopic metallographic structure. These physical changes to the metal allowed the investigators to narrow down the number of possible sites of the bomb. The distribution of fragments of the bomb was also a useful clue. In the end, it was decided that the bomb was placed in the left side of the forward cargo hold. The fact that the cockpit fell to earth in one piece, separated from the rest of the plane, reinforced this belief.

The gas chromatographic analysis of chemicals isolated from the various items showed that the Czech-made explosive, Semtex, was probably used in the bomb. Some items of clothing had appreciable quantities of compounds that are found in Semtex. A particularly interesting discovery was the finding of small pieces of a stereo system of a make called Toshiba "Bombeat", which is available only in the Middle East and North Africa, including Libya, upon which country suspicion soon fell. Another Libyan link was a microchip from the detonator circuit, of a kind identical to ones found on two Libyan agents in Senegal in 1986.

Fragments of detonators were also found and it became clear that a two-step detonator had been used. The first step was a barometer-detonator, which is triggered by the drop in temperature when the aeroplane reaches high altitudes. The second was an

ordinary timer-detonator. The presence of both detonators was probably the reason why the airport authorities failed to detect the presence of the bomb, since terrorists normally use a barometer-detonator only. When a suspicious item is tested at an airport, it is subjected to low pressure, which would detonate the bomb under controlled conditions. If the bomb on board Flight 103 had been treated this way, it would not have gone off.

Many people have asked why the pilot did not send a distress signal, which, normally, he would have had time to do. If the bomb had indeed been placed in the forward cargo hold, then the explosion would have damaged the electronics centre of the plane, rendering any attempt to send radio signals futile. The cockpit voice recorder registered a loud bang less than a second before the aircraft disintegrated. It is quite possible that the sound was that of a bomb exploding.

These are the most important basic facts of the investigation. Some alternative proposed causes are so unlikely as to border on the fanciful, for example the idea that magnetic disturbances were responsible. The most realistic alternative explanation was that the cargo door was defective – a defect known to exist in other aircraft (including other Boeing 747s) and which has caused air crashes.

How does this fit in with the rest of the evidence – the microchips, the Semtex compounds, the bang on the voice recorder, the Toshiba "Bombeat" stereo and the detonators? A certain microchip might mean that a person from the Middle East was involved in some way, but it does not mean that this person was a Libyan terrorist. This applies to the stereo system as well. The compounds (RDX and PETN) found on the various items are not only found in Semtex, but in other explosives and could have been there as a result of contamination. The bang on the voice recorder could have been the sound of the aircraft breaking, rather than the sound of a bomb.

The detonators are harder to explain away. Also, the cumulative nature of the evidence and the fact that the bomb scenario was much more inherently probable than the others compelled one to believe that the tragedy was an inhuman terrorist act.

Below: *Wreckage from Pan Am Flight 103. Libyan Abdelbaset Ali Mohmed al Megrahi was convicted of planting a bomb on the plane on 31 January 2001. On August 15 2003, Libya formally accepted responsibility for the bombing.*

There is something particularly awesome about documentary evidence. A few marks on a piece of paper can incriminate or exonerate, bring great happiness or great misery, inform us or reveal to us the extent of our ignorance.

Writing is so much taken for granted that we tend to forget the power of it. It is no wonder that, in days gone by, those who could read and write were looked upon as wizards. In this chapter we will consider what the written word or the image can tell us about a crime or a past event. We will also consider the spoken word, which, when taken in context, can reveal so much about a criminal's thoughts.

Handwriting Analysis

A person's handwriting is a very personal attribute and no two people share exactly the same style. This uniqueness is the basis of handwriting identification. However, this does not mean that the differences between the handwriting of different people are always obvious and clear-cut, since many of the differences are very small and subtle. There are variations, too, between the handwriting of a single person at different times. Changes in style take place with age – a child's handwriting is very different from that of an adult. As a child grows up, it will change its style considerably, but, even when that style has stabilised in adulthood, changes will still occur. Tiredness, illness, emotional state, position of

Below: *In 1932, the aviator Charles Lindbergh's baby son was kidnapped and murdered. Bruno Richard Hauptmann was accused, convicted and executed, partly as a result of handwriting comparisons between the ransom notes and samples of his writing.*

writing, the drinking of alcohol, among other things, will cause changes in handwriting. Nevertheless, the basic style usually remains detectable.

In forensic cases, the document examiner is usually asked whether a hand-written document was written by a particular suspected individual or not. Comparisons with other undisputed examples of that person's handwriting will have to be made. First of all, the gross differences are examined. Some people write the fifth letter of the alphabet thus: e. Others may write it like this: ε – the so-called Greek "e". Some may have a habit of curving the tail of the "y" at the end of a word, thus: y but others may leave it straight – y. These differences, although numerous, are finite and cannot be used to establish authorship, although they serve as a rough sorting exercise.

We can all recognise the form of someone's handwriting, but we would find it difficult to describe it in a fashion that would enable anyone to recognise it on sight, without having previously seen a sample of it. The document examiner tries to prepare a kind of visual description of the two sets of handwriting being compared. This can be done by comparing the relative positions of the highest points of the letters and the lowest points of the letters, giving us a picture of what we might term the "amplitude" of the writing.

One of the difficulties with identifying handwriting is that there is sometimes no undisputed sample with which it can be compared. In such cases the suspected author of the document is asked to write a piece of text dictated by the document examiner. The danger inherent in this is, of course, that the writer may deliberately alter his writing in order to deceive the investigators. In spite of this, however, certain basic aspects of handwriting style cannot be changed easily, since these are done automatically and the writer may not be aware of these subtleties.

At this point I must draw attention to a serious weakness in the methodology of handwriting specialists. Almost always the opinion given by them is based on a comparison of the suspect document with a known sample from a suspected individual. This is not a scientifically valid practice, since the possibility that there may be another author (i.e. other than the suspect) is not addressed. So, if the handwritings do not match, then the suspect is cleared, but if, in the opinion of the examiner, they do match, then the suspect is guilty. However, it is very difficult to say what, in fact, constitutes a match.

In general, forensic document examiners use a five-point scale in their conclusions about the possibility of whether a particular individual was the author of a document or not. It runs as follows:

1. Common authorship. One hundred per cent positive, written by the same person.
2. High probability. Very strong positive evidence; very unlikely to have been written by a different person.
3. Probably, or could well have been written by the same person.
4. Inconclusive.
5. No evidence. (This does not mean that the suspect did not write the document, merely that there is no evidence that they did.)

The subjectivity of this scale is obvious. To my mind, this, together with the lack of consideration of other possible authors of a document, weakens handwriting evidence considerably.

An Illustration with Apples

IT MAY NOT BE OBVIOUS why other possible authors should be considered, so let me present the argument in everyday terms. Let us say I give you a red apple, then take you to a tree and ask you whether you thought the apple came from that tree. Upon inspecting the tree and finding that it bears yellow apples, your answer will be that the apple could not have come from that tree.

But what if I had taken you to a tree bearing red apples? I suspect that your answer would have been that the apple could quite easily have come from that tree, but that you cannot be sure, since there are many red-apple trees in existence.

The proper course of action would have been for me to show you as many red-apple trees as possible and ask you which one of them the apple in your hand came from. Although you could find no fundamental differences between your apple and the ones on the single red-apple tree I showed you, you might well have found many small differences between the apples on the many different red-apple trees. This is because any description is incomplete; we describe only what we think is essential or relevant. And what we think is essential or relevant depends on what we are comparing the object with.

Forgery and Falsification

The forging of a whole document is not an easy process and most forgeries are alterations made on existing documents. Often, a word or words are removed by erasing them with a rubber, or by scraping them off with a razor blade. In crudely made alterations of this kind it is usually easy to see the changes with the naked eye, but sometimes such forgeries are done more expertly.

Erasures by a rubber eraser are often not easy to detect by eye. In such cases, lycopodium powder* is used to dust the document

Above: *As a crude first pass, suspected counterfeit notes are carefully examined under a magnifying glass for any obvious alterations before being subjected to further tests.*

while holding it at an angle. The excess is shaken off lightly, but some of the powder will adhere to small particles of rubber that remain on the papers after erasure. Unfortunately, the powder cannot be used to detect the use of plastic erasers.

Some forgers use chemical oxidising agents or solvents to obliterate words on a document, substituting another word.

Such changes are not visible to the naked eye, but microscopic examination will reveal a discoloration in the treated area. Also, if the ink used to write a substitute word is different from the ink used in the rest of the document, this may be detectable. Some inks can be rendered transparent under infra-red light; other inks do not react in this way, although they can often be distinguished from one another by the fact that some, when subjected to blue-green light, will radiate infra-red light, while others will not.

Those inks that absorb infra-red light differ in their ability to do so. Subjecting a document to infra-red light and recording the light reflected from it on to special film may show that different inks had been used. Chromatography can also be used to separate and identify the components of the inks used. A blunted hypodermic needle is used to remove a small sample of ink for laboratory analysis.

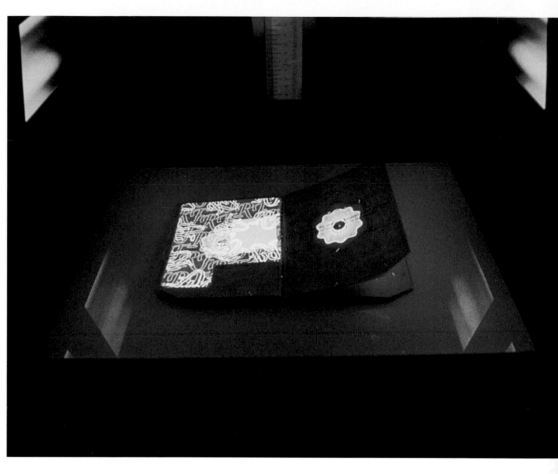

Above: *A passport in an anti-forgery detector that uses ultraviolet light to reveal the ordinarily invisible watermarks.*

It may seem strange to say that there are no reliable methods of either identifying or of dating inks. Most forensic work done on ink is concerned with comparing two samples, rather than the identification of specific makes. At least, this is the situation in most countries, including Britain, but the Secret Service Laboratory in Washington, USA, maintains a large collection of inks, which may be compared to inks from forensic cases for positive identification. Also in the USA, some manufacturers now add to their inks fluorescent dyes, which are changed every year or two, allowing the dating of these inks in the event of their criminal use.

When someone writes something on a piece of paper in a notebook, the paper underneath will, to a greater or lesser extent,

Forged Signatures

SIGNATURES THAT ARE suspected of being forged form a special category of handwriting examination. Most commonly, forged signatures are tracings of an original genuine one. Such tracings are often made in pencil and, since the inked-in signatures will not flow consistently over the pencil marks, some of these latter can be detected under microscopic examination, or even by the naked eye. However, more refined techniques are available to establish that a signature has been inked over. We have seen that many inks are transparent when viewed under infra-red light, while pencil markings remain opaque. This fact can easily be exploited to examine signatures that may have been forged.

Some forged signatures are not tracings and are done freehand. These flow more steadily from the writer's hand, unlike tracings, which betray a laboured, hesitant movement over the paper. Nevertheless, even the free-hand forger will hesitate, removing the pen from the paper at intervals, with the result that the end product lacks the fluency of the true signature.

Top: *The letter B on this passport appears normal when viewed under visible light.*

Bottom: *When viewed under light of a different wavelength in a spectral comparator, the genuine letter is revealed as an E.*

be indented. This fact allows investigators to discover what had been written on the top piece of paper if it had been torn out of the book. The indentation may not always be clear enough for decipherment, but a technique known as ESDA (Elesctrostatic Detection Apparatus) can highlight these indentations. Reading such indentations may be important if the writing on the uppermost sheet was, say, a blackmail note or a threatening letter.

ESDA makes use of a physical phenomenon that is not understood scientifically. When a piece of paper is indented, its dielectric properties (i.e. the extent to which it is a non-conductor of electricity) change. Why this happens, no-one knows, but it is useful to the forensic investigator. Essentially, ESDA is an apparatus that releases an electrostatic charge through the paper, which is kept tilted at an angle. A mixture of photocopy toner and small glass beads is sprinkled over the paper. The altered

electrical properties in the indented areas will attract the toner-covered beads, making the indentation legible.

Paper is much easier to date and identify than inks, due to the widespread use of watermarks. There have been attempts to forge watermarks, but these are easily spotted. A watermark is made during the manufacturing process and the image is visible because there are fewer fibres in it than there are in the rest of the paper. Attempts at forging a watermark are concerned with the addition of an image, which can easily be identified as such. The usual methods employed are either the printing of a mark, or the compression of the paper with a bossed design of the mark.

Other attributes of paper include the kind of fibre from which it is made (e.g. wood, cotton, synthetic) and whether or not it had been treated with chalk or fluorocarbons during manufacture, among other things. It is, therefore, often possible to narrow down the field of search quite considerably. Particularly important documents, such as banknotes or passports, are printed on paper that contains fluorescent fibres, special inks and other devices that make the process of forging difficult or impossible.

Charred papers are often encountered in forensic investigations, either as a consequence of a fire or as a result of the deliberate intention to destroy evidence. Charred bits of paper, as everyone knows, are extremely fragile and likely to crumble, but there are techniques that can be employed to preserve such material. Spraying the fragments with a three per cent solution of polyvinyl acetate in acetone will consolidate them, making them more amenable to flattening without breaking. The pieces of paper can then be floated on a 25 per cent solution of chloral hydrate, with 10 per cent glycerine in an alcohol solution. The papers can subsequently be photographed under ordinary or infra-red light. The whole process is by no means an easy one, but in the hands of an expert, much of the writing can be revealed. Another method is to sandwich pieces of charred paper between two photographic plates, which are then placed in a dark box for about two weeks. This is followed by the photographic developing of the plates, resulting in the "resuscitation" of the writing.

In principle, typewriters and computer printers can be linked to particular documents, due to the peculiarities of each individual machine – no two of which are exactly alike. In practice, however, it is much easier to achieve this with an old-fashioned typewriter than it is with any other machine.

The Hitler Diaries

A complex case of forgery came to light after the editors of the German magazine, *Der Stern*, announced on April 22, 1983, that they had acquired Hitler's diaries – all 62 volumes of them. Although many people seemed to accept them as genuine, forensic investigations soon showed them to be forgeries.

First, the bindings were held in place with polyester threads, a synthetic fabric not manufactured until after the Second World War. In other words, after Hitler's death and after the date of the last entry in the diary. The labels on the diaries were stuck by means of a glue that contained chemical compounds not in use until after 1945. The paper was of a kind not manufactured until 1955.

Other evidence included the fact that it was highly unlikely that Hitler, having suffered injuries during the 1944 attempt to assassinate him, would have been able to write so copiously well into 1945, as suggested by the diaries. His taste for fine book bindings was not reflected in the rather second-rate paper and imitation leather bindings of the diaries.

On the other hand, when the handwriting was subjected to analysis it seemed to match samples of Hitler's writing. However, the origin of these samples was suspect, as they came from the collection of Gerd Heidemann the *Der Stern* reporter who purchased the diary on behalf of his employers and who, together with Konrad Kujau, the dealer who sold him the diaries, was brought to trial and convicted. The two men were sentenced to prison terms of four years and eight months.

Below: *Adolf Hitler (1889–1945). In 1983 the magazine,* Der Stern, *claimed to have bought Hitler's diaries for the period 1932-45. Detailed analysis of the writing, ink, paper and bindings proved them forgeries.*

CASE HISTORY

The Murder of Julie Ward

Although the deliberate forging or falsification of documentary evidence is usually carried out with a certain amount of subtlety, there are cases in which the record has been altered in the most transparent way. An example of this occurred after the murder of Julie Ward, a young Englishwoman, who was on holiday in Kenya in the 1980s.

Julie Ward was murdered in the Masai Mara Game Reserve in southern Kenya in September, 1988. She disappeared early that month and her family in England began to grow concerned about her safety. Her father, John Ward, flew out to Kenya to look for her. He went to the Masai Mara and there had the horrible experience of discovering his daughter's remains himself. All that remained was her jaw and part of her left leg. A fire had been lit nearby.

The story of the horrific murder of Julie Ward has been told many times and I will not go over the whole ground here. Suffice to say that the Kenyan authorities did their utmost to cover up the murder. One way they tried to do this was by tampering with the report on the most important part of the evidence – the skeletal remains.

The leg and jaw were given to Dr Shaker, an Egyptian pathologist in the employ of the Kenyan police. In his post-mortem report he concluded that the remains had been "cleanly cut" with a sharp instrument and that there could be no doubt that foul play was involved. Before the report was released to John Ward, Dr Shaker informed him of its contents, adding, confusingly, that "I shall make sure that it cannot be tampered with".

Puzzled by this odd remark, Mr Ward waited to receive his copy of the report. There were delays. Another visit to Dr Shaker elicited the response that he could not supply a copy of his report, because the police had taken all the copies. Did he not keep a copy for his files? No, replied the doctor, he did not have a copy. Could he type a new report from his notes? No, said the doctor, since he kept no notes! Eventually, through the intervention of the British High Commission, a copy of the post-mortem report was obtained. It had been altered.

Where Dr Shaker had typed that the jaw was "cleanly cut", someone had typed "cracked" over it. The original typing was still discernible and the new typing was misaligned, appearing half a notch below the original. Further on, where the original stated that the left lower leg had been "cleanly cut", someone had typed a

Left: The site of Julie Ward's murder in the Masai Mara Game Reserve in southern Kenya.

series of Xs over the word "cut", erased the word "cleanly", then typed the word "torn". Where Dr Shaker had reported that there was a "sharp" wound on the calf of the leg, the word was altered to read "blunt".

Altered by whom? Before the report reached the British High Commission, Dr Jason Kaviti, Kenya's Chief Government Pathologist, had read it. Accompanied by Dr Shaker, who was in a state of fright, and John Ferguson, of the High Commission, Mr Ward paid a visit to Dr Kaviti at the Kenyatta Hospital. Slapping the report down on his desk, Ward asked the dumbfounded pathologist why he had falsified the report.

No immediate reply came. Eventually, he said that, while he was in the mortuary the previous day, he found the unfinished report and decided to make some "corrections" to Dr Shaker's English, for Dr Shaker's command of the language was not very good. He, Kaviti, simply "knew" that, when Dr Shaker typed "cleanly cut", he really meant to type "torn", so he felt obliged to "correct" the report.

The Kenyan authorities had been claiming that Julie's death had been caused by an attack by wild animals. In view of this, the most startling alteration in the forged report was its conclusion: "Blunt injuries with subsequent burning". In other words, the animals killed their victim, then lit a fire to burn the evidence! If the burning took place after the injuries, then foul play had to be involved. The report had not been altered well enough; it is hard to think of a more unsubtle attempt to falsify the documentary record.

Dr Kaviti was obliged by Mr Ward to initial and date the changes he made, thus admitting his guilt for all to see. As far as I am aware, no action was ever taken against the government pathologist.

A small, but interesting and relevant little event took place during Dr Shaker's investigations of the jaw. Julie Ward's dental charts were obtained from her dentist in England, albeit with some difficulty, since the dentist seemed strangely reluctant to reveal the document. The chart was needed to compare with the teeth in the jaw, in order to confirm that the jaw was, indeed, Julie's. When Dr Shaker examined the chart, he concluded that it matched the jaw and that the jaw did, indeed, belong to Julie Ward. And yet he was slightly puzzled. There was an extra filling on the chart, where there was no corresponding filling in the jaw. Perhaps it was an honest mistake. On the other hand, perhaps the dentist had been charging the National Health Service for fillings he had not performed; this would, at any rate, explain why he was so reluctant to hand over the records.

CASE HISTORY

The Turin Shroud

"Someone got a bit of linen, faked it up and flogged it". With these words, one of the most famous images to exercise the attentions of forensic scientists – the image on the Shroud of Turin – was dismissed by Professor Edward Hall of Oxford University. His comment came after his, and two other, laboratories arrived at the conclusion that the Shroud was a forgery made sometime between 1260 and 1390. The conclusion was based on radio-carbon dating methods.

Prior to this finding, analysis of pigment particles from the Shroud showed them to be red ochre and vermilion with collagen tempera medium, a paint composition common in the fourteenth century. In fact, the Shroud first came to light during that century, when it was in the possession of a French soldier, Geoffrey de Charny. After that, the Shroud changed ownership several times; by 1983, ownership had passed to the Pope, although the Shroud itself is kept in Turin.

So, carbon dating and pigment analysis indicated a fourteenth-century origin. In addition, it is interesting to record that the French church denied the authenticity of the Shroud when it first appeared. In fact, one bishop went so far as to write to the Pope, saying that he knew the artist who painted it.

Is this, then, the end of the matter? Has science disproved the authenticity of the Shroud? The startling answer is that the matter is as far away from resolution as ever. The Shroud is a length of linen cloth, measuring 14 feet and 3 inches (437cm) long by 3 feet and 8 inches (111cm) wide. It is woven in a tight herringbone pattern and it bears the front and back images of a person. The image is not at all clear; the well-known published photographs of it are, in fact, negatives, which show the image more clearly than do the developed prints. It is said that the images are those of Jesus Christ and that the cloth was the shroud in which he was wrapped after being brought down from the cross.

What supports this assertion? First, the herringbone weave is historically unusual and does not resemble any known mediaeval fabric. On the other hand, there are examples from Egypt, dating from Ptolemaic (i.e. Greek) times. The stitching, too is unusual, but it does resemble the stitching in some textiles from Masada, the Jewish fortress destroyed by the Romans in AD73. The shape of the Shroud – long and narrow – was certainly not typical of fourteenth-century France.

It has not been established how the image was made. There was only a minute amount of pigment on the cloth. In order to reproduce a similar image, modern science has had to resort to the use of techniques that were unavailable to mediaeval artists. The images most closely resembling the ones on the Shroud were produced by injecting a person with a short-acting radioactive isotope, then wrapping him in a cloth.

The Shroud was kept folded over for several centuries, yet the image did not soak through, as would have happened had the image been painted. Traces of blood were found on it, but, of course, no-one can tell whose blood it was. The image itself is strange; it seems to represent a man in a contorted position, with legs bent – a position that is very difficult to hold for any length of time, as would have been required from an artist's model. It has been suggested that the position is similar to that of a body, fixed in rigor mortis, that has been brought down from a cross.

Of particular interest is the pollen that was extracted from the cloth. The spores belonged to two plant species: *Zygophyllum dumosum*, which has a distribution restricted to the Jordan Valley and the Sinai Peninsula, and *Gundelia tournetfortii*, which is also restricted to the Middle East, although it has a wider distribution in the region. Small pieces of wood were found in the region of the image of the back of the head, and the suggestion has been made that these came from the cross itself.

Although it is true that there is no verified reference to the Shroud prior to the fourteenth century, earlier references to a shroud of the same kind are known. Sixth-century references to a cloth in Edessa (modern Urfa in Turkey) describe it as having the face or body of Jesus miraculously imprinted on it. It is said that this was taken to Constantinople in 944, but it disappeared from there after the sack of the city by the Crusaders in 1204. Interestingly, a manuscript in Budapest, dating from the 1190s, shows the body of Jesus being wrapped in a shroud that is very similar to the Shroud of Turin. The herringbone weave, as well as several distinctive tears to the cloth, suggest that the picture is of the Shroud of Turin itself.

If the Shroud had been forged, to what end would it have served? Geoffrey de Charny was a poor man and an undistinguished soldier. How he came to have it is a mystery, but it is possible that he was related to a Templar Knight of the same surname, who was put to death by King Philip IV, when he dissolved the Order of the Temple. If so, then – speculating wildly – Geoffrey may have inherited it from his more distinguished ancestor, who may have brought it to France from the Holy Land, if that is where it did, indeed, originate.

The evidence as a whole does seem to point to a pre-mediaeval, Middle Eastern origin, yet the radiocarbon dating and paint analysis results point the other way. In my view, the pigment analysis means very little, since the paint could have been added later. As for the radiocarbon results, the author Ian Wilson has suggested that bacterial and other contaminating matter may have confused the issue, resulting in a more recent dating. This kind of error has been known to happen in other cases.

Below: *A computer-generated image of the face on the Shroud of Turin.*

The Spoken Word

It is not only the written word or image that can point to the truth; the spoken word can also yield evidence. Take this fairly simple example. When the California police informed O.J. Simpson that his ex-wife had been murdered, Simpson immediately became hysterical. The police officer watched him with increasing bewilderment, for something was wrong: he had not told Simpson which one of his two ex-wives had been killed and Simpson hadn't asked.

On a more scientific level, attempts have been made to describe the individual human voice objectively, with the aim of identifying a person. These days threatening or obscene telephone calls seem to be increasing and, if these can be recorded and later compared with the voice of a suspect, an arrest could be made. Unfortunately, the state of the technology in this area is not yet highly developed.

We can all identify the voices of our friends and relations, although we may sometimes make mistakes. Nevertheless, there is a *prima facie* case for believing that voices ought to be as distinctive as many of our other attributes: our gaits; our faces; our fingerprints; our DNA. It was on the basis of this belief that the voice spectrograph was developed.

There are two types of spectrograph, each producing a different kind of voiceprint. The Bar Voiceprint records a 2.5 second segment of speech on magnetic tape. This is then electronically transferred to a stylus, which makes a trace on chart paper on a revolving drum. The resulting chart looks like a bar code fluctuating up and down. The denser the print, i.e. the closer together the bars, the louder the voice, thus:

Quiet voice: | | | | | | | | Loud voice: ||||||||||||||||

Below: *In 1971 Clifford Irving (1930–) claimed to have tapes, letters and manuscripts from Howard Hughes for an authorised biography. Hughes denied this and Irving was subsequently convicted of forgery.*

The general shape of the print is also said to be unique to an individual. Thus, two different voiceprints may be represented as follows (these representations are diagrammatic):

||||||||||||||||||||||||||||||||||||||||||||||||||||||||||||||||||||||||||||||||||||| and

||||||||||||||||||||||||||||||||||||||||||||||||||||||||||||||||||||

Another kind of spectrograph produces a contour voiceprint. These look like the contour lines on a geological map and are said to be unique to the individual.

I hope that the cautious manner in which this section is written is not lost on the reader. In this area of voice analysis, forensic scientists are still groping around in the dark. Having said that, some practitioners in the USA have claimed considerable success with this technique. For example, when Clifford Irving claimed to be publishing the autobiography of the recluse millionaire, Howard Hughes, a group of press, radio and television reporters met at Los Angeles, where a television company asked for a comparison to be made between Hughes' voice, as heard on the telephone, and an undoubted earlier recording of his voice. This showed that the refutation made by Hughes was, indeed, made by him, not an impostor, and Irving was later found guilty of forging the so-called "autobiography".

Another approach to voice identification is the technique of narrowing down suspects on the basis of regional accents. In Britain, Dr John French is a veritable Professor Higgins in this regard and has had a number of successes in identifying people. He employs what he calls "isoglosses", which are wavy lines on a map, showing where a particular accent merges with another. This is too specialised an area to discuss further here, but it seems to me to be a subject with a promising future.

* Lycopodium powder is composed of the yellow spores of the club moss, *Lycopodium clavatum*. It is used in the manufacture of fireworks and certain cosmetics.

Lie Detectors

ONE OF THE MOST famous pieces of forensic equipment, the polygraph or lie-detector, is also one of the least reliable. It cannot detect whether someone is lying or not; it can only tell us whether the person being tested is agitated or not. It gives us information about the physiological and psychological condition of the person, but it cannot tell us why the person is in that state. For example, a shy person may react adversely to the machine, when a more outgoing person may not. Similarly, a sick person may perform badly, although he may have done better had he been well.

A more recent innovation in the search for the truth in the spoken word is the voice analyser. Unlike the polygraph, the person tested does not have to be attached physically to the machine. It is said that sub-audible tremors during speech can be detected by the instrument; these tremors being, apparently, characteristic of people who are lying. Several similar devices are being marketed in the USA, but I view these developments with deep suspicion.

Finally, I must mention a story told me by Dr William Aulsebrook of South Africa. Apparently, the Zulu people have a fail-safe method of identifying a liar. The suspects are brought before a judge and each is fed a spoonful of flour, then asked to speak. Only the guilty man will have a dry mouth and the flour will fly about out of his mouth as he speaks, revealing his guilt. I cannot say that the system is in any way inferior to the polygraph; the reasoning is the same, but the conclusions are equally unreliable.

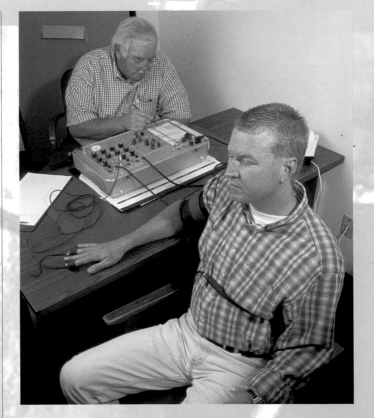

Above: *Lie detector. Sensors record the subject's autonomic system's reactions to questions and a chart is produced for interpretation.*

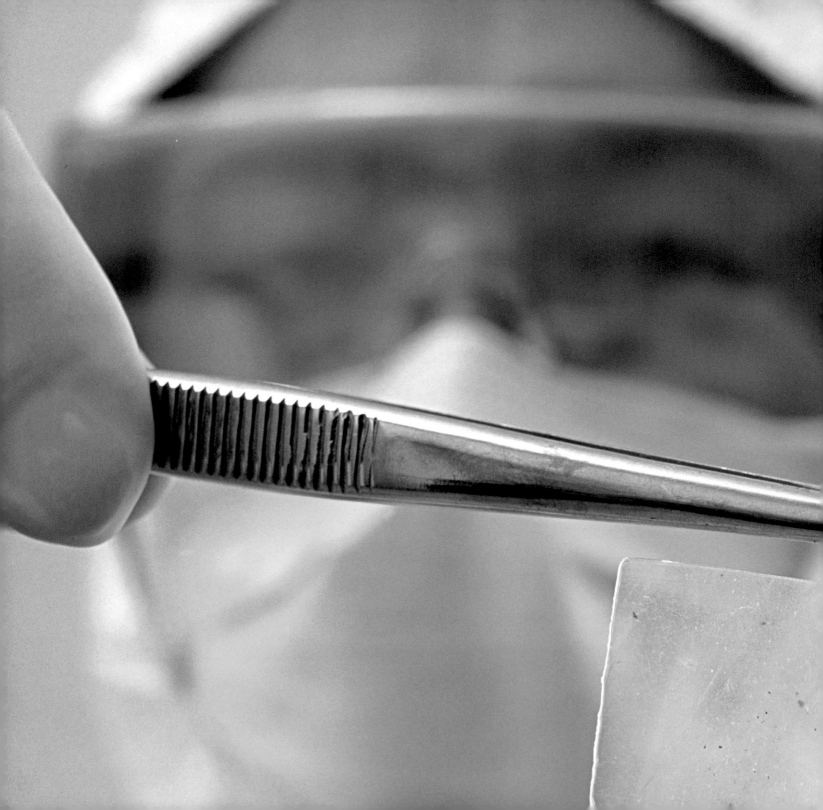

So often in forensic work, as in life in general, it is the minute little details – a scratch here, a smudge there – that are the most revealing. The smallest thing, if it is out of the ordinary, can tell us a great deal.

This chapter deals with those little pieces of evidence that keep cropping up in forensic cases – the sort of evidence with which Sherlock Holmes would have felt comfortable. One of the most frequently encountered pieces of such physical evidence is shattered glass, which is often found at the scene of a burglary, where a window was smashed, or at a murder, in which a bottle-fight resulted in death, or a shooting, where bullets were fired through a window. Many other situations can be imagined.

Glass has two very useful properties, from the forensic point of view. It refracts light and it has a certain density. Both these qualities can be measured and used as a means of identifying the fragments, i.e. to arrive at a conclusion about the origin of the glass – did it come from the smashed window at the site of the burglary? Did it come from the bottle found broken at the scene of the murder?. Often a suspected criminal will have fragments of glass adhering to his clothes or shoes; these can be compared with glass from the scene.

Refraction is the apparent bending of light when it moves from one medium into another. The most commonly experienced example is when a stick is immersed in water, making it appear as though it is broken at the point of entry. This happens because the speed with which light travels changes from medium to medium. The ratio of the speed of light in air to its speed in water is termed the refractive index of water. The speed of light through air is about 300 million metres per second, but when it enters water it is slowed down to about 225 million metres per second. Therefore, if we take the refractive index* of air to be 1, then that of water is 1.33, since:

$$300,000,000 \text{ divided by } 225,000,000 = 1.33$$

In glass, light is even more highly refracted since it moves more slowly through it – about 200 million metres per second – than through water. Consequently, the refractive index is higher, being around 1.5. The exact refractive index of any particular kind of glass will be slightly above or below this figure.

The refractive index of a glass fragment can be measured by immersing it in a drop of silicon oil and examining it under a microscope with a hot stage, i.e. a stage that can be heated slowly at a known rate. As the oil warms up, its refractive index will change, until it reaches a point when it equals the refractive index of the piece of glass. At this point it will disappear from view. Since the refractive index of the oil at different temperatures is

* More correctly, the refractive index is the ratio of the speed of light through a vacuum (rather than through air) and its speed through a medium. For our purposes, however, we can take the speed of light through air as our standard.

Left: *Reconstructing a car headlamp. Glass can be identified on the basis of its refractive index and its density. Both properties are useful for linking fragments from suspects and scenes.*

known, the investigator can conclude that the refractive index of the glass is equal to that of the oil at the temperature at which the glass became invisible.

The refractive index is not a unique identifying feature of glass, since most glasses have very similar indices. If the glass from, say, the clothes of the accused is compared with glass from the scene and found to be different, the accused may be eliminated from the inquiry. But if they are the same, it is no evidence of guilt; it simply means that we have to go further into the matter.

The density of the glass fragments from scene and suspect can then be determined. This is done by exploiting the fact that solid particles will float, sink or remain suspended in a liquid, according to whether they are less dense, more dense or equal in density to that liquid. The liquid most commonly used forensically is a mixture of bromoform and bromobenzene. The glass fragment (say, from the scene) is placed in this mixture and further amounts of bromoform or bromobenzene are added until the fragment remains suspended in the liquid. The glass fragments from the suspect's clothing can then be immersed in the

liquid to see whether they, too, will remain suspended. If they do, then both scene glass and suspect glass have the same density; if they float or sink, the two groups of fragments are clearly different in density.

Let us say that the two sets of glass we are comparing have the same refractive index and the same density. This will strengthen our belief that the two sets had the same origin, but it would still not be conclusive. Certain other examinations can be carried out, based upon the chemical composition of glass. Essentially, glass is made by heating a mixture of sand (silica or silicon dioxide, SiO_2), limestone (calcium carbonate, $CaCO_3$) and soda (sodium carbonate, Na_2CO_3). However, glass also contains various impurities, which are either deliberately or accidentally added during manufacture. For example, sheet glass often contains four per cent magnesia (magnesium oxide, MgO), while bottle glass usually contains about two per cent aluminium oxide

Below: *Scanning electron microscope. The specimen is placed in a small chamber and subjected to a beam of electrons. Three-dimensional images are produced by collecting the electrons scattered by the specimen.*

(Al_2O_3). Iron salts often occur in glass, but these are eliminated from the glass used to make milk bottles since they add a greenish tinge to the glass, which makes the milk look unappetising! (The iron salts are what make sheet glass look greenish when looked at side on.)

The presence of such impurities can be detected by the use of scanning electron microscopy, which uses a beam of electrons, rather than light, to magnify an object. Objects under the focus of an electron beam will emit radiations that are unique to the chemical elements contained in it. These chemical signatures can be isolated and monitored through the use of energy dispersive X-ray analysis, a technique that allows the determination of both the presence of certain elements and their respective amounts in the specimen. A more destructive method, emission spectrometry, can be used to detect the presence of trace elements in glass. Here, the material is burnt and the spectra emitted used to identify the elements. However, use of this method means that the item is destroyed and cannot be used for further forensic investigations.

While the above techniques depend on the use of sophisticated apparatus, some simple, common sense procedures are used in the examination of glass. If it is coloured glass, then the two samples in question can be compared by eye. It is also possible to determine whether the glass came from a flat sheet, or from a curved object like a bottle, simply by examining it. Slightly more complex is the matching of pieces of glass together, which can be done if fairly large pieces of glass are found. Glass fragments that appear as though they might fit together can be so fitted by hand, and perfect fits will hold together very tightly, strongly resisting separation.

The identification of a piece of glass as having a common origin with another piece of glass thus depends upon the number of attributes that both sets share and on the rarity of some of the attributes. For example, a glass with a particular refractive index may be so rare that the probability of finding two sets of fragments having the same index, but which do not have the same origin, must be regarded as being remote.

It is not only the fragments themselves that can yield useful information. The way in which a piece of glass broke can also be used as evidence. Consider, for example, what happens when a bullet – or a projectile travelling at very high speed – is shot through a window. The glass molecules at the point of impact will dislodge the molecules in front of it; this continues until the bullet emerges through the other side of the pane. The resulting hole will be crater-shaped, the larger end being at the point of exit of the bullet, the smaller at the point of entry (A). Of course, the presence of glass particles on the floor on the side where the bullet emerged will often betray the direction of the bullet, but such fragments can be very small and, in any case, they may have been removed in an attempt to conceal evidence.

If a projectile travelling at low speed hits a window pane, the crater-shaped hole will not form, but a star-like or radial pattern of fractures emanating from the hole will be evident (B). Circular, arc-like fractures can often be seen around a hole, connecting some of the radial fractures (C). These fractures will form on the

Right: *Glass damage, impact side, from a high-velocity bullet in a fatal shooting in Maryland. The round, crater-shaped hole is surrounded by a nearly symmetrical pattern of radial and concentric cracks.*

Below: *(A) Schema showing high velocity bullet hitting glass pane, (B) hole with radial fractures caused by low speed object, (C) concentric cracks, (D) schema of low speed bullet hitting glass pane, (E) two slow bullets.*

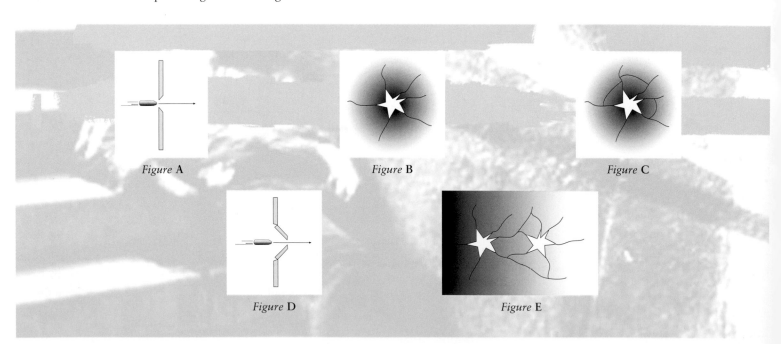

Figure A   *Figure B*   *Figure C*

Figure D   *Figure E*

outside of the window, i.e. the side struck by the projectile (D).

It is difficult to distinguish between a hole made by a high-velocity bullet and one made by, say, a pebble travelling at high speed. A window struck by a slow-moving stone will shatter in its entirety, as will one that is subjected to a close-range shot. However, the presence of gunpowder residues on the glass fragments will often indicate that a firearm was used. Of course, there is a gradation between the crater-shaped hole and the hole surrounded by radial and circular fractures. The latter can be caused by a bullet if it is travelling at lower speed.

Sometimes two or more bullets may pierce a window and, if radial fractures are present, it is possible to determine which shot was fired first. This is because the radial fractures caused by the second shot will end at the existing fractures caused by the first shot (E). It is clear that the hole on the left resulted from the first shot, the one on the right having been made later.

Above: *As hair grows, it can incorporate traces of the chemicals produced when drugs or poisons are metabolised. These remain in a fixed position in the hair shaft and act as a diary of poison/drug abuse.*

Hairs, both human and animal, are often found at crime scenes. In principle, they ought to be very good evidence, routinely used, but, in practice, this is not the case. We know that human hair differs from animal hair and that the hair of different animal species differ from one another. Also, human hairs differ from person to person and from one part of the body to another. Unfortunately, few systematic studies have been carried out. Another problem is that hair shows great morphological variation, even within the same individual. Of course, this does not mean that we cannot make more general statements on many occasions. For example, the hairs of black people and those from white people are quite easily distinguished from one another; and animal hairs are easily very different from human hair. The hairs of black and Far Eastern people, although they differ greatly between the two groups, are remarkably uniform within each group. Conversely, the range of variation among people of European origin is very great. Nevertheless, in most cases in which hair is used as evidence, the investigation involves a comparison between hairs found at the scene and those from a suspect.

The structure of a hair is quite simple. It consists of an inner core, the medulla; a surrounding layer, the cortex; and a covering "skin", the cuticle. This structure has been compared with that of a pencil: the lead represents the medulla; the wood the cortex; and the paint the cuticle. Sometimes, however, the medulla is absent. When it is present, it may occur in a continuous, uninterrupted line along the length of the hair, or it may be interrupted or fragmented in various patterns, thus:

————————

Continuous

——— ——— ———

Interrupted

——— —— ———

Fragmented

In most human races the medulla is rarely continuous, although it is the norm in people from the Far East (China, Japan and South-east Asia). The shape or pattern of the medulla can also be distinctive and can readily be seen under the light microscope. Another attribute of a hair is its medullary index, which is the ratio of the width of the medulla and the width of the whole hair shaft. Typically, the figure is less than 0.3, whereas in most animals it is at least 0.5.

The hair cuticle is not smooth like a continuous skin, but arranged as overlapping scales, like those of a fish. Again, the pattern of these scales can be of diagnostic value. These and other characteristics of hair should, one day, allow us to produce a complete atlas of hair forms, both human and animal, but, until this is achieved, most investigations will have to depend on comparisons made on a case-by-case basis.

This is, perhaps, the moment to mention that work-horse of the forensic scientist's armoury – the comparison microscope – which enables one to view two objects simultaneously. This is used to compare all sorts of items, from bullets to pieces of vegetation, but nowhere does it come into its own as when it is used to compare hairs and other fibres.

Hairs found at a scene can yield other kinds of information. For example, it is possible to say whether a hair was forcibly removed from its owner or not. This is because a hair torn out of the scalp will have pieces of tissue adhering to the root, whereas hair falling out naturally will have a root, but no adhering tissues. Also, hair roots can be used as a source of DNA for fingerprinting. Even the hair itself (i.e. minus the root) will contain mitochondrial DNA, which could be used to determine maternal relationships.

It is sometimes possible to say whether a hair came from a child, because children's hair is finer than adult hair, although this is not always the case. Bleached or dyed hair can be so identified and the period since the last bout of bleaching can be gauged from such evidence.

Right: *Coloured scanning electron microscope of a blonde Eurasian human hair shaft, magnification x 680. The outer cuticle is formed from overlapping plates or scales.*

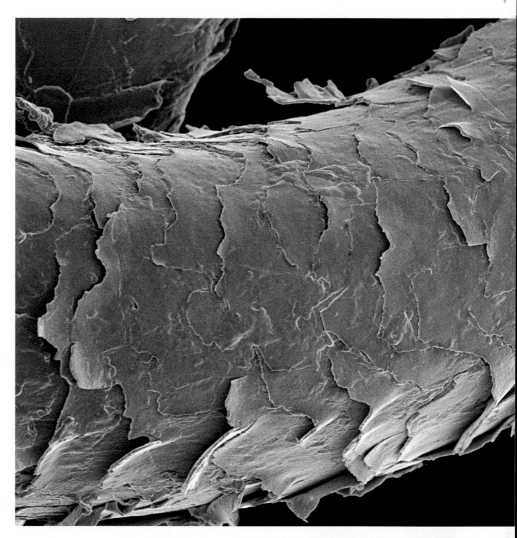

CASE HISTORY

The Evidence Of Dog Hairs

In May, 1968, an eight-year-old boy, Christopher Sabey, was found murdered – strangled – in the village of Buckden in Huntingdonshire, England. After a very intensive investigation, during which 4,000 statements were taken, suspicion fell on a young man named Richard Nilsson. It was then decided to take a further look at some seemingly trivial clues found on Christopher's body. They were three hairs, which looked as though they might have come from a dog.

Laboratory examination revealed them to be, indeed, dog hairs. They were white, tinged with fawn and could not have come from the Sabeys' black dog. Hairs found on Nilsson and hairs taken from his dog were of a similar colour. Neutron activation analysis showed that all three samples – from Christopher, from Nilsson and from Nilsson's dog – had very similar trace element characteristics. This was strong evidence, but it became stronger still. The police took hair samples from every dog in the village – all 144 of them – and sent them to the Home Office Forensic Science Laboratory in Nottingham. Most were eliminated because they were the wrong colour, but 54 dogs did have the right colour. The trace element tests on these samples showed that the hairs on Christopher's body could have come from only three dogs, one of which was Nilsson's dog. Further evidence established Nilsson's guilt. At his trial, he was found guilty and sentenced to life imprisonment.

Textile Fibres

Allied to hairs are, of course, textile fibres. These are usually classified as being either natural or synthetic, although some fibres are manufactured from the cellulose derived from natural fibres and can, therefore, be regarded as being intermediate. Although there are many kinds of

Below: *Textile analysis. This FBI specialist is collecting fibre samples. Since the dress is multi-coloured it is important to take a number of samples from the various patterns for future comparisons.*

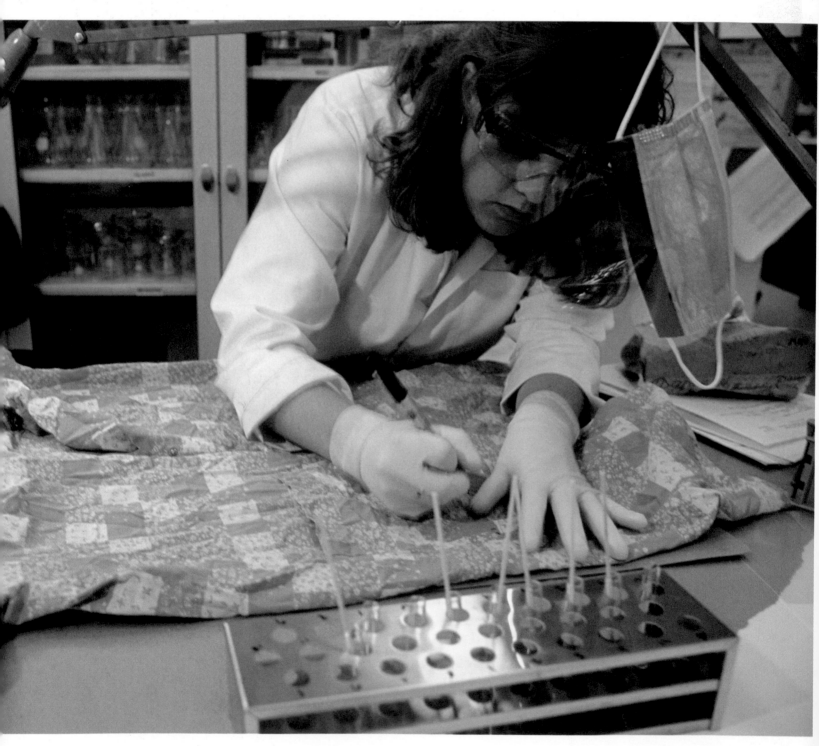

natural fibre, cotton is easily the most common. Nowadays, however, synthetic fibres are more widely used.

In the television adaptation of *The Holy Thief* by Ellis Peters, the mediaeval monk-sleuth Brother Cadfael was able to identify a murderer by showing that a gold-and-red fibre found at the scene matched those from the fine raiment of the aristocratic suspect. There was no poetic licence in this drama, since this kind of scenario often happens in forensic cases today.

Textiles are usually much easier to identify than hairs, because it is easier to maintain, or have access to, reference collections; although there are very many natural and synthetic fibres in use, these are finite in number and information about them is easily gained from the manufacturers. Also, textile fibres have characteristics that hairs do not possess, such as being dyed in all sorts of colours and woven in various patterns. Synthetic fibres have particular chemical compositions, which can be analysed in the laboratory.

Often, part of a garment is found at a scene and there is usually no great difficulty in identifying it as being of a certain make; the date of its manufacture can be ascertained by simple inquiries to the manufacturer. It is sometimes necessary to compare such a fragment with the garment of a suspected person, part of whose garment has been torn, in order to see whether the fragment came from that garment. This is, of course, a simple operation and it possible to say immediately whether or not the two parts fitted one another.

Two fibres may appear to have the same colour to the human eye, although the dyes used in each one may be different. In order to determine whether or not this is the case, organic solvents can be used to extract the dyes, which are then identified by the use of chromatography. However, such treatment would destroy the fibre as a piece of evidence and it often happens that there is very little material, perhaps just one short fibre, from the scene. In such cases microspectrophotometry is used.

A microspectrophotometer is a microscope linked to a spectrophotometer, which is a device that measures the wavelengths of light. When light is transmitted through the fibre under the microscope, some wavelengths will be absorbed and others not. The pattern of wavelengths that pass through the fibre is recorded as a graph on the computer screen of the spectrophotometer. This spectrogram, as it is called, is essentially a description of the dyes in the fibre and can be compared with a database of spectrograms of a very wide range of fibres. This technique does not destroy the fibre.

The diameter, or width, of the fibre may also be an identifying attribute. This can be measured very easily under a microscope. In fact, colour and diameter are the two basic features that must

be determined at the outset, since if these are compared with those of the suspect fibre and found to be different, there is little point in pursuing that line of evidence. On the other hand, if they do match, then there is every reason to go more deeply into the matter.

The next step is to establish the chemical composition of a fibre. In order to understand how this is done, it is necessary to say some words about the way synthetic fibres are made (natural fibres are often identifiable on the basis of their structure, much like hairs, although the other techniques discussed in this chapter may be used). Fibres are made from chemical substances called polymers, which are very large molecules made of repeated,

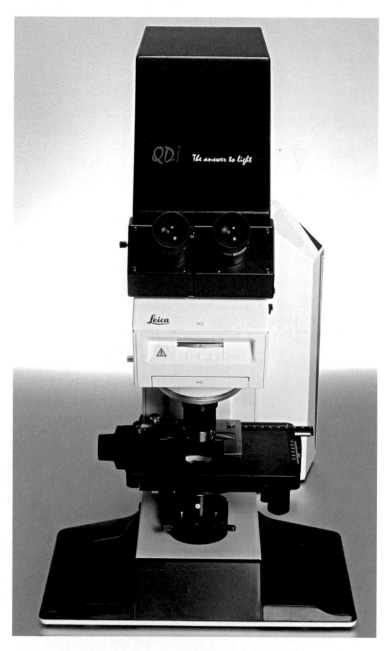

Above: *Microspectrophotometer. This is used to measure the transmission of light through individual fibres. This varies according to their colour and is useful for matching samples taken from suspect and scene.*

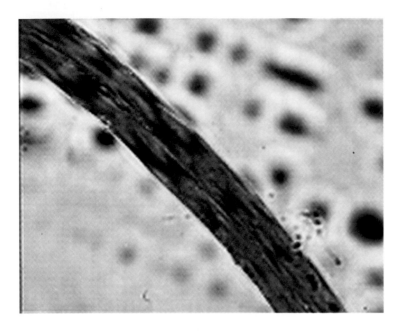

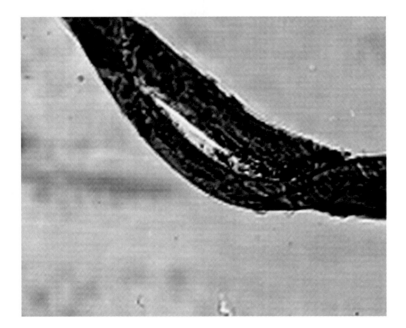

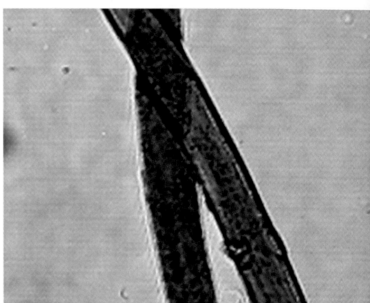

Above: *Textile fibres. Light microscope images (micrographs) of several types of clothing fibre from the same scene. The width and colour of these textile fibres is used for matching purposes.*

identical units known as monomers. So, if we designate a monomer as ∞ then a polymer would look like this:

∞∞∞∞∞∞∞∞∞∞∞∞∞∞∞∞∞∞∞∞∞∞∞∞∞∞∞∞∞∞∞∞∞∞

This picture is intended merely to illustrate the point; a real polymer is made up of thousands of monomers. Polymeric fibres are made by melting a polymer (either manufactured or natural, such as cellulose), or by dissolving it in an organic solvent. The polymer is then passed through the very fine holes of a spinneret, from which it emerges as numerous filaments, which harden into the fibres that are used to weave the cloth. The polymers have a

regular arrangement along the long axis of the fibre. This regularity endows the fibre with the properties of a crystal and it is what imparts strength to it.

Unfortunately, from the point of view of the forensic scientist, polymers of this kind are not at all easy to dissolve, so, in order to discover the chemical composition of a fibre, it is not possible to subject it to gas chromatography in the normal way. The fibres must be heated to a very high temperature, decomposing the fibre into gases, which can be used in this technique. However, the technique is even more destructive than the one discussed above in relation to the chemical analysis of dyes. Happily, another technique, based on the optical properties of fibres, is available.

Light waves vibrate in all directions at right angles to the direction in which the light is travelling. However, when light passes through certain materials, including synthetic fibres, it emerges polarized, i.e. some of the vibrations will be at right angles and some will be parallel to the length of the fibre. This results in the light being refracted in two different ways. If a crystal of a kind that polarizes light is placed on this page, two images of the print beneath will be seen. The difference between the two refractive indices, which is usually very small, is known as the birefringence. Birefringence values of most synthetic fibres range from 0.001 to 0.18 and are specific to the various fibres, so they can be used to identify them. Thus, acrylic has refractive indices of 1.524 and 1.520, so the birefringence is 0.004; whereas Dacron, a kind of polyester, has a birefringence of 0.175.

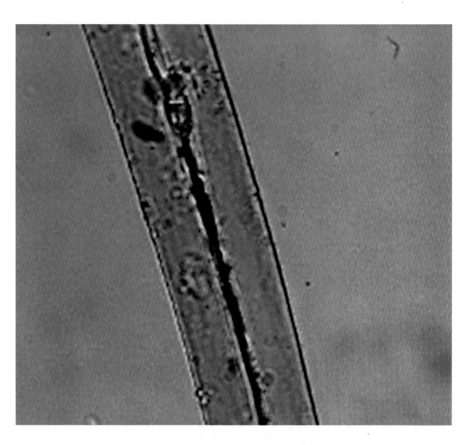

Right: *Light micrograph of a fibre. The central shaft (dark) indicates that this is a natural fibre (hair). The width will help with identification: it varies on different partsof the body.*

CASE HISTORY

A Case Solved with Fibre Evidence

A case investigated by the American forensic scientist, Richard Saferstein, shows how fibre evidence can be used in criminal detection. The body of a woman was found in an alleyway in East Harlem. She was identified as a local church member, who used to sell church literature in the area. Beside the body lay a large flower box and plastic liner, which were sent to Saferstein, together with the victim's clothing.

Light-brown wool fibres, navy blue wool fibres and red acrylic fibres were found in the box and the liner. These were compared with fibres from the victim's clothes, when it became clear that they all came from that source – light-brown overcoat, navy blue wool/polyester slacks and red acrylic sweater. However, additional fibres were found in the box and the liner. These were light blue nylon fibres and brown rabbit hairs. Significantly, fibres and hairs of the same kind were found on the deceased's overcoat, as well as some red nylon fibres.

This information was supplied to the police, who then learned that a man had recently sold a brown rabbit hair coat to a local man. They managed to obtain the coat from the purchaser and handed it over to Saferstein. The rabbit hairs from the coat were indistinguishable from those Saferstein had found in the box, the liner and on the victim's overcoat. The police felt they had sufficient evidence to obtain a warrant to search the suspect's apartment. There they found two rugs – one blue, the other red. Samples of these were sent to the laboratory, where examination revealed them to be made of nylon; and they were indistinguishable from those found on the victim's overcoat and, in the case of the light blue fibres, in the box and liner.

On the basis of this and other evidence, the man was arrested, put on trial, found guilty of murder in the second degree and was sentenced to life imprisonment.

Traces of Blood

O ne fact of which murderers seem totally unaware and about which, if they were aware of it, they can do nothing, is the fact that it is almost impossible to

Below: *Assassination in Corsica. The pool of blood marks where the victim finally fell, but many smaller stains (1–6) have been found. The pattern of bloodstaining can often be a valuable clue.*

eradicate all traces of blood completely. Even after many years, very small traces of blood can be detected at the scene of a murder, if any blood had been shed at the time. Of course, burning a building in which a murder had been committed will destroy all such evidence, but, short of that, some bloodstain evidence will remain for a long time. Even smooth surfaces, such as bathroom tiles washed clean, will retain traces of blood.

At the scene of a brutal murder, large quantities of blood will be splashed all over the place. There will be drops and pools of blood on the floor, splashes on the walls, smears of blood here, smudges there, perhaps even a trail of blood leading somewhere else. All this has to be interpreted in an attempt to reconstruct events.

The interpretation of the pattern of bloodstaining is so dependent upon the experience of a forensic scientist that it is not possible to give more than a general idea of the kind of thing that is done. When a drop of blood falls to the floor, it will remain more or less spherical, if the floor surface is smooth, as in the case of linoleum or tiles. If the surface is rough or irregular, it will assume a star shape. However, care must be exercised when making interpretations of this sort, since a star shape will also form if the drop falls from a great height.

When a drop of blood strikes a wall at right angles to it, it will remain round in shape, but if it strikes the wall at, say, an angle of 20 degrees, it will form an elongated, oval shape. In fact, it is possible to determine the angle from which the drop came on the basis of its distortion, i.e. the extent to which it deviates from the circular form.

Blood falling at an angle, either on the floor or on a wall, will splash further on striking the surface, resulting in further stains beyond it. In other words, the smaller splashes lie on the side opposite to that from which the drop came. This can be shown diagramatically in the following way:

Direction of travel

Pools of blood may occur in two places at the scene, a fact that reveals that the victim moved, or was moved, from the place of initial attack to another place while still alive. The spurting of arterial blood over walls, and even ceilings, will reveal the place in which the victim was attacked, since the blood ceases to flow after death and the heart will not be able to pump it.

The Blood Trail that Defied Gravity

Some bloodstains can provide startling evidence. A sensational murder, the full story of which has not, even now, been fully revealed, occurred in the Bahamas during the Second World War, when the Duke of Windsor was governor of the islands. Sir Harry Oakes, probably the wealthiest baronet in the British Empire, was found bludgeoned to death in his bed. He was lying on his back. An attempt had been made to burn his body. In spite of the initial assumption that Oakes died in his bed, a tell-tale sign was discovered that suggested that his body had been moved. This sign became known as the blood trail that defied gravity, for blood from an injury above the baronet's left ear moved upward, over his cheek to his nose, then over the bridge of the nose and down to the other cheek!

Left: *Sir Harry Oakes (1874–1943) Born in Maine, USA, he struck gold beneath Kirkland Lake, Ontario, Canada, in 1918. Moving to the Bahamas in the 1930s he donated large sums to help the islands and was knighted by King George VI in 1939.*

After a very bloody murder, the murderer will sometimes try to conceal the body and clean the scene. Clothes may be washed, walls may be cleaned and floors may be scrubbed, but still a trace will remain. If it is suspected that blood had been spilt in, say, a particular room, a minute investigation of it should reveal some traces of blood. Any stain or discoloration, however faint, that looks as though it might be blood, should be examined further. Often a microscopical examination will reveal some red blood cells adhering to an object, although, to the naked eye, it may appear quite free of blood.

When the presence of blood is suspected, some preliminary tests can be carried out. One of the best known of these is the Phenolpthalein or Peroxidase Test, of which there are several variations, the most widespread being the Kastle-Meyer Test. The suspect substance is removed by rubbing with a piece of tissue or filter paper and placed in a watch glass, whereupon 130 mg of phenolphthalein, 1.3 gm of potassium hydroxide and 100 ml of distilled water are added. This is boiled till clear; 20 gm of powdered zinc is added while boiling. A few drops of hydrogen peroxide is then added. If the solution turns pink, the result is positive. The test is sensitive even at dilutions of up to 15 million.

Other methods of detecting blood involve the use of certain sprays that either turn the stain a particular colour, or cause it to fluoresce. The spray luminol is used in dark conditions to detect blood on, say, a wall; if blood is present, fluorescence will occur. Leucomalachite green (which is, in fact, colourless) will appear as a green stain if blood is present. Spraying phenolpthalein mixed with orthotolidine will result in a pink colour in the presence of blood.

Earlier, I used the word "preliminary" to describe these methods of blood detection. By this I meant that a positive result indicates that the substance present is most probably, but not certainly, blood. For example, the Kastle-Meyer Test will give a positive result if used on potatoes. Such tests are called presumptive tests by scientists. They serve to indicate that further work is necessary if a positive result is obtained; in the case of a negative result, however, one can conclude that blood is absent.

In order to confirm the presence of blood, a precipitin test is carried out. This is based on the immunological phenomenon in which antigens are formed in the blood of an animal when an antibody enters the system. Antigens react with antibodies, rendering them harmless. An antigen will react with only one kind of antibody, in other words, for each kind of antibody, a particular kind of antigen is needed. The way this is used as a means of identifying a substance as being human blood is to inject a rabbit, or other laboratory animal, with human blood. This causes the rabbit to form antigens in its own blood, with which to combat the foreign blood. A sample of blood is then taken from the rabbit and the blood serum isolated, which, because it contains antigens to human antibodies, is called human antiserum.

The antiserum is placed in a very fine capillary tube and an extract from the suspected bloodstain is added to it. If the extract contains human blood, a cloudy band will form at the area where the two liquids meet. If no reaction takes place, then the extract does not contain human blood, but it may well contain the blood of an animal. If this is suspected, the process can be repeated, using dog or cat blood (or blood from whatever animal is thought to have shed the blood) with which to inject the rabbit.

Nowadays, the test extract and the antiserum are usually placed in wells at opposite ends of a plate coated with agar, a gelatinous substance derived from certain species of seaweed. The two sera will move toward one another and a precipitate will form where they meet. A variation of this technique is the use of an electric current to make the two substances move faster toward one another.

Left: *Blood analysis. This automatic sampler analyses and counts the different blood cell types present in a sample and displays the results on the monitor (right).*

Little Items of Evidence

IT IS OBVIOUS THAT so many little items of physical evidence can be used to reconstruct events; and space does not allow the consideration of all of them. Soil found on a shoe; a leaf stuck to clothes; paint smeared on a jacket; oil on a glove; all these things can link a person to a place. The principle is straightforward enough, the practice specialised and time-consuming. A specialist botanist may be needed to identify that suspicious leaf-fragment; a specialist geologist will have to be consulted about that strange reddish soil; and so on. There is, theoretically at least, no end to the kinds of clues one might find.

Tools often leave their "fingerprints" – the jemmy will make in impression on the wooden frame of a window, or a pair of scissors may have been used to cut a piece of paper, showing that it had not been torn. Great issues, as Sherlock Holmes might have said, may hang on such things. Much of the case for the murder of Julie Ward in Kenya (see page 162) was based upon the conclusive demonstration by Professor Austin Gresham that the bones had been cut with a heavy blade, not bitten through by a lion or a leopard, as was alleged by the Kenyan authorities.

Any forensic case is made up of little details. The task of the scientists involved is to try to reconstruct events; and if all the evidence seems to point one way, one has a scenario that is compelling. A story supported by many different lines of evidence will have a strength and integrity that is difficult to shake. However, one must be careful not to interpret the evidence in such a way that it is made to point one way only; often evidence can point many different ways. The probability of one's interpretation of the evidence – all of it – must be assessed. This is not always done, and I am bound to say that miscarriages of justice are known to happen as a result. The following case is an example of what can happen when bad forensic science, prejudice and confused thinking come together to perpetrate injustice.

Below: *Bagged and labelled items are removed from a murder suspect's home for investigation.*

A Cautionary Tale

Michael and Lindy Chamberlain arrived at Ayer's Rock from their Queensland home on the evening of August 16, 1980. They set up camp east of the Rock. With them were their three children: Aidan, six; Reagan, four; and Azaria, a baby girl of nine and a half weeks. The Chamberlains were known to be people of good character.

Shortly, before eight o'clock the following evening, Mr and Mrs Chamberlain were at the barbecue area preparing a meal. Aidan and Azaria were with them; Reagan was asleep in the tent. After nursing Azaria, Mrs Chamberlain returned to the tent with Azaria and Aidan, where she put the baby to bed. Aidan then said that he was still hungry, so Mrs Chamberlain went to the car and fetched a tin of baked beans, then returned to the barbecue area with Aidan. Later, the time that elapsed between her leaving the barbecue area with Aidan and the baby and her return with Aidan and the tin of baked beans was estimated at being between five and 10 minutes. The other campers noticed nothing odd about Mrs Chamberlain's manner on her return.

A short while later, Azaria was heard to cry by Mr Chamberlain and other campers. Mrs Chamberlain starting walking back to the tent to attend to the baby. She suddenly stopped and, according to

her own account, cried out: "That dog's got my baby!". Mrs West, one of the campers, later said that she heard the growl of a dog from the vicinity of the Chamberlains' tent and Mrs Chamberlain cry out: "My God, my God! A dingo has got my baby!". Mr West also said he heard the growl. Another camper, Mrs Lowe, said that the cry definitely came from the Chamberlains' tent and that it was the cry of a baby, not of a child. She also said that the cry was loud and sharp and that it seemed to stop abruptly.

Mrs Chamberlain said she saw a dingo emerging from the tent, shaking its head. She could not see its snout properly, because it was below the light level and her view was obscured by shrubs and the railing that surrounded the camping area. She did not see the baby in its mouth, but guessed at the time that the animal might have had a shoe in its jaws. When she entered the tent, the baby was not in its bassinet. Mrs Chamberlain made a quick search of the tent, satisfying herself that Azaria had not simply fallen out of her cradle.

The alarm was raised and a frantic search began, but Azaria was not found. Drag marks were seen on the sandy ground and Aborigine trackers said that the marks were associated with dingo tracks. The police constable, who had arrived at the scene, and the park ranger, also saw the tracks. At length, the search was abandoned.

These, in brief, are the undisputed facts about what happened that night. At the trial, the prosecution asserted that, after going back with Azaria and Aidan to the tent, Mrs Chamberlain changed into a pair of track suit trousers, took the baby to the car, slit its throat, placed the body in a camera bag in front of the passenger seat, returned to the tent, removed the trousers, put on the clothes she had been wearing earlier, washed her hands (there was no water in the tent), then returned with Aidan and the tin of baked beans to the barbecue area, where she appeared perfectly calm and collected. These events were supposed to have taken place during a period of five to 10 minutes. The prosecution could not suggest a motive for the murder.

The prosecution alleged that, after Azaria was killed, Mr and Mrs Chamberlain buried the body somewhere in the vicinity. Yet nobody saw either of them with digging implements or behaving oddly during that evening. They appeared shocked and distressed. There was a great deal of vegetational fragments and soil on Azaria's clothes when they were discovered about a week after the tragedy, four kilometres away from the Rock, near some dingo dens. A study of this evidence suggested that the body had been dragged through the various vegetational and soil types between the camping site and the place of discovery.

What was the physical evidence that was used to make a case

Left: *Ayers Rock/Uluru in the Uluru–Kata Tjuta National Park, Australia is the world's largest monolith and an Aboriginal sacred site. This majestic arkose (a feldspar-rich sandstone) outcrop rises 318 metres above the desert floor and is a favourite tourist spot.*

Above: *The Dingo (*Canis lupus dingo*) is a wild dog found in Australia. It hunts in small family groups, pairs or alone.*

from the normal use of a family car. I should point out that the unreliability of the blood tests and the less-than-efficient manner in which they were carried out came to light only after the trial. At the trial, the jury believed that a large amount of specifically baby's blood was discovered in the car.

The prosecution's professional witnesses stated that the damage to Azaria's clothes was carried out with scissors and could not have been done by a dingo's teeth. However, the specialists in this field disagreed with one another and it eventually became clear that it could not be stated that a dingo could not have made the cuts in the clothing.

The prosecution alleged that the fact that the baby had been removed from its clothes was evidence of human involvement, since a dingo could not remove a body from clothes in such a manner as to damage them only slightly. However, experiments carried out at Adelaide Zoo, using a dead goat kid dressed in clothes, revealed that dingoes could remove clothes in this manner, albeit with somewhat greater damage, and the Park Ranger, Mr Roff, with practical knowledge of dingo habits, maintained that a dingo would have no difficulty in removing a baby from its clothes in this way.

against Mrs Chamberlain? First, there was the evidence of the blood; there was a certain amount of blood in the tent. The blankets covering Azaria were stained with blood, as were several other items. The track suit trousers that Mrs Chamberlain was supposed to be wearing when she committed the alleged crime had some marks that resembled, but were not shown to be, blood stains; these were on the front and below the knee. The Crown concluded that the blood on the trousers came from Azaria when she was killed in the car and that the blood in the tent came from Mrs Chamberlain's clothes when she returned there after the "murder". No evidence was presented to prove these assertions.

The prosecution alleged that there was blood in the car, especially under the dashboard and in the camera bag. However, it was shown that the forensic tests used to detect the blood were faulty. The very small amount of genuine blood that was detected – inconsistent with what one might expect after a baby's throat had been slit – could have come from a Mr Lenehan, an accident victim, whom the Chamberlains had rescued in that same car. The amount of blood traces in the vehicle were what one might expect to result

The prosecution alleged that dingoes are unlikely to attack people and kill children. In fact, frequent attacks on children and adults by dingoes were known from the Ayer's Rock area. Before the Azaria tragedy occurred, Mr Roff had written to his superiors about the dangers to people from dingoes, writing that "children and babies can be considered possible prey". Shortly before the Chamberlains visited the Rock, a dingo had removed a pillow from beneath the head of a camper.*

In short, there was no evidence against Mrs Chamberlain. Much of the forensic evidence was discredited. But the jury at the trial, probably unduly influenced by the blood evidence, returned a verdict of "Guilty".

On October 29, 1982, Alice Lynne Chamberlain was convicted on a charge of murder by the Supreme Court of the Northern Territory. Her husband, Michael Leigh Chamberlain, was convicted of being an accessory after the fact. The convictions were subsequently upheld by the High Court. Both Mr and Mrs Chamberlain persistently denied the charges made against them. After five years in prison, Mrs Chamberlain was released, when a Royal Commission of nquiry concluded that there were "serious doubts and questions as to the Chamberlains' guilt".

In his report, the Royal Commissioner, Mr Justice Morling, commented on the forensic evidence adduced at the trial:

The question may well be asked how it came about that the evidence at the trial differed in such important respects from the evidence before the Commission. I am unable to state with certainty why this was so. However, with the benefit of hindsight it can be seen that some experts who gave evidence at the trial were over-confident of their ability to form reliable opinions on matters that lay on the outer margins of their fields of expertise. Some of their opinions were based on unreliable or inadequate data. It was not until more research work had been done after the trial that some of these opinions were found to be of doubtful validity or wrong. Other evidence was given at the trial by experts who did not have the experience, facilities or resources necessary to enable them to express reliable opinions on some of the novel and complex scientific issues which arose for consideration. It was necessary for much more research to be done on these matters to determine whether the opinions expressed at the trial were open to doubt.

t is the fact that every piece of evidence was interpreted by the prosecution in the most damning, if unconvincing, way that is the real cause for concern. But the story of Lynne Chamberlain tells us a great deal more about the nature of evidence. This innocent woman, having lost her daughter in dreadful circumstances, was accused of her murder on the basis of – what? Nothing whatsoever. There was no evidence against her, no *prima facie* case to answer at all. Why, then, did all this happen?

The Chamberlains were Seventh Day Adventists, which made them unpopular with certain sections of the community. There was readiness to believe the worst about them and it was even suggested, needless to say in the absence of any evidence, that Azaria was ritually slaughtered.

But this is not the worst of it. The case against Mrs Chamberlain was based entirely on the belief that the dingo story was false. If there was no dingo, then Mrs Chamberlain was guilty, in spite of the fact that she had no motive and no opportunity, since what she was supposed to have done, in the company of her son, in five to 10 minutes, is simply not credible.

Let us suppose, for the sake of the argument, that Azaria had not been taken by a dingo. Why does it follow that Mrs Chamberlain murdered her? Yet the forces of law and order managed to make a case against her. Why was it never suggested that someone else could have committed the murder? Surely this is the most likely explanation, if it could be shown that the dingo did not exist. Yet this suggestion was never made.

* Since the Chamberlain case, several attacks by dingoes on adults have been recorded.

Below: *Lynne (Lindy) and Michael Chamberlain on their way to court. In 1982 Lindy was convicted of murdering her baby Azaria. She was pardoned in 1987.*

The reader may wish to read more deeply about the various aspects of forensic science discussed in this book. The following are some suggestions for further reading. They have been grouped under the chapter headings for ease of reference. However, a very useful and up-to-date general compendium on the subject is:

Siegel, J., Knupfer, G., & Saukko, P.J. [eds.] (2000). *Encyclopedia of Forensic Sciences*. Academic Press.
General texts on forensic science:
White, P. [ed.] (1998). *Crime Scene to Court: The Essentials of Forensic Science*. Royal Society of Chemistry (Cambridge).
Saferstein, R. (1995). *Criminalistics: An Introduction to Forensic Science*. Prentice Hall (New Jersey).

LOCARD'S PRINCIPLE AND THE FORENSIC MIND

As far as I am aware there is no popular book that deals with the assessment of evidence in forensic science, but a good, albeit very advanced text is:

Robertson, B. & Vignaux, G.A. (1995). *Interpreting Evidence*. John Wiley and Sons.

SPIRIT OF PLACE

Vanezis, P. & Bustill, A. [eds.] (1996).
Suspicious Death Scene Investigation. Arnold Hunter (London) and Oxford University Press (New York).
Hunter, J., Roberts, C. & Martin, A. (1996). *An Introduction to Forensic Archaeology*. Batsford (London).

TIME WILL TELL

General:
Aitken, M.J. (1990). *Science-based Dating in Archaeology*. Longman (London).
Zimmerman, M.R. & Angel, J.L. [eds]. (1986). *Dating and Age Determination of Biological Materials*. Croom Helm (London).
Insects in forensic dating:
Greenberg, B. (2001). *Flies as Forensic Indicators*. Cambridge University Press. [An academic text].
Erzinçlioglu, Z. (2000). *Maggots, Murder and Men*. Harley Books (Colchester). [A more "popular" account.]

A QUESTION OF IDENTITY

DNA:
Krawczaj, M. & Schimidtke, J. (1994). *DNA Fingerprinting*. Bios Scientific Publishers (Oxford).
Anthropology:
Reichs, K.J. [ed.] (1986). *Forensic Osteology*. Charles C. Thomas (Illinois).

Facial Reconstruction:
Prag, J. & Neave, R. (1997). *Making Faces*. British Museum Publications.
Iscan, M.Y. & Helmer, R.P. [eds.] (1993) *Forensic Analysis of the Skull*. John Wiley & Sons (New York).
Fingerprints:
Lee, H.C. & Gaensslen, R.E. (1991). *Advances in Fingerprint Technology*. Elsevier Science (New York).
Identities:
Gray, M. (1998). *Blood Relative*. Gollancz (London).

CAUSES

Knight, B. (1996). *Forensic Pathology*. Arnold (London).
Wilkison, F. (1977). *Firearms*, Camden House (London).
Di Maio, V.J.M. (1985). *Gunshot Wounds: Practical Aspects of Firearms, Ballistics & Forensic Techniques*. CRC Press, (Inc) Florida.
Payne-James, J., Smock, W. & Busuttil, A. [eds.] (2002). *Forensic Medicine: Clinical and Pathological Aspects*. Greenwich Medical Media (London).

POISON

Ferner, R.E. (1996). *Forensic Pharmacology: Medicines, Mayhem and Malpractice*. Oxford Medical Publications (Oxford).
Gough, T.A. [ed.] (1991). *The Analysis of Drugs of Abuse*. Wiley (Chichester).

DESTRUCTION

Cooke, R.A. & Ide, R.H. (1992). *Principles of Fire Investigation*. Institution of Fire Engineers (Leicester).
Bailey, A. & Murray, S.G. (1989). *Explosives, Propellants and Pyrotechnics*. Brassey (London).
Roblee, C.L. & McKechnie, A.J. (1981). *The Investigation of Fires*. Prentice-Hall (New Jersey).

WORDS AND IMAGES

Ellen, D.M. (1989). *The Scientific Examination of Documents*. Ellis Harwood (Chichester).
Brunelle, R.L. & Reed, R.W. (1984). *Forensic Examination of Ink and Paper*. Charles C. Thomas Publisher (Illinois).
Wilson, I & Scwartz, B. (2000). *The Turin Shroud*. Michael O'Mara.

LITTLE DETAILS

Robertson. J. (1992). *Forensic Examination of Fibres*. Ellis Horwood (Chichester).
Mac Donnell, H.L. (1993). *Bloodstain Patterns*. Corning (New York).

Index

Picture Credits

The publishers would like to thank the following sources for their kind permission to reproduce the pictures in this book.

AKG London: Paul Alamsy: 9t

Associated Press: Vassar College, Brian McAdoo: 40

Bridgeman Art Library: Private Collection: 103

Corbis: 102, 148b; /Jean-Pierre Amet: 20; /Archivo Icongrafico, S.A.:81; /Arte & Immagini Srl: 56; /Bettmann: 36, 43, 97, 109t, 118, 135, 161, 166; /Bob Collier Photos: 85; /Ed Bock: 9b; /Bradford T&A: 93; /Christophe Calais: 45; /Jerry Cooke: 72; /Jim Craigmyle: 74; /Firefly Productions: 171; /Guardian: 17; /H.Prinz: 154–55; /Hulton-Deutsch Collection: 8, 42, 125b; /Kostin Igor: 63; /Imagehunters: 158; /Ed Kashi: 46; /Kent News & Pictures: 120; /Kim Little: 112; /Lawrence Manning: 124; /Raffy Martin: 96; /Will & Deni McIntyre: 16; /Wally McNamee: 26–27; /Spingler Michel: 33t; /Vivane Moos: 29b; /Alain Nogues: 170; /Mark Peterson: 73, 177; /Matthew Polak: 38; /Eric Robert: 123; /Chris Rogers: 64–65; /Royalty Free: 18, 83; /Ron Sachs: 173; /Shaul Schwarz: 76; /Ron Slenzak: 29t; /Horacio Villalobos: 77; /William Whitehurst: 33b

Craic Technologies: Picture courtesy of CRAIC Technologies: 177

Getty Images: 82, 98; AFP/Joel Nito: 58; /IDF: 151

Photos12.com: Siny Most: 119

Rex Features: 39b, 117, 162; /Chris Martin Bahr: 33b; /Steve Bell: 21; /Denis Cameron: 51; /J.K. Press: 152–53; /Nils Jorgensen: 61t; /Luigi Nocenti: 30; /Shout: 75; /Sipa Press: 145, 150, 180; /Paul Watts: 39t; /Kevin Weaver: 47

Science Photo Library: /Robert Brook: 138; /Dr. Jeremy Burgess: 35; /Scott Camazine/K.Visscher: 139; /Stephen Dalton: 90–91; /Tim Davis: 114t; /Alain Dex, Publiphoto Diffusion: 115; /Michael Donne: 133t, 133b, 136–37, 140, 142, 143t, 143b, 146, 148t, 160b, 160t; /Ken Edward: 86; /Mauro Fermariello: 2, 14, 15, 25t, 25b, 28, 31, 54, 67b, 69b, 71, 73, 87t, 88, 105t, 107, 125t, 168–69, 176, 178, 179, 182; /Vaughan Fleming: 132; /Simon Fraser: 92; /Pascal Goetgheluck: 6–7, 50, 80; /Steve Horrell: 130; /John Howard: 11; /James King-Holmes: 62; /Laguna Design: 129; /Dr. P. Marazzi: 94b; /Maximilian Stock Ltd.: 134; /John McLean: 84; /John Mead: 184–85; /Peter Menzel: 22, 61b, 79; / Constantino Margiotta: 1, 48–49; /Michael Viard, Peter Arnold Inc.: 104, 106, 144, 159; /Volker Steger, Peter Arnold Inc.: 10; /PHT: 100; /Philippe Plailly: 68; /Harvey Pincis: 59; /Dr. Jurgen Scriba: 89; /Lauren Shear: 94t; /Sovereign, ISM: 12–13, 105b; /Stanley B. Burns, MD & The Burns Archive: 66, 67; /TEK Image: 4–5, 110–11, 113; /G. Tomsich: 126; /Geoff Tompkinson: 87b; /Jim Varney: 23, 122; /VVG: 175; /Zephyr: 101

Topfoto.co.uk: 37, 95, 109b, 127, 156, 181, 186, 187; /Imageworks: 167; /FNP-Star: 19; /Firepix: 141; /Fortean: 164; /PressNet: 183

Every effort has been made to acknowledge correctly and contact the source and/or copyright holder of each picture and Carlton Books Limited apologizes for any unintentional errors or omissions which will be corrected in future editions of this book.